DATE DUE

Splendors of
Latin Cinema

Funded

By

The Chancellor's Office,

California Community Colleges
Governor's Career Technical Education
Initiative (SB 70)

SPLENDORS OF LATIN CINEMA

R. Hernandez-Rodriguez

PRAEGER

An Imprint of ABC-CLIO, LLC

A B C CLIO

Santa Barbara, California • Denver, Colorado • Oxford, England

Library of Congress Cataloging-in-Publication Data

Hernandez-Rodriguez, R.
    Splendors of Latin cinema / R. Hernandez-Rodriguez.
       p. cm.
    Includes bibliographical references and index.
     ISBN 978–0–313–34977–5 (hard copy : alk. paper) — ISBN 978–0–313–34978–2 (ebook :
alk. paper) 1. Motion pictures—Latin America—History—20th century. 2. Motion pictures
—Latin America—History—21st century. 3. Motion pictures—Spain—History—20th
century. 4. Motion pictures—Spain—History—21st century. I. Title.
✓ PN1993.5.L3H48 2010
791.098—dc22   2009033316

14 13 12 11 10   1 2 3 4 5

This book is also available on the World Wide Web as an eBook.
Visit www.abc-clio.com for details.

ABC-CLIO, LLC
130 Cremona Drive, P.O. Box 1911
Santa Barbara, California 93116-1911

This book is printed on acid-free paper (∞)

Manufactured in the United States of America

Contents

Preface

Latin cinemas have recently enjoyed a high degree of international attention, led by the successes of Spain, Mexico, Argentina, and Brazil—something that makes all Latin cinemas very optimistic about their future. This book provides an introduction to the vitality and diversity of these cinematic traditions. Rather than focusing on one country or a strictly chronological order, this volume offers a general view of the cinemas of Spain and Latin America; it therefore encompasses two continents and for the most part two languages (Spanish and Portuguese), although some films in other languages will certainly be mentioned.

All through their existence, the cinemas analyzed in this book have been considered marginal both in their distribution and in that the kind of films known outside these countries have been very limited in their scope—predictably the most popular are the ones addressing social and political issues considered typical of underdeveloped nations, such as poverty, migration, crime, corruption, and repression by fascist military governments. And although these problems are important in the history of many Latin countries, to assume that films dealing with such issues are the only kind produced in the region is not accurate—especially if we consider that most of these countries developed film industries long ago, with genres and star systems that reflected the diversity of their own societies. These cinemas also all enjoyed success at some moment in their history, although were not always able to compete with Hollywood. Nevertheless, Latin cinema has long been viewed as essentially marginal.

Fortunately, this view has begun to change in recent years thanks to a general interest from international audiences and academics alike—as well as by the collective efforts of production and distribution of many Latin countries, most significantly through Ibermedia, a multinational organization created with the intention of supporting the cinema of its members. All this has brought Latin cinemas closer than ever to a global audience, while helping to create a considerable amount of written materials on the subject. This volume seeks to contribute, albeit modestly, to such an enterprise.

In the following pages, we discuss some of the most important, fascinating, and popular films from Spain, Mexico, Brazil, Cuba, and Argentina, as well as the significant attempts produced in Venezuela, Colombia, Chile, Peru, Bolivia, and Uruguay, with a special focus on the most recent releases—and those most likely to be available to an American audience. All of these films are discussed in historical and cultural context, but are also connected to their national film traditions, which in most cases go back to the beginning of the twentieth century. In the cases of Spain, Mexico, Brazil, and Argentina, this tradition includes period pieces, experimental films, films with a strong social content—particularly during the 1960s and 1970s—as well as comedies, melodramas, political thrillers, and the musicals that dominated most of the 1940s and 1950s.

Among the directors mentioned or analyzed in the volume are consecrated figures such as Luis Buñuel, Humberto Mauro, Emilio Fernández, José Luis Garci, Juan Antonio Bardem, Roberto Gavaldón, Carlos Saura, Juan José Bigas Luna, Fernando Trueba, Leopoldo Torre Nilsson, Arturo Ripstein, Glauber Rocha, Nelson Pereira dos Santos, Suzana Amaral, Tomás Gutiérrez Alea, Jorge Sanjinés, Miguel Littin, and Pedro Almodóvar, as well as some of the most exciting young directors that have reclaimed the international screens for Latin movies and have already contributed to one of the most exciting chapters of the history of world cinema, such as Alejandro Amenábar, Guillermo del Toro, Lucrecia Martel, Alfonso Cuarón, Fernando Meirelles, Alejandro González Iñarritu, Walter Salles, José Padilha, Pablo Trapero, Lucía Puenzo, Carlos Reygadas, and Daniel Burman—to mention but a few.

A volume like this one represents the difficult undertaking of talking about cinemas from several cultural traditions and social and political circumstances united sometimes by language, and sometimes by geography or ethnicity. Nonetheless, this is a great opportunity to introduce the diversity, originality, and creativity of the films produced in Latin America and Spain. It is also, I hope, an opportunity to understand the possibilities of this particular medium, and a window to these parts of the world.

Acknowledgments

I want to acknowledge the support of the Latin American Institute of the University of California, Los Angeles, and particularly of its director, Professor Randal Johnson, for a most-needed summer research grant that allowed me to visit the libraries of that institution and gave me access to the collection of the UCLA Film & Television Archive. This book would not have been possible without their generosity and support.

Introduction: Cinema in Latin America and Spain

Latin American and Spanish cinemas have gone through a long history of splendor and crisis. Considering that cinema arrived early in the Latin world—a few months after the invention of the medium in most cases—and that soon after that moving pictures started to be made all over the region, we can say with certainty that Latin cinemas are among the oldest in the world. Yet relatively few people elsewhere know them very distinctly, in part because of the difficult conditions these societies have endured during the past century and in part because, as Luisela Alvaray put it, "Different film industries move at different paces and are contingent to distinct social and political processes. Hence, Venezuelan, Peruvian, or Chilean cinemas, just to mention three contrasting examples, have achieved a lesser dimension than the three major industries—those of Mexico, Brazil, and Argentina."[1] In recent decades, however, and thanks to more stable social and political circumstances, most Latin cinemas have been enjoying a degree of international popularity—led by Spain, Mexico, and Brazil—which makes all of them optimistic of their future. Globalization has helped, without a doubt, inasmuch as it has increased awareness about other cultures in audiences from different regions—especially in the United States, an audience traditionally reluctant to accept foreign films.

But globalization has been fruitful in another way—in the agreement formed between American and local producers and distributors that has resulted in an increase in the number of venues receptive to Latin American films (now distributed worldwide by companies such as Columbia, Sony, or Twentieth Century Fox). This has also improved directors' visibility and thus their ability to cross over to mainstream Hollywood. "Paradoxically, however difficult it is for a smaller industry to compete with hegemonic Hollywood corporations in an unregulated market, it is also true that coproduction and distribution by larger corporations are contributing to increase both the number of works and the exposure of regional cinemas into the extensive global arena."[2] Examples of this are the success of such films as *Diarios de Motocicleta* (*The Motorcycle Diaries*, Walter Salles, 2004)—the second-most-watched Latin film in the United States, after *Como Agua para Chocolate* (*Like Water for Chocolate*, Alfonso Arau, 1992); *Amores Perros* (Alejandro González Iñarritu, 2000), a movie that became one of the most important films of the new millennium; *Cidade de Deus* (*City of God*, Fernando Meirelles and Kátia Lund, 2002), a film that circulated in art cinemas all around the world to great critical success; and *Y Tu Mamá También* (Alfonso Cuarón, 2001), the coming-of-age comedy that was the "highest-grossing Spanish-language film ever in the United Kingdom."[3]

For years these cinemas, including Spanish cinema, were considered marginal in their global distribution, but also in that the films that were better known in other latitudes were those addressing issues crucial to marginal societies, either the so-called "third-world" countries or those nations underdeveloped or under a fascist military government. Thus, Latin American cinemas became known mostly as a cinema of revolution, a cinema of political activism and good intentions, if not always a cinema of quality; in fact, quality was intentionally not an issue for many of these directors who saw in technical perfection a reactionary position more appropriate for the bourgeois cinema of Hollywood. This is all true, of course, but only of the movement called the New Latin American Cinema, which in its most extreme propositions advocated a cinema of "garbage" or proclaimed an aesthetic of hunger as a reaction to an imposed and fast "modernization" that was trying to incorporate them to a capitalist market. As Scott L. Baugh has suggested, "several film manifestoes from the formative period of the New Latin American Cinema refute this modernizationist conceptualization of development in Latin America and offer alternative models of social change that rely heavily on the alliance of Latin American socio-politics, economics, and the arts."[4] Something similar happened to Spain, a country under a repressive fascist military government for almost 40 years, commanded by Francisco Franco.

However, to assume that this is the only cinema produced in the region is not accurate; on the contrary, as we mentioned before, such countries as Argentina, Mexico, Spain, and Brazil developed early on a real film industry with genres and star systems that reflected the diversity of those societies; these cinemas also enjoyed relative success at some moment of their history, but were not always able to compete with the Hollywood machine. Trying to remedy this situation and to promote and disseminate their cinematic production, Iberian and Iberian American countries came together in Brasilia in 1977 to study the possibility of mutually supporting their production and opening a free, common market, something proposed by Roberto Farias of Brazil. Despite the fact that officials from the Mexican, Brazilian, Spanish, and Argentine governments were present, the conclusions and findings of the meeting were presented only as recommendations, and none of them was really reinforced officially or aggressively. Six years later in Madrid, at the Encuentro de Cine Iberoamericano (Iberian American Cinema Encounter), the issue of a common market of Latin cinemas resurfaced, but with no better luck than it had had in the previous meeting. Finally in 1997, fourteen heads of state of the region created El Fondo Iberoamericano de Ayuda, Ibermedia (The Iberian American Fund of Help, Ibermedia), an organization that aimed to support production and distribution of films as well as to establish a shared market that could support the local production. This time the results have already been remarkable if we consider that Ibermedia has been instrumental in the production of films such as *Machuca* (Andrés Wood, 2003), *Sin Dejar Huella* (*Without a Trace*, María Novaro, 2000), *La Ciénaga* (*The Swamp*, Lucrecia Martel, 2001), and *El Crimen del Padre Amaro* (*The Crime of Father Amaro*, Carlos Carrera, 2002).

The recent success of Latin cinemas is remarkable and refreshing and offers a more accurate view of the diversity, originality, and creativity of the films produced in Latin America and Spain. It also offers new ways of understanding the possibilities of the medium and provides a window to these parts of the world. Nonetheless, the fact remains that most people do not know the history of all the Latin cinemas and that until recently very little had been written on the subject. This, fortunately, has changed in the last few years—several books have appeared focusing either partially or totally on Latin America and Spain. Some of them are collections of essays analyzing genres, films, or the importance of some actors or directors for their national traditions; some look at Latin American and Spanish cinemas as important, needed chapters of world cinema; and others focus on individual national film traditions, Spain, Mexico, and Brazil being the ones favored by critics. Titles such as *Mexican Cinema* (1995) by Paulo Antonio Paraguaná, *Mexico's Cinema* (1999) edited by Joanne Hershfield and David R. Maciel, *Popular Cinema in Brazil, 1930–2001* (2004) edited by Stephanie Dennisson and Lisa Shaw, *Contemporary Brazilian Cinema* (1984) by Dennis West, and *Spanish Cinema, The Auteurist Tradition* (1999) edited by Peter William Evans are but a few examples.

Still volumes like the one presented here are rare because of the difficult undertaking of talking about cinemas from several cultural traditions and social and political circumstances united sometimes by language, sometimes by geography or ethnicity, and that expand for a century in some cases. To make it even more difficult, the task of summarizing each tradition has to be accomplished in a few pages. Nonetheless, the necessity of introducing Latin cinema is as urgent as ever because of the undeniable presence of these national film traditions in the international cultural scene, and in the United States in particular. It is also necessary because of the quality of the films emerging from those traditions, which reveal new and exciting possibilities of the medium, and also show that films like these can be possible only if they belong to a longer tradition of making films—vibrant, colorful, diverse traditions that have been until very recently unknown outside of the Iberian and Iberian American world. As Danilo Trelles writes, "Latin American cinema has managed to survive against all odds [...] which demonstrates the vitality of the region."[5]

This book, then, is an introduction—an incomplete introduction, inevitably—to the cinemas of Latin America, but also of Spain, with the intention of showing some of the vitality and fertility that characterizes them and that has become more evident in recent years. It also aims to excite the readers' curiosity and invite them to continue watching these films, exploring their themes ideas, and, of course, engaging their history. It aims as well to offer a more impartial and concise view of Latin cinemas and their historical and cultural context in order to assist the public in its further investigation of the subject. In 1990, an Argentine critic, for example, complained that in almost a hundred years of motion pictures, most Latin cinemas have not even developed into industries and that the "cinematic exchange of Latin America with the rest of the world could not even be called uneven [since it was] actually, nonexistent."[6] And yet, two years later *Como Agua para Chocolate* became the single most-watched foreign film in the United States and received numerous awards all over the world, marking the beginning of a boom of Latin cinema that has continued until now. In the 1980s most critics considered Spanish cinema dead, and yet those are the years that saw the emergence of Pedro Almodóvar, perhaps the most famous and international Spanish film director ever.

This book assumes that there are enough reasons to be optimistic of the future, although it is important not to forget that there is still much to do, especially since the lack of information on Latin American and Spanish cinema allowed a series of misconceptions to become accepted as true. In his book *How to Read a Film* (2000), for example, James Monaco affirms that it was not until the 1960s and 1970s that the world "saw the extension of film culture beyond the boundaries of the U.S., Japan, and Europe into the developing countries."[7] And when he refers to Latin America, in only a few pages, he mentions some Chilean directors, Cuban cinema, and Brazilian *cinema novo*; yet in reference to Mexico, a country with one of the longest and most important film industries in the region, he mentions only Spanish expatriate Luis Buñuel: "Mexico, like Brazil, produces more than fifty features per year. For many years Mexican cinema was dominated by the imposing figure of Luis Buñuel."[8] He concludes with this quick assessment that unfortunately says nothing: "Other Latin American countries contributed to the repertory of Third World classics on a more limited scale. Notable were *Blood of the Condor* (Bolivia, Jorge Sanjinés, 1969) and *The Hour of the Furnaces* (Argentina, Fernando Solana and Octavio Getino, 1968)."[9]

This, as we already said and as we see in the following pages, is inaccurate at best. And yet such stereotypes are common. That is why a book that reviews the development of the different Latin cinemas in their historical context, as this one does, seems relevant and important at the present time when films such as *Amores Perros*, the Oscar-nominated *El Laberinto del Fauno* (Guillermo del Toro, 2006) and *El Crimen del Padre Amaro*, or the winners of the Golden Bear at the Berlin Film Festival, *Central do Brasil* (1998) and *Tropa de Elite* (José Padilha, 2007), not to mention the films of Pedro Almodóvar or Alejandro Amenábar, have brought back these cinemas to a prominent position in the world. They have given enough reason to critics and the public alike to hope for a golden age of Latin cinemas with their own styles, their own development, and their own particular social and political circumstances; these traditions, although independent, have often interacted with each other. It is particularly important, then, to realize that in order to understand the present and future of these cinemas, we need to have a better understanding of their history, richness, and diversity, and also of the way they interact with each other.

As Michael T. Martin writes in the introduction to his *The New Latin American Cinema*, "Cinematic traditions have not developed autonomously, spontaneously or evenly in Latin America (nor in other regions of the Third World). Similarly, the representation of national cinemas in the volume is uneven."[10] And, as he mentions as well, until the 1960s most critics from Europe and the United States ignored the cinemas produced in Latin America, something that has changed since "film scholars have generated, in recent years, a substantial corpus of criticism."[11] In the following pages, therefore, we discuss some of the most important, fascinating, and popular films to come out of Latin America and Spain in the last few decades. We connect them to a long tradition of filmmaking that goes back to the beginning of the twentieth century and even earlier, a tradition that includes periods of experimentation and social commitment, particularly during the 1960s and 1970s, as well as a period of classic comedies, melodramas, and musicals during the 1940s and 1950s. We discuss films, directors, and stars from Mexico, Cuba, Brazil, Argentina, Peru, Spain, and Chile who have contributed to one of the most interesting chapters of the history of world cinema.

Chapters 1 and 2 of the volume are dedicated to the cinema of Spain. The reason for this is really arbitrary. It aspires, however, to offer a solid and concise introduction to an industry that in the last few decades has emerged as one of the most diverse and free in matters of sexuality and progressive social issues today. It also aims to structure the book in a chronological and comprehensive way that would seem more logical to an American reader. Chapter 1, consequently, is an overview of the development of this national film industry, an industry that often has been considered in crisis, but that has demonstrated in the past 20 years that it is one of the most vibrant of Europe and definitely the most stable of all the Latin traditions. The chapter starts with a review of this industry's latest accomplishments and goes back to its origins. Chapter 2 focuses on the films of Pedro Almodóvar—the most famous Spanish director today—providing the reader with a general examination of his major films, as well as his importance for the revitalization of Spanish culture after the death of Francisco Franco and his role in the *la movida* cultural movement, a movement that confirmed modern Spain as a society truly democratic and liberated.

Chapter 3 focuses on Mexico, a country historically with the strongest Latin American film industry, an industry that developed and established early and that at its peak enjoyed a level of success that was unprecedented for a Latin American country, becoming second only to Hollywood in the region. This chapter, then, reviews the development of Mexican cinema, focusing first on the last two decades of its production, and moving back to the films produced during the 1980s, 1970s, and 1960s, including the tradition of an independent cinema, or cinema of auteur, represented by directors such as Felipe Cazals, Luis Alcoriza, and particularly Arturo Ripstein. Paying special attention to the films made by Guillermo del Toro, Alfonso Cuarón, and Alejandro González Iñarritu, but also to those produced by independent directors such as Carlos Reygadas and Julián Hernández, we analyze one of the most diverse cinemas in the world. These Mexican directors have been so successful that for the past 10 years critics have been proclaiming a new golden age.

If critics talk of a new golden age, logically this means that there was a previous golden age of Mexican cinema, which is the subject of Chapter 4. In this chapter, we review mainly the Mexican movies of the 1940s and 1950s, the period considered the best of that industry, but also films from the 1930s when the industry was really established. The chapter looks into the most popular genres of the industry—melodramas, comedies, and musicals—as well as the importance of the revolution and an idealized view of the countryside for cinema, and modern Mexican society in general. It also reviews the emergence of an urban culture that was a sign of the changing times and that found in film the perfect vehicle for the explorations of a new sensibility. The nation's struggle with a fast modernization that brought changes meant also that the traditional values were changing and that the traditional society was giving pass to a new society with new values that forced society to form a different picture of its national identity. This chapter is by necessity an inclusive introduction to this period of Mexican cinema, rather than a detailed and chronological history.

Chapter 5, similarly, analyzes the development of the other great film industry in Latin America, Brazilian cinema. From the success of such films as *Tropa de Elite*, *Central do Brasil*, and *Cidade de Deus* to the importance of film in the transition to democracy in the 1980s or the presence of a popular cinema that incorporated television, sexuality, and dance into a longer tradition of massive celebrations and carnival, Brazil has had a solid cinematic presence in the world. This presence includes the creation of film genres that are unmistakably Brazilian, the importance of samba and Carmen Miranda as well as the production of the most important film studios in South America. However, it is the radical, innovative, adventurous propositions of Brazilian cinema of the 1960s and 1970s that really gave not only international notoriety, but also prestige to this country as a producer of film. These films are known generally as *cinema novo*, and *cinema novo*, for better or for worse, has represented for a long time and for a lot of people Latin American cinema in general.

That is why Chapter 6 is dedicated to Brazilian *cinema novo*. One of the most ambitious and accomplished film movements to come out of Latin America or even the Iberian Peninsula; *cinema novo* ingeniously mixes radical aesthetic propositions with history, cultural and popular manifestations, as well as politics in order to address the most important social issues of its time. In the process it creates an allegorical cinema of great beauty and intellectual depth. Dealing simultaneously with censorship and a violent political repression, cinema in Brazil during the late 1950s and 1960s attempted to focus on issues that were of importance to the nation in such films as *Barravento* (Glauber Rocha, 1962) or *Rio 40 Graus* (Nelson Pereira dos Santos, 1955) before turning the camera to the middle classes in the 1970s to meditate on the failure of the leftist intelligentsia that had tried to change the social conditions of the Brazilian population. In the end, *cinema novo* made possible the appearance of even more radical propositions, such as *estética do lixo* (aesthetics of garbage) and *estética da fome* (aesthetics of hunger), that rejected technical perfection and a polished style as markers of oppression and imperialism, mainly associated with Hollywood and the American intrusive politics in the region.

Chapter 7 focuses on the other great film industry in South America, Argentine cinema. Contemporary of the Brazilian, Mexican, and Spanish industries, the Argentine film industry can even be regarded as the first one of them considering that the production of films in that country precedes the others by a few months. However, by the 1930s the four industries were competing in equal terms, and soon after that it became evident that Mexico had won the race by establishing a presence in the region with a level of production and even quality of films like no other Latin nation. Nonetheless, Argentine cinema has been all though its history a consistent and worthy rival of the Mexican and Spanish film industries as well as a producer of excellent films and even film movements that have characterized Latin cinema internationally. This chapter tries to assess this film tradition in a succinct and fair way by taking into consideration that like many other Latin cinemas, the Argentine industry has been affected by social, political, and economic problems that have resulted in a pattern of periodic crisis and reemergence. However, with a reputation for quality and intellectual depth, it is important to mention that Argentine films have always had a solid international presence only reconfirmed in the last decade.

Chapter 8, like the previous chapter, tries to summarize in a few pages a whole national film tradition—that of Cuba. It is true that the Cuban film industry, which goes back to the 1950s, is younger than the Argentine film industry and therefore has fewer movements, films, genres, and directors to review; however, since the first years of the triumph of a revolution that transformed that Caribbean nation into the first socialist state in the hemisphere, film has been at the center of its cultural and social programs. Convinced of the importance of mass communication, and of film in particular, to disseminate its ideology and to promote education and social programs, the Cuban government placed film in a privileged position as a priority of the new administration. Consequently, in a few years this country managed to develop one of the most liberated, interesting, and consistent cinemas in Latin America.

The last chapter, Chapter 9, is even more wide-ranging since it tries to give the reader an overview of the most important films and directors that have kept some cinematic tradition alive in countries such as Colombia, Venezuela, Chile, Peru, and Uruguay, which did not develop a national film industry with the same resonance, consistency, or impact outside of their national boundaries, but which have nonetheless produced interesting and important films with some regularity. Recently, however, all of these countries have been able to maintain a more consistent presence in international film festivals and even an occasional film that manages to attract enough attention in other countries to give them some commercial distribution in such cities as New York, Los Angeles, London, or Paris. This, as stated before, offers enough reasons to be optimistic of the future not only of Latin cinema, but of cinema in general because the sooner Latin American and Spanish cinemas are recognized as important chapters of world cinema, the sooner we can get a more complete picture of the history of film as a medium of mass communication as well as a manifestation of human identity. "To tell a story is a mysterious thing," wrote

Maurice Blanchot.[12] And that is what film reveals so clearly; to be human is to tell marvelous stories to each other.

Finally, I want to mention that there is one obvious omission in this book, that of the cinema of Portugal. A country with a rich culture and a highly regarded film tradition, Portugal is one of the founding countries of Ibermedia and has produced one of the great Latin cinemas, a cinema that has gained international attention and praises with figures such as the master Manoel de Oliveira and João César Monteiro, as well as more recently with the excellent João Pedro Rodrigues. Unfortunately, however, there is even less circulation of films and a greater lack of information about this national cinema outside of Portugal. New York, San Francisco, Los Angeles, and Chicago have regular film festivals showcasing the films of Latin America and Spain, but even there Portugal is often not included. Therefore American audiences have had even less exposure to the films from that small European country. In order to write about Portuguese film, even briefly, it becomes indispensable to travel to that country and spend several months researching and watching films, something beyond the scope of this book. The situation seems to be changing for the better with recent books on the subject such as Alberto Mira's *The Cinema of Spain and Portugal* (2005) and more recently with Randal Johnson's *Manoel de Oliveira* (2007). So it is possible to hope that a future edition of this book or future projects like this one would be able to include a chapter on the cinema of Portugal.

NOTES

1. Luisela Alvaray, "National Regional and Global: New Waves of Latin American Cinema," *Cinema Journal* 47 (Spring 2008): 49.

2. Ibid., 55.

3. Ibid., 54.

4. Scott L. Baugh, "Manifesting La Historia: Systems of 'Development' and the New Latin American Cinema Manifesto," *Film and History* 34 (2004): 57.

5. Danilo Trelles, "El Cine Latinoamericano en la Batalla de la Cultura," *Cinemas d'Amerique Latine* 7 (January 1999): 165.

6. José Agustín Mahieu, *Panorama del Cine Iberoamericano* (Madrid: Ediciones de Cultura Hispánica, 1990): 20.

7. James Monaco, *How to Read a Film: Movies, Media, Multimedia* (New York: Oxford University Press, 2000), 332.

8. Ibid., 334.

9. Ibid.

10. Michael T. Martin, *The New Latin American Cinema. Volume Two* (Detroit: Wayne State University Press, 1997), 28.

11. Ibid., 17.

12. Maurice Blanchot, *The Infinite Conversation* (Minneapolis: University of Minnesota Press, 1993), 381.

CHAPTER 1

The Cinema of Spain

A SUCCESS STORY

To reduce the cinematic tradition of an entire nation to only one or two names is unfair. That, however, seems to have been the fate of Spain, a nation with not only a long tradition of making movies, but strictly speaking, one with several traditions if we consider the Catalonian, Basque, and Galician regional cinemas, cinemas that have also contributed significantly to the production of Iberian films in languages other than Castilian. Spain's cinema has been at various moments in its long history, particularly for foreigners, the films of José Luis Sáenz de Heredia, the official director of Franco's Spain; the films of Juan Antonio Bardem; the films of Carlos Saura; or even the surreal films of Luis Buñuel. But this does not take into consideration that the latter actually made only a couple of films in his native Spain and the majority of his career was developed in Mexico, the county of which he became a citizen toward the end of his life.

The most recent case of this reductionism of Spanish cinema, and perhaps the most obvious for the contemporary reader, is the one represented by Pedro Almodóvar, an Oscar-winning director whose rich and colorful career goes back to the early 1980s, a decade of great social, political, and economic changes in Spain. Those are also years of crisis in this country's film industry, which according to many critics was in desperate need of help. Even as late as 1991, John Hopewell writes that this cinema had almost always been in crisis; in fact, he argues, "the Spanish cinema was in crisis even before it existed."[1] Therefore, the force, originality, and perfect timing of the movies of

Almodóvar, which coincided with the beginning of the emergence of
Spain as a democratic, modern, finally European nation, give some
validity to the claims of crisis and of spectacular recovery of its film
industry; they also provide us with the perfect point of departure to
talk about Spanish cinema.

We will return to Almodóvar's career and significance in the next
chapter, but for now I want to emphasize that despite the originality
of this filmmaker, Spanish cinema is much more diverse than what is
usually acknowledged. It is perhaps the concurrence of Almodóvar's
sensibility and the changes that his country was experiencing after
the death of Francisco Franco in 1975 that made his films so quintessentially "Spanish." These changes were expressed mostly through an
explosion of social and cultural freedom known as *la movida*, a movement that subverted the stereotypical representations of Spanish
culture (flamenco music, bullfighting, Madrid's night life, religious
festivities, etc.). The 1980s represented a moment of change for Spanish
cinema that mirrors the social and political changes the country had
been undergoing since the late 1970s. This is particularly visible in the
overwhelming feeling of social freedom and an exaggerated interest in
countercultural movements as well as experimentation with drugs, alternative music, literature, and sexuality.

All this can be seen almost point by point in Almodóvar's first
features and particularly in his *Pepi, Luci, Bom y Otras Chicas del Montón*
(*Pepi, Luci, Bom and Other Girls on the Heap*, 1980). This movie, despite
all its flaws, can be considered a landmark of the period if only because
it had wide circulation among young people at a moment when Spanish
cinema "lacked a really effective system of protection" against foreign,
mostly Hollywood films, according to film historian Fernando
Méndez-Leite. In a way, this movie showed that, just as the years after
Franco's death had promised to the young generation, a new world of
liberties unheard of in previous decades was there for the taking by
those brave and adventurous enough to claim it. So with this attitude,
"many interesting films were made, in general filmed with limited
resources and little experience by a group of young directors that had
had their first opportunities to make films in those hopeful years of the
transition."[2] Those years saw the beginning of the careers of many
directors, some of whom would become in time the most recognized
Spanish filmmakers of the new millennium. Although none of them
became as famous and as popular as Almodóvar, nonetheless they do
represent a new generation of professional directors with commendable
achievements such as the works of Manuel Gutiérrez Aragón,

Pilar Miró, Jaime Chávarri, or José Luis Garci, whose *Volver a Empezar* (*To Start All Over Again*) won an Oscar in 1982 and whose *El Abuelo* (*The Grandfather*, 1998), *Asignatura Aprobada* (*Course Completed*, 1987) and *Sesión Continua* (*Uninterrupted Session*, 1984) were also nominated for the same award.

Not all the films made in the 1980s had high artistic aspirations, and only a few were of good quality. So if the years of *la movida* were the years of carefree experimentation and flirting with alternative cultures, they were also the years of an explosion of popular culture and particularly the years of "the S movies, a sort of soft-porn genre, as well as of the comedies of Mariano Ozores [a director of light, popular comedies], of the movies of Parchis [an ephemeral teen-idol musical group], of residual terror films, and of bad co-productions of action films."[3] The signals were mixed and the crisis seemed more and more pronounced. According to Hopewell, "Spanish films' share of their domestic box-office has dropped disastrously from 29.76% of total theatrical gross in 1977 to a mere 7.67% for the first eight months of 1989."[4] He attributes this drop to the bad quality and the limited production of films, the backwardness of Spanish industrialization, which started late compared to other Western nations,[5] and to the lack of moneyed middle classes, not to mention the increasing popularity of Hollywood's understanding of films primarily as a form of entertainment.

In general, the circumstances in which the industry had functioned until then—all this according Hopewell[6]—were almost preindustrial and improvised. However, the filmmakers were not the only ones to blame, but their audiences as well. Traditionally, Spain had never really had a receptive public of cinephiles like France, where Buñuel had to take his *Un Chien Andalou* (*An Andalusian Dog*, 1929) to be appreciated. It, therefore, had to struggle constantly to establish an industry that could be considered really national. If a portion of the public was interested in film as an artistic or cultural medium that carried some sort of national soul, including idiosyncrasies and rules of conduct—something Franco understood and exploited very well—the majority saw cinema more and more as a form of entertainment and as a spectacle. In addition, there was an increasing disinterest from the part of the government that had previously been supportive of film, treating it as a matter of national culture to the point that by the last decades of the twentieth century Hopewell can claim, "There has been no official Spanish Film School in Spain since the Escuela Oficial de Cine was run down by Franco's government in the early

1970s ... The number of cinemas in Spain has dropped drastically from 2,640 in 1986, to 2,234 in 1987, to 1,882 in 1988."[7]

That situation has changed today. Many film schools and centers have opened recently, and the Spanish government has shown a renewed interest in the industry. Movies have been made, directors have emerged, and Spanish cinema has had an international projection as never before to the point that the perceived crisis of the 1980s has been transformed into one of the most astounding recoveries in film history. Méndez-Leite sees in Almodóvar and Alejandro Amenábar the parameters of this success. He observes that in 1980 Almodóvar had to struggle to finish and, even more, to show his first feature, but by the year 2000 he "parades his movie *All About My Mother* in every single gala and festival around the world, where he wins trophies never before within reach of Spanish cinema," while Amenábar "prepares to film his third picture, *The Others*, a production made possible with money from the multinational Miramax, starring Nicole Kidman and with Tom Cruise as executive producer. There is no doubt that many things have changed in those twenty years."[8] Considering this, it is not surprising that by 2008 both Amenábar and Almodóvar have already won Oscars and continue careers that have been amply recognized internationally.

Garan Holcombe, a British critic, echoes this sentiment in a recent article published in the *California Literary Review*. For him it is undeniable that "in the last few years all things Latino have been in increasing vogue,"[9] particularly cinema. He names Mexican hearththrob Gael García Bernal, who at the time had already gained international notoriety without having made a single film in English, and Colombian actress Catalina Sandino Moreno, as well as "most significantly of all, at least in terms of the exposure guaranteed, two Spanish filmmakers [who] have won the Best Foreign Film Oscar in the last few years, Pedro Almodóvar and Alejandro Amenábar."[10] Like previous critics, Holcombe considers that something very important has happened in Spanish cinema in the last 20-something years, but he thinks it is a global phenomenon, so he goes further to declare that if Almodóvar was the king of the foreign films circuit all through the 1980s and 1990s, there is a new contender to the title, Amenábar: "Now, it seems, the King has lost his crown."[11]

Similarly, Méndez-Leite considers that between 1980 and 2000, "Spanish cinema has produced much more interesting films than in all of its previous history."[12] This is a very provocative statement. Yet what it shows is that, like Mexican or Brazilian cinema, Spanish cinema went through a similar pattern of crisis and reemergence, albeit it met with more favorable economic circumstances. Toward the end it received the support of a more politically stable and prosperous society that had benefited from joining the European Union in 1986. Spain has been, therefore, better positioned than Mexico or Brazil to carry the renaissance of its film industry to a higher, more secure place, at least for now. To speak of a resurgence of Spanish cinema makes sense only if we take into consideration its circumstances, the diversity of its talent, and if we acknowledge the efforts and contributions of all the directors working in that industry at least since the 1970s.

In general, these directors constitute a generation that distinguishes itself from the previous ones. One thing in particular that sets these directors apart is that the themes that have occupied them from the late 1970s on have been heavily centered in the recent history of their country; not surprisingly, many films focus on the Republic, the Civil War, and the Postwar, seeing their recent past with a very critical eye. However, they have also paid attention, with more or less success, to the glorious past of Baroque Spain and have used some of the best works of its literature, including modern and classic authors. These directors, nurtured by their national cultural traditions, take those very same traditions to the extreme and exercise very little restrictions. This makes their cinema, and culture in general, one of the most liberating and prejudice-free in the world at the present time. All these cultural changes have been influenced and favored strongly by the first socialist governments of the early 1980s, according to Méndez-Leite, favor that has not gone without criticism and opposition.[13]

While history is important, other contemporary issues have also been at the center of concern of Spanish filmmakers; issues such as terrorism, homosexuality, and immigration have been treated with a frankness rarely seen in other cinemas. Interestingly enough, many of the directors from earlier generations, such as Luis García Berlanga, Juan Antonio Bardem, and Fernando Fernán Gómez, as well as many more from the so-called New Spanish Cinema of the 1970s, such as Carlos Saura, Mario Camus, Vicente Aranda, Francisco Regueiro, José Luis Borau, and Víctor Erice, kept active all through the end of the twentieth century and even now, influencing and being influenced by the young directors. In some cases they produced some of their best works in their later years. Perhaps to better appreciate this phenomenon, it would be helpful to review the last few decades and their most significant films.

THE LAST THREE DECADES

With an international reputation, an Oscar, and successful films in Spanish and English, Amenábar can be considered the most representative Spanish director of the new millennium; even though Almodóvar continued producing films and collecting praises and prizes in 2000, nobody can claim a decade his or hers more than he can claim the 1980s. But the decade of the 1990s is perhaps the most exciting in the history of Spanish cinema. The 1990s saw a variety of approaches to a tradition that is constantly reinventing itself to the point that a veteran director such as Juan José Bigas Luna, who began his career in the 1970s, manages only then to become an internationally recognized filmmaker with the success of *Jamón Jamón* (*Ham Ham*, 1992), a film that in many ways summarizes the Spanish attitude of that particular moment. *Jamón Jamón* is a revision of Spanish excess and an honest look at this culture. As Celestino Deleyto puts it, it is an "explicit attempt to present a cultural tapestry of Spain in the last decade of the twentieth century"[14] through an exploration of machismo and violence and their relationship to sex, particularly as embodied in the persona of Raúl (Javier Bardem), a young man who exudes sexuality.

From the opening of the film we are presented with two very important aspects of Spanish culture that will prove to be more than symbolic: the landscape of the region where the movie takes place—an arid region that brings to mind immediately *Las Hurdes: Tierra sin Pan* (*Land without Bread*, 1933), Buñuel's surreal documentary about an impoverished region of Extremadura—as well as the constant presence of stereotypical cultural markers, from the prominent presence of the Osborne bull (an old ad for brandy), whose black shape we see partially at the beginning of the film while the camera pulls back and reveals more of the anatomy of the animal (its monumental testicles to be exact), to food (which is in the title itself), to bullfighting, the national pastime, to Goya, particularly in the fight between Raúl and José Luis with two ham legs that evokes the painter's famous *Duelo a Garrotazos* (*Duel with Cudgels*). Also symbolic is the powerful and ambivalent figure of the mother, another presence in many tragic literary works and films from Spain that can be considered a challenge to the discourse of sanctity of family and motherhood abused by the Franco regime.

Bigas Luna seems to be offering through outrageous comedy and melodrama a revision of traditional Spain and a disarticulation of its cultural identity. That the movie came out in 1992 when the country was preparing to celebrate in a big way the 500-year anniversary of the discovery of America does not seem to be a coincidence, adding another layer to the already multiple meanings of the film. This is also the case of another movie of the same year, *Belle Epoque* (1992), by Fernando Trueba, another veteran. This movie executes a similar revisionism of national identity through over-the-top parody. Winner of an Oscar for best foreign language film, *Belle Epoque* tells the story of Fernando (Jorge Sanz), a young soldier who deserts the army during the civil war and wanders through the countryside until he eventually finds refuge with Don Manolo (Fernando Fernán Gómez), a self-proclaimed anarchist and artist, and his three daughters. With them Fernando lives an idealized, carefree existence full of enlightenment and sexuality. Unlike *Jamón Jamón*, *Belle Epoque* is easy, fun, with just enough postmodern elements to make it look deep and contemporary, while remaining foreign audience–friendly (perhaps that explains the fact that it won the Oscar).

However, both films are concerned with what seems to be a Spanish obsession—sex. If Bigas Luna is more open and frank in the sweaty and lethal possibilities of sex, Trueba is more perceptive in his observations of the minor, comic possibilities of mismatched encounters and attractions that in the end constitute life. *Belle Epoque* is set in some of the hardest times in Spanish history, right before the country became engaged in World War II, but it is so charming and disarming in its naïveté that for moments it makes us forget the tragedy of war with both comic and tender scenes while it encourages us to shamelessly enjoy its freshness. *Jamón Jamón*, on the contrary, takes us to the other extreme, to the ridiculous and grotesque aspects of Spanish society at the end of the millennium, to make Spaniards, and audiences in general, wonder if things have changed at all in a century. The omnipresence of sexuality does not surprise if we consider, as we said before, that this society is among the most liberated and free in the world, in part because it endured decades of repression.

This is not unique to these films; sexuality is, in one way or another, at the center of such films as *Amo Tu Cama Rica* (*I Love Your Cozy Bed*, Emilio Martínez Lázaro, 1996), a twist on the boy-meets-girl-boy-loses-girl story set in the Spain of the end of the millennium with very predictable situations; *Malena Es un Nombre de Tango* (*Malena Is a Name for a Tango*, Gerardo Herrero, 1996), a story of sister rivalry and an exploration of the old battle of the sexes; and the redundant *Entre las Piernas* (*Between the Legs*, Manuel Gómez Pereira, 1999), about two sex addicts, their passionate relationship, and the consequences of such relationship in their lives and the lives of others. Others include *Tranvía a la Malvarrosa* (*Tramway to Malvarrosa*, José Luis García Sánchez, 1996), a story about a young man who gives up his desire to be a writer and becomes a lawyer to please his father and in the process meets, and loses, the girl of his dreams, only to learn about love from a call girl; *Tesis* (*Thesis*, Alejandro Amenábar, 1996), where sex and violence merge with the voyeuristic pleasures of film; *Nadie Hablará de Nosotras Cuando Hayamos Muerto* (*Nobody Will Mention Us Girls When We Are Dead*, Agustín Díaz Yanes, 1995), a movie that combines film noir and pulp fiction-like cinematography; and *La Mujer Más Fea del Mundo* (*The Ugliest Woman in the World*, Miguel Bardem, 1999).

La Mujer Más Fea del Mundo is a typical product of the cinema of the end of millennium. Using big names, lots of money, and an aggressive publicity campaign targeting young audiences, the movie is a cross between a sci-fi flick and a Hollywood thriller, mixed with nostalgic nods to camp films of the 1970s or even the 1940s. *La Mujer Más Fea*, like *Nadie Hablará de Nosotras*, boasts a combination of past and present styles and Hollywood genres, one being its most obvious references to Quentin Tarantino's *Pulp Fiction* (1994), as well as old-fashioned Spanish movies, particularly the kind of soft-porn flicks that existed under Franco. What is interesting in these two movies is that, like what happened in Hollywood in the 1990s, the cinema of the end of the century in Spain is highly "postmodern"—that is, it seeks and exhibits the most influences, while deconstructing genres, topics, and ideologies.

Nadie Hablará de Nosotras is closer to an American noir complete with violence, sexuality, and Mexican drug dealers around a very simple plot: Gloria (Victoria Abril), a Spanish prostitute working in Mexico City, is somehow mixed with a gang of drug dealers. During a police ride she escapes, returns to Madrid, is chased by the drug dealers, and has to fight them while trying to dismantle their operations in Spain. She also tries to reconnect with her comatose husband and an ex-militant leftist mother. There is a lot of blood, violence, and melodrama in this picture, but it does not possess any of the irony of *Pulp Fiction*, a movie that had been released a year earlier and is a clear influence. *Nadie Hablará de Nosotras* is interesting, however, not only because it won several Goyas (the Spanish Academy Awards), but also because it represents a new style in which it has became more and more common to mix old and new genres, techniques, and styles. Rob Stone has traced some connections between Gloria and women characters from earlier Spanish films, such as the heroines of Juan Antonio Bardem's *Calle Mayor* (*Main Street*, 1956) and Saura's *Ana y los Lobos* (*Ana and the Wolves*, 1972), because they are women who do not fit the stereotypical norm. These women "were clearly exceptions from dissident film-makers, whose films utilized the suffering female as a metaphor for those who endure marginalization."[15] That is also the case of Lola (Elia Galera), the main character of *La Mujer Más Fea*, except that because this movie is a comedy, it is easier to read its characters as parodies, therefore rendering Lola as a more modern and yet paradoxically less revolutionary character than Gloria.

Something similar can be said about another set of films about male homosexuality, a subject that reemerges in the 1990s, but that had already been treated with very interesting results in the 1970s. Many films deal with this subject; their plots cover almost every imaginable aspect of this form of sexuality: from perversion to free, careless sex to AIDS to tender tales of first sexual experiences treated sometimes with irony, sometimes with cynicism or sentimentality, but almost invariably with a sense of entitlement, reinforced by self-absorbed characters so full of themselves that it makes it difficult sometimes to see what they have to add to the discussion. These films, with few exceptions, such as Almodóvar's *La Ley del Deseo* (*Law of Desire*, 1986) or *La Mala Educación* (*Bad Education*, 2005), seem rather conventional if not antiquated in their views, particularly when compared with earlier films such as *El Diputado* (*The Congressman*, Eloy de la Iglesia, 1978) and *La Muerte de Mikel* (*The Death of Mikel*, Imanol Uribe, 1984).

Of the gay films of the end of the millennium, perhaps the best known are *Segunda Piel* (*Second Skin*, Gerardo Vera, 1999) and *Sobreviviré* (*I Will Survive*, Alfonso Albacete and David Menkes, 1999). *Segunda Piel* has an excellent cast of first-rank actors including Cecilia Roth, Javier Bardem, Jordi Mollà, and Ariadna Gil, but the plot is a little melodramatic and implausible, particularly after all the freedom in matters of sexuality that Spanish cinema has accustomed its audiences to expect from it and considering that gay marriage is legal in Spain. The plot is very simple: elusive Alberto (Jordi Mollà) has a sexual relationship with openly gay surgeon Diego (Javier Bardem). Alberto, confused and unsure about his feelings and his sexuality, is also married and in love with his wife Elena (Ariadna Gil). He becomes even more confused and scared when he realizes that his affair with Diego is becoming something more serious for his lover.

Elena eventually finds out her husband is having an affair, although she does not realize at first that it is with a man. However, when she confronts him and discovers the truth, she reacts in shock despite remaining calm and supportive. Alberto, clearly divided between the love he feels for his wife and his homosexual desires, declares that he is just going through a phase and that he will overcome this problem. Nonetheless he continues seeing Diego; when he suddenly goes to meet him for what will be the last time, Diego confronts him and demands that Alberto make up his mind and accept his homosexuality. Alberto, unable to do so, reacts very predictably and melodramatically by driving away on his motorcycle only to crash and die in the accident. After Alberto's death, Diego meets Elena, and they bond in grief as well as in the love the two of them felt for Alberto.

Equally implausible is the plot of *Sobrevivré* in which Marga (Emma Suárez), a beautiful girl who is pregnant and happy, loses her fiancé and the father of her baby in a car accident. With emotional and monetary problems, she is forced to get a job at a video store where she meets Iñaqui (Juan Diego Botto), a handsome gay man. They are attracted to each other instantly, although not sexually; they start seeing each other more often until their friendship becomes a love relationship. Iñaqui is open about his sexuality from the beginning, so nobody seems to be deceiving anyone. That is also why it is hard to accept that all of a sudden they are a perfect couple, and he even manages to avoid gay "temptation" a time or two before proposing to Marga. The end of the film, it is true, denies the assumption that gay men—or at least some gay men—are gay until they meet the right woman. Still it is hard to accept this simplistic story coming from one of the very few countries in the world where homosexuals can legally marry. That a man who has consciously accepted his life as a homosexual wants to run to the bed of the first available woman he encounters just because he had a bad breakup is less than credible. Not that it is impossible for gay men and women to be attracted to the opposite sex or that they would not be able to perform with or love their heterosexual counterparts in real life, but there are just not enough elements in the plot of the film to justify their relationship.

That is the same problem with *Cachorro* (*Bear Cub*, Miguel Albaladejo, 2004), a film about homosexuality, AIDS, and the gay bear subculture. The movie opens with a corpulent gay couple making love and a third partner, Pedro (José Luis García Pérez), walking in the room after taking a shower to hurry them up. He, we learn, is expecting company—his sister and her hippie partner are coming by on their way to India to drop off her young son so he can take care of him while they are away. There are no taboo topics in this family, so when the sister arrives the conversation soon turns to boyfriends, pot, sexual relations, and psychoanalysis with some predictability. Pedro does his best to adapt to his new role and tries to be very cautious in his relationships and conversations with friends around his nephew Bernanrdo (David Castillo), but the precocious boy makes it clear that he knows everything about sex and particularly about his uncle's sex life. What started as a simple favor for his sister becomes a life commitment when she is imprisoned in India for drug possession. The uncle now has to care for his nephew but first has to fight the boy's rich paternal grandmother who also wants to take care of the boy and who threatens him with revealing to the boy that he is HIV-positive.

The uncle gives in and tells the boy he really does not want him around, the boy cries, and the rich, old woman sends the "cub" to a boarding school. Later in the movie, when the boy knows the reason why his uncle gave up on him, he tells his grandmother he knew about his uncle's condition and still wanted to be with him. Years go by, the old woman dies, and the uncle and the nephew, now an adolescent, finally reunite in a tearful scene at her funeral in what wants to pass for the happy culmination of a family love that transcends all obstacles. "I did not want to stay with you at first," tells the boy to his uncle at some point in the movie, "but now is different." Now is different because the boy loves his uncle and the carefree, happy life he has with him—that seems to be the point of the movie. The problem, however, is that nothing on screen really justifies such a transformation or makes us understand the origins of that profound love, which certainly cannot be explained by the few rather dull days the boy spent with his uncle after his mother left him there. Arguably that would leave room for a more complex interpretation that insinuates incest, but that is not clearly expressed in the film. It is more likely that the director tried to make his story a contemporary one more by saying it than showing it.

Movies are not real life, of course; they are abstractions, fictions we create and use to entertain each other, to meditate on some aspects of life, or to explore political, cultural, and social issues. They are, therefore, individual observations of the world inasmuch as they are loaded with the views and experiences of whoever is responsible for their creation. Because of that, they are unavoidably more charged with ideology. Compared with earlier films touching on the same subject, such as *La Muerte de Mikel* and *El Diputado*, we sense a lack of depth in the movies made in the late 1990s—although this could very well be because those earlier films had additional political and even terrorist subplots. Nonetheless, with these films Spanish cinema managed to place itself, soon after the country's return to democracy, at the forefront of social issues conveying progressive messages.

The same applies to such movies as *Kilómetro 0* (*Kilometer 0*, Yolanda García Serrano and Juan Luis Iborra, 2000) and *Amor de Hombre* (*The Love of a Man*, Yolanda García Serrano, 1997) where the closeness between a gay man and his female best friend is jeopardized by his meeting another man and falling in love with him. This also can be said about *Más que Amor, Frenesí* (*Not Love, Just Frenzy*, Alfonso Albacete and David Menkes, 1996), perhaps the most outrageous of these films, in which the spirit of Almodóvar seems to be hovering around, and *I Love You Baby* (also by Albacete and Menkes, 2001), yet another story about a gay man becoming "straight," this time after he is hit on the head by a disco ball, and the desperate attempts of his boyfriend to "rescue" him from the arms of a woman. *Krámpack* (*Nico and Dani*, Cesc Gay, 2000), on the other hand, is a warm and touching coming-of-age story that rests too heavily on the freshness and charm of its two adolescent protagonists Dani (Fernando Ramallo) and Nico (Jordi Vilches) and cares little about story, plot, or conflict—unless our idea of conflict is minor heart breaks, secret desires, and sex between two confused youths. The film, however, manages to capture the atmosphere and the charged emotions of first sexual discoveries.

That Spain changed and developed perhaps too rapidly without having the opportunity to adjust to the consequences of such progress and prosperity is evident in a genre that has had increasing presence in Spanish cinema—illegal immigration. As in the case of the movies centering on homosexuality, these movies mostly about North African and Caribbean immigrants in search of a better life reveal a society that does not know how to face the challenges of a new global order. Examples of this are movies such as *Las Cartas de Alou* (*Alou's Letters*, Montxo Armendáriz, 1990), a story about a Moroccan immigrant who, while living illegally in Spain and surviving against all odds in a hostile land, finds solace in writing letters to his family back home depicting a happy life; *Bwana* (Imanol Uribe, 1990), a movie about the encounter between a typical Spanish family and two illegal African immigrants, a situation that brings to the surface all the tension and misunderstandings of a society that traditionally has not been on the receiving end of the migration phenomenon and seems unable and unwilling to understand its new role of receptor of cheap labor, rather than exporter of it; and *Saïd* (Llorenç Soler, 1998), which tells the story of a young undocumented Moroccan worker in Spain who befriends a girl from an upper middle-class family who decides to help him to overcome the obstacles of racism and discrimination.

More interesting is *Poniente* (*West*, Chus Gutiérrez, 2002), a movie that treats the issue of recent African immigration to Spain in a more balanced and honest way by acknowledging that Spaniards themselves were doing the same thing just a few decades earlier. *Poniente* tells the story of Lucía (Cuca Escribano) who returns to her small town after the death of her father to take care of his farm. There she meets Curro (José Coronado), her father's accountant. Curro is the son of Spanish emigrants himself who returns to the land of his parents in search of his own roots. Together Lucía and Curro confront the hostile attitude of the townspeople toward the migrant workers and join forces with them to fight prejudices and discrimination, adding much needed historical perspective and humanity to a situation that many see as a threat and a problem. *Flores de Otro Mundo* (*Flowers from Another World*, Icíar Bollaín, 1999) and *Princesas* (*Princesses*, Fernando León de Aranoa, 2005) deal with the same phenomenon but in relation to Caribbean cultures. *Flores de Otro Mundo* is the story of a group of middle-age men from a provincial Spanish town trying to marry young girls from "another" world, in this case Cuba and the Dominican Republic, who are in turn desperately trying to start a new life away from poverty even at the cost of marring older strangers to whom they have no sentimental or affective connection. *Princesas* also deals with women working illegally in Spain as prostitutes and the vulnerability in which they find themselves in a society that discriminates against them.

THE YEAR OF THE TRANSITION

Between 1975, the year of Francisco Franco's death, and 1982, the year in which the Spanish Socialist Workers Party (PSOE) came to power, is the period known as the transition, the transition from a fascist dictatorship to democracy and from an almost preindustrial economy to one of the fastest-growing European nations and the 12th most important economy in the world, just behind Mexico, the 11th, and Brazil, the 10th, according to the latest information released by the World Bank.[16] These years represent also a transition for Spanish culture and cinema going from heavy censorship to a freer environment that was in a hurry to show all kinds of movies that had been censored under Franco, regardless of their quality. Those are also the years of Cine España, an organization dedicated to promote Spanish cinema abroad. Even though there was a constant production of films in the years under Franco, in the 1970s there was a desire to produce "serious" films with sometimes-provocative themes and a reemergence of a variety of genres.

One of the first movies of the decade, *El Jardín de las Delicias* (*The Garden of Delights*, Carlos Saura, 1970), is a very acid and lucid look at the Spanish society of its time, with some surreal overtones and some nods, not so much to Buñuel but to Hieronymus Bosch, the fifteenth-century painter of nightmarish scenes that inspired the title of this film that seems ominous of the end of the Franco's regime. Rich businessman Antonio (José Luis López Vázquez) lost his memory and is paralyzed as the result of a car accident; unable to access Antonio's fortune in a Swiss bank, his relatives try to help him recover his memory through shock therapy so he can remember the number of the Swiss account. One by one they recreate several scenarios of traumatic moments in his life with the hope that he would react. The act of revisiting the traumatic past is a very clear metaphor of Spain under Franco, the national patriarch represented by Antonio, the family patriarch unable to move, yet at the center of several interpretations of the collective past.

The other big successes of the early 1970s, both in Spain and abroad, were two very different movies that deal with childhood, *Adiós, Cigüeña, Adiós* (*Goodbye, Stork, Goodbye*, Manuel Summers, 1971) and *El Espíritu de la Colmena* (*The Spirit of the Beehive*, Víctor Erice, 1973). *Adiós, Cigüeña* is a comedy about the end of innocence for a group of Spanish teenagers. Paloma (María Isabel Álvarez), a 12-year-old girl, gets pregnant by her boyfriend Arturo (Francisco Villa), who is 14. When they decide to find all the information they can about childbirth, they get a little help from their classmates. All the youngsters do their best to keep the pregnancy a secret from their parents and teachers. The comic situations resulting from trying to conceal Paloma's pregnancy are intelligent and never excuses for the cheap laughs one can expect from a coming-of-age teen movie. In the end, they learn much about life, love, and where babies come from. Similarly, *El Espíritu de la Colmena*, although with a more serious tone, deals with the world seen through the eyes of two young girls,

Isabel (Isabel Tellería) and Ana (Ana Torrent). The world they see and try to understand is post-civil war Spain. Ana becomes obsessed with Frankenstein after attending a screening of the film and believes that the monster's spirit lives in the old barn behind her house. When Ana finds a fugitive soldier hiding in the barn, she mistakes him for the monster and befriends him, mixing real life with a vivid fantasy.

This critical view of the last years of Franco's Spain is continued by Carlos Saura in two movies produced after *El Jardín*: *Ana y los Lobos* (*Ana and the Wolves*, 1972) and *La Prima Angélica* (*Cousin Angelica*, 1973). *Ana y los Lobos* is the story of a beautiful stranger, Ana (Geraldine Chaplin), who arrives at an austere Spanish mansion inhabited by an old-fashioned family composed of an old, atrocious mother and three brothers. One of the brothers is married and is the most authoritarian; the second is obsessed with the military; the third one tries to follow a fanatical, ascetic religious life. The hypocrisy and sexual repression of the men represent what Saura sees as the three biggest problems of Francoist Spain, particularly when it ends with their raping and killing of Ana. *La Prima Angélica* tells the story of a middle-aged, successful businessman from Barcelona, Luis (José Luis López Vázquez), who has to travel to the south of Spain to bury his dead mother in the family crypt. The movie is as much a trip across Spain as it is a symbolic journey to the past, in which Luis reminisces about his childhood and his obsessive relationship with his cousin Angélica, whom he idealized as a child. The story is about revisiting and "correcting" one's own past as much as it is about remembering the civil war from the perspective of the Republican side.

With the death of Franco in 1975, filmmakers managed to touch subjects that directly criticized the regime or the traditional Spanish values of family, patriarchy, and Christianity upon which that regime rested. With Franco gone, they had a lot less restrictions and censorship was relaxed, conditions that fostered a new cinema. *Furtivos* (*Poachers*, José Luis Borau, 1975), a film about the killing of the mother, is perhaps the first product of this new cinema. In love with a reform-school runaway named Milagros (Alicia Sánchez), Ángel (Ovidi Montllor) takes her home to meet his mother, Martina (Lola Gaos), a solitary woman living in the woods with whom he has a very strange relationship. Milagros, as it turns out, is actually in love with her ex-boyfriend, an escaped convict, who appears looking for her, but before they can run away together, Milagros is killed by Martina. The young man then becomes determined to kill his mother for murdering his wife. It is interesting to note that the other important movie of the same year, *Pascual Duarte* (Ricardo Franco, 1975), is also a story about matricide. Pascual Duarte (José Luis Gómez), a peasant whose alcoholic father beats his intolerable mother constantly and whose sister becomes a prostitute, goes on a killing spree before he is captured and executed by the police. The film is based on the 1942 novel *The Family of Pascual Duarte* by Nobel laureate Camilo José Cela, but unlike the novel, it centers not on the family but on Pascual, somehow turning him into an abstraction of the system.

Cría Cuervos (*Raise Ravens*, 1975), Saura's first movie after Franco, is similar to *Furtivos* and *Pascual Duarte* in that it involves a real or symbolic killing of a parent. Ana (Ana Torrent) may or may not have killed her abusive father who mistreated Ana's mother (Geraldine Chaplin), whose ghost haunts the house where Ana lives as a grown woman with her sister, aunt, and grandmother. *Cría Cuervos* is also related to *El Espíritu de la Colmena* in that a tragic world is seen through the eyes of a little girl. The fact that Ana's father dies and her mother has been dead all along makes it possible to draw comparisons between the movie and the historic moment where the father is Franco, the dead mother is the Republic, and Ana is the new Spanish generation. Intended or not, these connections are inevitable when we place the movie in its historical context.

The other notable movies of the decade are, in somehow chronological order, *La Ciudad Cremada* (*The Burned City*, Antoni Ribas, 1976), *A un Dios Desconocido* (*To an Unknown God*, Jaime Chávarri, 1977), *Camada Negra* (*Black Brood*, Manuel Gutiérrez Aragón, 1977), *Bilbao* (Bigas Luna, 1978), *El Crimen de Cuenca* (*The Crime of Cuenca*, Pilar Miró, 1979), and *El Diputado* (*The Deputy*, Eloy de la Iglesia, 1979). These last two films are of special importance because of their repercussions in Spanish society. Miró's film was one of the biggest hits of the decade, becoming a true favorite of the audience, and *El Diputado* succeeded in its treatment of sexuality and politics. As Alejandro Melero Salvador writes,

> It would be a mistake to ignore the fact that films like *El diputado* were seen by large audiences, and normally shown in neighborhood cinemas [...] And de la Iglesia did succeed in reaching a mass public. His movies transpired to be the most successful of their day and their popularity would endure, as is attested to by the fact that, ten years after it was made, fifteen million viewers saw *El diputado* when it was aired on Spanish national television.[17]

The decade of the 1980s began with an interesting metafilm, *Gary Cooper Que Estás en los Cielos* (*Gary Cooper, Who Art in Heaven*, Pilar Miró, 1980), that tells the story of a movie director (Mercedes Sampietro) confronting her own mortality and revisiting her own work and past. Also of that year were *Opera Prima* (*First Work*, Fernando Trueba, 1980), a story about first attempts in music and love; *La Muchacha de las Bragas de Oro* (*The Girl with the Golden Panties*, Vicente Aranda, 1980), a movie about a writer who retires to the country to write his memoirs and the relationship he develops with his niece and her friends, while exploring human relations, passion, and art; *El Proceso de Burgos* (*The Trial of Burgos*, Imanol Uribe, 1979), which is a part documentary, part pamphlet film that documents the activities of Euskadi Ta Askatasuna (ETA), the Basque group seeking independence from Spain; and, as we already mentioned, the first feature film of Almodóvar, *Pepi, Luci, Bom y Otras Chicas del Montón*.

The following year, Saura presented his first film of the dance series, *Bodas de Sangre* (*Blood Wedding*, 1981), inspired by the play of García Lorca, and Imanol Uribe continues his explorations of ETA and its conflictive relationship with the Spanish government in *La Fuga de Segovia* (*Escape from Segovia*, 1981), the fictitious story of 30 Basque "terrorists" who escape from prison and seek refuge in France before they are pardoned in 1970 by King Juan Carlos. *Patrimonio Nacional* (*National Patrimony*, Luis García Berlanga, 1981) is also a movie about the nation and its old institutions—its decrepit aristocracy in this case. *La Colmena* (*The Hive*, Mario Camus, 1982), based on a novel by Cela, and *Demonios en el Jardín* (*Demons in the Garden*, Manuel Gutiérrez Aragón, 1982) turn an unforgiving eye to everyday life under Franco with its treasons, lies, and the struggles. *Volver a Empezar* (*To Begin Again*, José Luis Garci, 1982) is one of the most important movies of the decade because it was the first one to be awarded an Oscar for best Foreign Language Film. Also interesting is *Maria Antonieta* (1982), a film paid for by the Mexican government as an attempt to revitalize its national cinema using the name of this prestigious Spanish director; the film was a biography of Antonieta Rivas Mercado, a free-spirited, aristocratic Mexican beauty who, rejected by her lover during the Mexican Revolution, killed herself in Notre Dame Cathedral in Paris at the age of 30.

Carmen (1983) is the second and perhaps the most popular of the dance films of Carlos Saura; the title says it all. *Las Bicicletas Son Para el Verano* (*Bicycles Are for Summer*, Jaime Chávarri, 1983), *El Sur* (*The South*, Víctor Erice, 1983), and *Los Santos Inocentes* (*The Holy Innocents*,

Mario Camus, 1984) continue the tradition of social criticism of Spanish life under Franco with a focus on class struggles and the new versus an old bourgeoisie. *La Linea del Cielo* (*Skyline*, Fernando Colomo, 1983) is an interesting, funny movie about a Spanish émigré in New York City, a movie that dissects and mocks the Spanish male psychology and his artistic aspirations, as well as cultural misunderstandings, with tasteful discretion. *Tasio* (Montxo Armendáriz, 1984), almost an anthropological view to the life of a Basque peasant and the life and culture of the village, is an excellent example of regional and realistic cinema. If *El Dipiutado* pushed the envelope in the 1970s by mixing politics and alternative sexualities, *La Muerte de Mikel* (*Mikel's Death*, Imanol Uribe, 1984) went even further by adding terrorism, misogyny, transexuality, and separatism to the already volatile cocktail, making it really explosive. Politically active, married, and member of a prominent local family headed by a matriarch, Mikel (Imanol Arias) has to confront ancient prejudices when he gets sentimentally involved with a transvestite. When he appears dead one morning, wife, mother, party, and church are all suspects since they all had enough reasons to want to get rid of him. Uribe has said that it is no mystery that Mikel was killed by his mother, which the last scene confirms. Nonetheless, the possibility that it could have been somebody else adds richness to the film.

La Corte del Faraón (*The Pharaoh's Court*, José Luis García Sánchez, 1985) brings back some of the old genres, particularly zarzuela and popular comedy, to the big screen with a serious purpose—to criticize and mock the censorship prevalent during Franco's regime. In the same revisionist vein, we find *El Año en que Murió Franco* (*The Year Franco Died*, Gonzalo Suárez, 1985) and an excellent exploration of psychological terror, the thriller *Tras el Cristal* (*In a Glass Cage*, Agustín Villaronga, 1985), a film that can be seen very easily as a reference to Franco's Spain in its exploration of sadism, authoritarianism, and sexual perversion. The same year Saura made his third dance film, *Amor Brujo* (*Love, The Magician*, 1986); Vicente Aranda brought to the screen the famous novel by Luis Martín-Santos, *Tiempo de Silencio* (*Time of Silence*, 1986); and Fernando Fernán Gómez presented *Viaje a Ninguna Parte* (*Trip to Nowhere*, 1986), a modern picaresque story in which we see alive and well the same old spirit of the tradition of the Spanish pícaro and his adventures that gave us such classics as Don Quixote and Sancho Panza.

Other important films produced in the decade of the 1980s are *El Crack* (*The Crash*, José Luis Garci, 1981), *La Vaquilla* (*The Calf*,

Luis García Berlanga, 1985), *Sé Infiel y no Mires con Quién* (*Be Unfaithful Regardless of Whom*, Fernando Trueba, 1986), *Lola* (Bigas Luna, 1986), *El Dorado* (Carlos Saura, 1987), *El Lute: Camina o Revienta* (*Run for Your Life*, Vicente Aranda, 1987), *La Casa de Bernarda Alba* (*The House of Bernarda Alba*, Mario Camus, 1987), *Asignatura Aprovada* (*Course Completed*, José Luis Garci, 1987), *Divinas Palabras* (*Divine Words*, José Luis García Sánchez, 1987), *Si Te Dicen que Caí* (*If They Tell You I Fell*, Vicente Aranda, 1989), *¡Ay Carmela!* (Carlos Saura, 1990), *Las Cosas del Querer* (*The Things of Love*, Jaime Chávarri, 1990), *El Vuelo de la Paloma* (*The Flight of the Dove*, José Luis García Sánchez, 1990), and *Las Edades de Lulú* (*The Ages of Lulu*, Bigas Luna, 1990).

THE YEARS OF FRANCO AND BEFORE

Even though cinema arrived early in Spain, it is perhaps not until the decade of the 1950s that we can talk about a real film industry. The first film shown in Spain was on May 15, 1896, at Madrid's Festival of San Isidro, and the first Spanish moving picture appeared that very same year called *Salida de Misa de Doce en la Iglesia del Pilar de Zaragoza* (*Leaving Midday Mass at the Church of Our Lady of Pilar in Zaragoza*) filmed by Eduardo Jimeno. These pictures, like many other first attempts elsewhere, had to do with filming everyday life and customs in order to amuse citizens with images of themselves. By 1908 there were enough moving pictures and fictional films with plots and characters that we can properly call them narrative films. The first movies were adaptations of literary works and plays such as *El Hotel Eléctrico* (*The Electric Hotel*, Segundo de Chomón, 1905) and adaptations of José Zorrilla's *Don Juan Tenorio* (Ricardo Baños, 1908), as well as the first version of *Don Quijote* (Narciso Cuyàs, 1908). Following these films, versions of Pedro Calderón de la Barca's *El Alcalde de Zalamea* (*The Mayor of Zalamea*, 1915) and Miguel de Cervantes's *La Gitanilla* (*The Little Gypsy*, 1915) appeared, both adapted for the screen by Adrià Gual.

Not only were the classics of the language adapted to the silent screen; also adapted were more modern literary works and examples of pop culture, such as Vicente Blasco Ibáñez's *Sangre y Arena* (*Blood and Sand*, 1916) and zarzuela, the typical Spanish musical genre, with the first version of *La Vervena de la Paloma* (*The Carnival of the Dove*, José Buchs, 1921). Two of the most important directors of early Spanish cinema made their debut in those years, Florián Rey with

La Revoltosa (*The Mischievous Girl*, 1925) and *Lazarillo de Tormes* (1925) and Benito Perojo with *Boy* (1926) and *El Negro Que Tenía el Alma Blanca* (*The Black Man Who Had a White Soul*, 1927). Other films were produced during the first two decades of the twentieth century, but without a doubt the most important Spanish silent film is the surrealist collaboration of Luis Buñuel and Salvador Dalí, *Un Chien Andalou* (*An Andalusian Dog*, 1928). With this collection of absurd images, some of the most memorable in cinema history, such as the eye being cut or the ants invading a hand, Spanish silent film comes to the end. After that, Buñuel would film only one more film in Spain, his documentary *Las Hurdes, Tierra sin Pan* (*Land without Bread*) in 1932, before he could return with the film *Viridiana* in 1961, a film that could not be seen in Spain until 1977 despite winning the Palm D'ore at the Cannes Film Festival.

Florián Rey continued making movies including his interesting *La Aldea Maldita* (*The Cursed Village*, 1930); *Nobleza Baturra* (*The Nobility of the Peasantry*, 1935), a movie that with his folkloric characters and situations as well as its sentimental view of the country folk became a sensation; and *Morena Clara* (*Brunette, Not Too Dark*, 1936), which also became a huge box-office hit and solidified the career of Imperio Argentina, whose launching he had actually helped with *La Hermana San Sulpicio* (*Sister San Sulpicio*, 1928). Perojo's movies of the period were *Susana Tiene un Secreto* (*Susana Has a Secret*, 1933) and his sound version of *El Negro Que Tenía el Alma Blanca* (1934). The following year he did another version of *La Verbena de la Paloma*, but this time with sound. Perojo was interested in musicals and *La Verbena* was perhaps one of the most accomplished films of the period, a film in which the characters and scenes were more convincing in their theatricality and, unlike those of *Nobleza Baturra*, not mere folkloric excuses. Perojo recreated the Madrid of the nineteenth century and made it believable; he "was convinced that the operetta was an expression of living popular culture, representative of the public and capable of reaching it, even when the librettos were bad or the music of average quality."[18]

Along with Perojo and Rey, the other important pioneers were José Buchs and Fernando Delgado as well as José Luis Sáenz de Heredia who made his debut in 1934 with *Patricio Miró una Estrella* (*Patricio Saw a Star*). This director is important above all because eight years later he produced the quintessential Francoist film *Raza*, a film that stands alone as the only political movie of the first decades of Spanish cinema, which were marked by folkloric comedies and musicals.

The decade of the 1930s was also the decade of the Spanish Civil War (1936–1939), and in those few years there was no film production, with the exception of some documentaries, many of which were made by foreigners fighting for or sympathizing with the Republic. However, soon after Franco came to power, film production resumed. During the years of Franco, Spain kept a very active film industry; however, most of its films, particularly during the first couple of decades, were films that purposely or not ignored political issues, except some propaganda films. Most of the productions were folkloric comedies or family dramas seeking to reinforce the values of the dominant ideology of family, country, and Catholicism.

Of those considered "propaganda," the most famous are *Los Últimos de Filipinas* (*The Last Ones in the Philippines*, Antonio Román, 1945), a grandiloquent epic of a group of soldiers during the Spanish-American war, and *Raza* (*The Spirit of a Race*, José Luis Sáenz de Heredia, 1942), the story of a traditional Spanish family disintegrated by the Civil War when the four brothers follow different paths either in the army, the church, and fighting for or against the Republic. Grave and pompous, these films praise the most stereotypical Spanish values. *Raza* is famous in addition because it was written by Francisco Franco himself under the assumed name of Jaime de Andrade and for containing vaguely autobiographic elements. Besides Román and Heredia, it is important to mention Juan de Orduña and Rafael Gil as some of the most active film directors of the postwar years, years of a cinema that only now is being revised and seen as more complex. Orduña directed some of the most popular films of the 1940s and 1950s, among them *Locura de Amor* (*The Craziness of Love*, 1948), *Alba de América* (*The Dawn of America*, 1953), and *El Último Cuplé* (*The Last Song*, 1957).

Alba de América subscribes to the Francoist ideology of a heroic Hispanic spirit that transcends all obstacles in its messianic mission during the discovery and colonization of the Americas. But *El Último Cuplé* was the movie that made him famous beyond Spain and that catapulted Sarita Montiel to stardom. By the end of the decade of the 1940s, and with the same spirit of Hispanism, some coproductions were made, mostly with Mexico. In the words of Fernando Alonso Barahona, the musical genre was enriched thanks to "collaborations with the great myths of Mexican music," particularly Jorge Negrete who made the successful *Jalisco Canta en Sevilla* (*Jalisco Sings in Seville*, Fernando de Fuentes, 1948) and *Teatro Apolo* (*Apollo Theater*, Rafael Gil, 1950), "as well as the great Pedro Infante, an excellent singer and actor who made *Gitana Tenías que ser* (*You Had to Be a Gypsy*)"[19] in 1953.

As Steven Marsh and Parvati Nair write in the introduction to *Gender and Spanish Cinema*, the general view of the films made in the first years of the dictatorship of Franco is that of mere propaganda; however, this is a preconception that is "not only founded on misinterpretation [but that] ignores the potential for pluralistic readings of the films of the 1940s."[20] Nonetheless, we can agree with them in that "Spanish cinema of 'quality' commenced after 1950 with the emergence of the first promotion of the Madrid Film School, among whose most celebrated members were Juan Antonio Bardem and Luis García Berlanga."[21] Previously to the 1950s, the film industry in Spain was "concerned with topics that met the approval of successive Francoist governments: military heroism, Spain's grandiloquent history, a dated religiosity, revived anti-communism, or the golden-egg laying goose of tourism," according to José Luis Borau, who mentions as well that the themes chosen were very distant from the audiences. "The order of the day was either zany Hollywood-style comedies, stilted imitations of Mexican melodramas, or hard-hitting neorealist narratives,"[22] styles that were highly admired.

The 1950s saw a shift in the themes and production of films. If the previous decades were signaled by musicals, comedies, historic epics, imitations of Hollywood films, and coproductions with Mexico, the 1950s saw a resurgence of a sort of social themes and an interest in Italian neorealism. Since the 1940s some directors were already suggesting a far more democratic society. But it was at the beginning of the 1950s when, perhaps without even knowing it, García Escudero, a member of the most progressive group of the regime, who was also the general director of the Department of Cinema, "took an administrative decision that ended the exaggerated nationalism and the pompousness of Cifesa," according to John Hopewell, when he allocated a small amount of money for a film called *Una Cubana en España* (*A Cuban Girl in Spain*, Luis Bayón Herrera, 1951),[23] a movie that signaled a tiredness with the pretentiousness of the official films or even the light coproductions with Mexico.

It seems as if the Spanish public was ready for a more realistic look at its everyday life; therefore, films such as *Surcos* (*Furrows*, José Antonio Nieves Conde, 1951), *Esa Pereja Feliz* (*That Happy Couple*, Luis García Berlanga, 1951), or *Día tras Día* (*Day after Day*, Antonio del Amo, 1951) seemed more appropriate. But it was Luis García Berlanga's *¡Bienvenido, Mister Marshall!* (*Welcome, Mr. Marshall*, 1953)—

a satirical view of the dreams and needs of the inhabitants of a dusty town so desperate to get help from the American Marshall Plan for the reconstruction of Europe after World War II that they decided to perform their Spanishness according to what they thought was expected of them—the film showed the possibility of being critical of Spanish society and still be commercially successful. As Borau writes, "In Spain it was precisely the auteurs who, above all, after the screening of ¡Bienvenido Mr. Marshall! in the spring of 1953, accepted responsibility for guiding and redefining the film industry to which they belonged,"[24] redirecting, that is, the cinema of Spain.

If ¡Bienvenido, Mister Marshall! had already shown the possibilities of a new cinema, its consolidation became official with La Muerte de un Ciclista (The Death of a Cyclist, Juan Antonio Bardem, 1955), a film that denounced the hypocrisy of the decadent bourgeoisie. On their way back home after a secret love encounter, married beauty María José (Lucia Bosé) and playboy Juan (Alberto Closas) run over a peasant man riding along the road on his bicycle. Afraid that their love affair could be known if the incident becomes public, they decide not to stop and leave the man to die on the road. Soon they forget the incident and continue their frivolous life with the confidence that nobody saw them; however, an anonymous letter reveals that there was a witness. The movie then turns into a game of cat and mouse that will show only the ugliest side of this class. Equally critical of the period are other movies, such as Calle Mayor (Main Street, Juan Antonio Bardem, 1956), El Cochecito (The Little Car, Marco Ferreri, 1960), and Los Golfos (The Hooligans, Carlos Saura, 1960). The two exceptions to this social concern are two very popular films in and out of Spain that represent the two extremes of the cinema that was predominant in the previous years: Marcelino, Pan y Vino (Marcelino, Bread, and Wine, Ladislao Vajda, 1955) and El Último Cuplé. If El Último Cuplé can be considered an "españolada," or an exaggerated folkloric piece, Marcelino is the oversentimentalized view of faith. Marcelino (Pablito Calvo), an orphan who was raised by a group of monks in a monastery, finds by accident, while playing, a crucifix in the attic of the chapel. Moved by compassion, the little boy takes Jesus off the cross and begins to care for him, visiting in the afternoons, bringing him bread and wine, and carrying on conversations with him. When one of the monks decides to spy on the boy to find out where he disappears all afternoon, he witnesses a miracle—the boy being taken to heaven.

During the next two decades, Spanish cinema begins imitating the cinema being produced elsewhere in Europe, particularly in places more progressive such as France and Scandinavia, but without the freedom of those societies in matter of sexuality or political and social equality. The so-called New Spanish Cinema of those decades, according to Román Gubern, "was one of the first and more relevant sub-genres in our production because it pretended to be auteur cinema."[25] And this auteurist tradition, we could say, had begun with the films of the 1950s. Interestingly enough, for Gubern this is far from being a triumph because in other European nations a "new cinema" meant freedom of expression and experimentation, but in Spain it meant a mixing of genres and styles with the chief purpose of eluding censors. "Lacking *Last Tango in Paris*, *Emanuelle*, or *Contes Immoraux*, films in which men and women get naked and have sex the 'the way God intended them to do,' Spanish cinema has been constrained to exploit to the fullest sexual perversions as caricatures and jokes."[26]

Not everybody agrees with this view of the Spanish cinema of those years, and such critics as Ronald Schwartz consider everything produced before 1950 less authentic. It is not until the 1950s, according to him, when a "New Spanish Cinema was borne as a protest over General Francisco Franco's policies [and to the] imitative Hollywood 'white telephone' school of Spanish cinema."[27] Schwartz is talking about the mainstream films that are considered the beginning of classical Spanish cinema, not to the New Cinema of the 1960s and 1970s, particularly those represented by Carlos Saura, Víctor Erice, Gutiérrez Aragón, and Chávarri. In any case, it is clear that the films of the 1960s and particularly the 1970s confirmed the status of Spanish cinema as a world cinema and paved the way for the latest success of directors such as Almodóvar and Amenábar.

NOTES

1. John Hopewell, "Art and Lack of Money: The Crisis of the Spanish Film Industry, 1997–1990," *Quarterly Review of Film and Video* 13 (1991): 115.

2. Fernando Méndez-Leite, "De Almodóvar a Amenábar," in *Las Generaciones del Cine Español*, ed. Juan Cobos (Madrid: España Nuevo Milenio, 2000), 93.

3. Ibid., 94.

4. Hopewell, "Art and Lack of Money," 115.

5. If it started in the 1950s as Hopewell says, it is true that it started with force, since already in 1966 an article in *Time* magazine mentions Spain as one of the fastest-growing countries in Europe; nobody is more surprised

than Franco: "For until six years ago, Spain was isolated from most of the world, brooding, stewing in its evaporating juice. Foreign investment was unwanted and restricted, and Franco was as openly anticapitalist as he was anticommunist." "The Awakening Land," *Time*, January 21, 1966, http://www.time.com/time/magazine/article/0,9171,835066-2,00.html.

6. See Hopewell's "Art and Lack of Money" where he writes, "The key factor determining the fragility of the Spanish film industry has been the belatedness of the country's industrial revolution, which only really takes off in the late 1950s. Without a moneyed middle class and a finely calibrated, continuous social scale, class differences in early twentieth century Spain, became gaping class divides," p. 115.

7. Ibid., 118.

8. Méndez-Leite, "De Almodóvar a Amenábar," 94.

9. Garan Holcombe, "Spanish Cinema: Almodóvar and Amenábar," *California Literary Review*, March 26, 2007, http://calitreview.com/topics/movies/27/.

10. Ibid.

11. Ibid.

12. Méndez-Leite, "De Almodóvar a Amenábar," 96.

13. Critic Fernando Alonso Barahona writes, "The sociocultural policies of the socialist government of Felipe González have been characterized by its tendencies to rigid and manipulative thinking as well as by a scandalous distribution of subventions to entities with a similar ideological affinity," 109 (my translation).

14. Celestino Deleyto, "Motherland: Space, Femininity, and Spanishness in *Jamón, Jamón* (Bigas Luna, 1992)," in *Spanish Cinema. The Auteurist Tradition*, ed. Peter William Evans (Oxford: Oxford University Press, 1999), 270.

15. Rob Stone, "¡Victoria? A Modern Magdalene," in *Gender and Spanish Cinema*, ed. Steven Marsh and Parvati Nair (Oxford: Berg, 2004), 167.

16. Roberto González Amador, "México: Undécima Economía, pero Ocupa Lugar 76 en poder de compra," *La Jornada*, April 12, 2008, http://www.jornada.unam.mx/2008/04/12/index.php?section=economia&article=023n1eco.

17. Alejandro Melero Salvador, "New Sexual Politics in the Cinema of the Transition to Democracy: de la Iglesia' El diputado (1978)," ed. Steven Marsh and Parvati Nair, *Gender and Spanish Cinema*, 96.

18. See Román Gubern, "Benitos Perojo's *La Verbena de la Paloma*," in *Modes of Representation in Spanish Cinema*, ed. Genaro Talens and Santos Zunzunegui (Minneapolis: University of Minnesota Press, 1998), 50.

19. Fernando Alonso Barahona, *Biografía del Cine Español* (Barcelona: Centro de Investigaciones Literarias Españolas e Hispanoamericanas, 1992), 30.

20. Marsh and Parvati, *Gender and Spanish Cinema*, 4.

21. Ibid., 5.

22. José Luis Borau, "Prologue: The Long March of Spanish Cinema towards Itself," in *Spanish Cinema, The Auteurist Tradition*, ed. Peter William Evan (Oxford: Oxford University Press, 1999), xix.

23. John Hopewell, *El Cine Español Después de Franco* (Madrid: Ediciones El Arquero, 1989), 14.

24. Borau, "Prologe," xviii.

25. Román Gubern, "Benito Perojo's *La Verbena de la Paloma*," 12.

26. Román Gubern, "Prólogo," in Equipo Cartelera Turia, *Cine Español, Cine de Sugéneros* (Valencia: Fernando Torres Editor, 1974), 14.

27. Ronald Schwartz, *The Great Spanish Films* (Metuchen, NJ: The Scarecrow, 1991), xiii.

CHAPTER 2

The Films of
Pedro Almodóvar

On June 17, 2008, the British newspaper the *Guardian* (Manchester) published a brief article by scholar and renowned British Hispanist Paul Julian Smith titled "The Curse of Almodovar,"[1] in which the author declared that even though Spain produces some 100 films a year, British audiences still keep associating its cinema with only one name—Pedro Almodóvar. Therefore, he continues, any movie from Spain that does not come with the "slogan" identifying it as a product of Almodóvar is very hard to sell. It is ironic, according to Smith, that "one super-sized name can capsize a national film industry by monopolizing international interest."[2] This statement provoked the wrath of Almodóvar who immediately responded with a letter to the daily asking it not to blame him for what was clearly a British problem. "It is unfair and very stupid to blame me for the lack of Spanish movies in the screens of the United Kingdom," he declared, particularly when we consider that the quota of movies in languages other than English in that nation is only 1.3 percent.[3] He admits that his name could help to promote Spanish films, but is firm in pointing out that the responsibility for making movies available to the British audiences is that of the distributors, not of the moviemakers.

In his letter, Almodóvar thanks Smith for writing about him and for using his name to call attention to a problem—which was exactly what the scholar had set out to do—however, he reiterates that this could have been done in a less sensationalistic way and without damaging his image. What is interesting about this incident is the immediate reaction of the director considering that the mentioning of his name is restricted to the first lines of the article and the rest of the text is about promoting the 2008 London Spanish Film Festival, which offered a variety of films, including homage to Fernando Fernán Gómez. In fact, Smith was more interested in pointing out the diversity of Spanish films demonstrated by the year's festival, which included a combination of idiosyncratic stories that showed a clear influence from Hollywood, to the point that he asks rhetorically if Spanish cinema is at the service of "exotic local color or transnational genre pics." The answer, of course, is that "Spanish cinema can successfully serve both." Smith's provocative intention is, obviously, to encourage the British public to look for Spanish films and to take a glance at "what lies beyond planet Pedro," not to suggest that people stop watching the films of Almodóvar.[4]

However, the idea of Almodóvar's predominance in Spanish cinema is by no means rare, as we mentioned in the previous chapter. Fernando Méndez-Leite had already observed in 2000, for example, that "[t]oday, Spanish cinema is identified with Pedro Almodóvar, who after his first attempts came close to perfection with his *¿Qué He Hecho Yo para Merecer Esto?*, a skillful combination of comedy and melodrama in which he offers a lively portrait of a 'maruja' beaten by life in the heart of a typical working-class neighborhood of Madrid."[5] What prompted Almodóvar's response to Smith's article seems a mystery and, in the opinion of many, an overreaction. Why did he react so defensively to an article that only briefly mentioned him, and that by no means was disrespectful or offensive? Reading his response, one cannot help but wonder if Almodóvar is mistakenly thinking he needs the extra publicity, something clearly absurd if we consider that he is at the peak of his career and as active as ever.[6]

On the other hand, his attitude seems very consistent with the picture we can draw from Marsha Kinder's account of an encounter with him in November 2003 when she was invited to a conference co-sponsored by Almodóvar's production company El Deseo and organized "to launch the new Almodóvar studies center at UCLM, a relatively new Spanish school located near his native village in La Mancha."[7] On this occasion, he seemed a self-centered, self-promoting man obsessed with success who tried to manipulate the public opinion about his work and "to demonstrate his status as a major world-class auteur to those Spanish critics and scholars who, despite (or perhaps because of) his enormous commercial and critical success worldwide, are still reluctant to take his work seriously.[8] To the event were invited the most important international scholars who had already written favorably about Almodóvar, including Paul Julian Smith himself. According to Kinder, "What was most fascinating about the conference was the way Almodóvar and his production company were blatantly controlling the auteurist discourse surrounding his films. This conference revealed their masterful negotiation of a complex network of local, regional, national, and international relations within the changing global film scene and the several ironies this mastery generates."[9]

For her, this manipulation of the discourse was obviously proof of globalization and the postmodern condition of contemporary cinema, despite the fact that Almodóvar "has remained committed to making movies only in Spanish and only in Spain, where he has total artistic control."[10] This is something that, ironically, does not make his work insular, particularly because of its intertextuality with Hollywood films and his connection with Latin America. Some of the characters in his movies, for example, are Cuban or Argentine émigrés to Spain, and some of the leading roles of his movies have gone to Latin American actors such as Cecilia Roth and Gael García Bernal, not to mention his constant use of Mexican and Cuban music. In this way, Almodóvar seems to be ahead of his contemporary fellow Spaniards by remaining global and competitive and yet faithful to his Spanish roots. That he is capable of making headline news if he writes a letter to a British newspaper is further testimony of this global condition and of the importance of the persona he has been cultivating for decades, a persona that is impossible to separate from his own movies. That alone is a wonderful testimony to filmmaking and to the intimate relationship between memory, life, and representation that all directors have dealt with one way or another, but that only few have been able to manipulate without sounding preachy or snobbish. As David Denby writes in *The New Yorker*, "Surely there has never been a world-famous director whose work is essentially camp"; therefore, we can assume he is "something unprecedented in movie history."[11]

In the previous chapter we mentioned that it was unfair to consider only one person the representative of an entire nation, culture, or industry. And it seems a contradiction that the second chapter of this book is dedicated to Almodóvar. However, the case of Pedro Almodóvar is unique, and it would be impossible not to take his huge presence as a point of reference in any meditation on Spanish film. For starters, no other Spanish director, and very few from other countries, has been at once a summary and point of departure in his or her national film traditions. Local and international, essentially Spanish and pluricultural, melodramatic and postmodern, camp and deeper in his understanding of human condition; Almodóvar has shown a particular ability to build not only a body of cinematic works that transformed his culture, but a brand name that allows him absolute control of his work and his creativity, while maintaining a commercial image that has proven to be as profitable as the likes of say Madonna or Michael Jackson. While it is important to keep in mind that Almodóvar is not the only Spanish director active today, he is a unique case not only in the history of Spanish film, but also in the history of world cinema.

AN ESTHETICS OF BAD TASTE

Films and life are often intertwined in the works of Almodóvar. But it is the movies themselves that make us pay attention to him; therefore, they are the first and foremost things to analyze when writing about this Spanish director. As we mentioned before, the feature film that inaugurated Almodóvar's prolific career was *Pepi, Luci, Bom y Otras Chicas del Montón* (*Pepi, Luci, Bom and Other Girls on the Heap*, 1980), a movie that presents almost point by point the effervescence of Spanish society in the 1980s. This being also the first exercise that would develop a style, it is also inevitably a movie that looks and feels amateurish and improvised, although we could argue that this carelessness could have been on purpose. Almodóvar's characters and dramatic situations are often introduced as caricatures that, then, develop in unexpected ways: "From its opening shot, *Pepi, Luci, Bom* reveals its deceptively simple yet irreverent approach to making meaning and to film-making itself,"[12] according to Ernesto Acevedo-Muñoz. The story is simple, although complex in its ramifications, Pepi (Carmen Maura) is an average girl who enjoys rock music and comic books and is saving her virginity to sell it for a considerable amount of money. Like any girl of her generation, the movie suggests, Pepi likes marijuana, which she grows in her own apartment. When a neighbor who is a cop enters her apartment using the excuse of the marijuana, he rapes her not before an outrageous exchange of words.

Pepi, furious because she will not be able to sell her virginity, as she had hoped, decides to avenge her wrongdoing. In the process she introduces the audience to "the emancipated atmosphere of a post-Franco Madrid populated by gays, lesbians, and transvestites, all of whom implicitly reject the phallocentric political and social order"[13] of the old Spain represented by the rapist cop. Caricatures or not, what is evident from that first film is that something new was going on in Spain and that this movie was mirroring those changes.

Exaggerated, outrageous, and drawing heavily on the 1980s punk sensibility, the movie presents a Madrid that only a few years earlier would have been unthinkable, an underworld of sex, drugs, defiance to authority, and political apathy, much in synchrony with the rebelliousness against authority and the establishment of the earlier British punk scene, albeit as the result of different historical circumstances.

This influence has been mentioned before numerous times, noticing how important the punk scene was for the Madrid of *la movida*. In fact, scholar Mark Allinson has called this time a time in which Spaniards had too much time and no political convictions or responsibilities.[14] In this case of course, whether it is openly acknowledged or not, the attitude of frenzy is a response to the world of authority and repression of the previous system, a sort of getting back at them, and therefore can be considered a political statement. When Pepi seeks vengeance, she gets help from her friend Bom (Alaska) who seduces Luci (Eva Siva), the wife of the cop who raped Pepi, who turns out to be a repressed masochist who tells Bom she likes to be treated "like a bitch" after she urinates on her. These are no longer the suffering mothers or innocent, provincial virgins of previous years; these are women who find solidarity among themselves and among the alternative cultures of the city.

In fact, the city is important because it clearly opposes itself and the culture it fosters to the Francoist discourse of the true Spain, the Catholic, patriarchal Spain of the small towns. As Marvin D'Lugo points out, "Characters like Pepi, the heroine of Almodóvar's first film, and Riza, the hero of the second, have come to Madrid looking for a freedom obviously denied them elsewhere."[15] This is a theme we see again and again in Almodóvar's films, a theme that is summarized in the tension between small town life and family versus big city (notably Madrid) and personal freedom. The characters of Almodóvar's first films are men and women who fight back and gang up against injustice and abusive authority, thanks to the sense of solidarity the city provides to the outcasts and to anybody who is different and who has been isolated in his or her village. This is true particularly in *Laberinto de Pasiones* (*Labyrinth of Passion*, 1982), *Entre Tinieblas* (*Dark Habits*, 1983), and *¿Qué He Hecho yo para Merecer Esto?* (*What Have I Done to Deserve This?*, 1984), but remains visible all through the master's career.

These films belong to the formative period of the director and are the ones that more virulently react against the previous Spain, setting the norm for the future Spanish culture. Time and time again any critic or scholar who has written about Almodóvar has mentioned the statement of the director that he makes movies as if Franco never existed, something that only confirms that he is directing and writing against him only because he did exist. These films share similar characteristics, such as an obsession with sex, drugs, and Madrid, the hedonist capital of self-indulgence. and therefore a symbol of freedom. That has prompted Acevedo-Muñoz to call it an aesthetic of bad taste. There is another element they have in common and that they share with the movies from his next phases: an interest in old American melodramas, particularly the tearjerkers or women's pictures. Rather than turning to the recent past of his country, as most of his contemporaries, Almodóvar turns to Hollywood for an alternative—and very personal—imagination more in tune with his gay sensibility.

He finds this sensibility in old melodramas, something in itself very subversive since, according to Kathleen M. Vernon, "his importation of *American* melodrama into *Spanish* film cast the light of suspicion onto the way both film industries have mythified the representation of historically contingent categories (such as gender and socioeconomic class) as natural, essential 'identities' in their implicit construction of a larger, national self-identity."[16] However, far from just taking these melodramas at face value, Almodóvar takes apart every single piece of the crying machinery to try to understand how it works, with the curiosity and perversion of an evil child prodigy. "Grounded in a moral and thematic Manichaeism, melodrama has often been read as constructing a fictional world of unambiguous absolutes, of villains vs. victims, shadows vs. light."[17] Almodóvar, on the contrary, uses it to explore "the breakdown of old hierarchies and the resulting dissolution of barriers and boundaries in a post-patriarchal, post-religious Spain."[18] Perhaps he said it best in an interview he gave to Marsha Kinder in 1987 in which she mentions how she finds fascinating the ability of the director to move quickly from one genre to another, to which he responds, "Just as you say, in my films everything is just at the border of parody," since as he adds, speaking of melodrama, "I don't respect the boundaries of the genre, I mix it with other things."[19]

LAWS OF DESIRE

This particular use of melodrama is the key to understanding much of the genius of Almodóvar. On the one hand, he uses the conventions of the genre to establish the story and its exaggeration to allow the audience to keep its distance through irony, but on the other when it seems that the movie is nothing but a postmodern parody that disarticulates—or deconstructs, to use a term in vogue—melodrama, it suddenly sends us back to square one by taking it seriously. If this is evident since the first movies of Almodóvar, the ones that took it to extreme are *Matador* (1986), *La Ley del Deseo* (*Law of Desire*, 1987), and *¡Átame!* (*Tie Me Up! Tie Me Down!*, 1989). In *Matador* we see, as in his previous films, a display of two stereotypes of Spanish culture: machismo and bullfighting. The twist here is that the sexuality and violence associated with this manly Spanish pastime are reverted to the main female character, who turns out to be one of the two *matadores* (killers) in the film. This picture, which focuses on the popular images of the bullfighter, according to Marvin D'Lugo, "Instead of repeating trite stereotypes reformulates the bullfighter clichés into a new Spanish myth, one in which passion and death are given a contemporary meaning."[20] It is more significant that a woman, not a man, behaves in a predatory way.

At the opening of the film we see a man masturbating in front of a television set while he is watching women being killed and dismembered. These horrific scenes are opposed to those of the same man, Diego (Nacho Martínez), a matador, teaching his pupils how to kill a bull and referring to it as an art of seduction. One of these young men, Ángel (Antonio Banderas), gets so aroused listening to his master that he even looks at his instructor's crotch with excitement and confusion. Strict religious upbringing and repressed sexuality become central themes in the story with the introduction of Ángel. But the real subversive element is the parallel story of a woman serial killer, María Cardenal (Assumpta Serna), who, like Diego, gets turned on with violence; she kills her victims as if they were bulls sticking a long hairpin in the back of their necks at the moment of orgasm. It is just a matter of time before María and Diego meet each other and realize that their perversions complement each other. When that happens, they are determined to kill each other at the moment of orgasm in what seems the perfect end for both of them. "They seemed so happy," the police officer in charge of the murder investigation says of their corpses. The film "ends in an overly dramatic, clichéd romantic setting that is clearly a parody of itself."[21]

Equally dependent on the tension among power, sexuality, and violence, *¡Átame!* was hugely controversial when it came out because of its subject—the rape and kidnapping of a beautiful woman who ends up falling in love with her captor. In reality, what was more controversial was the fact that the film almost seemed to validate the acquiring of love and family by any means possible, even if it involved violence and rape. Or as Rob Stone has written, the film is the story of Marina (Victoria Abril), a "reformed degenerate in a thriller/horror film, redeemed by the awakening of her innate romanticism."[22] But the same can be said of Ricky (Antonio Banderas), the young man who, obsessed with Marina, kidnaps her and takes care of her. An ex-mental patient, Ricky leaves the asylum that has been his home all his life to "work and have a family, like any normal guy," according to his answer to his psychologist. The desperation with which he seeks this bourgeois ideal of a family and a decent, normal job is clearly a parody of the middle-class aspiration in Spain under Franco. At the same time it is very sincere in its desire of love and happiness.

In the end Marina, Ricky, and Marina's sister, Lola (Loles León) become a family, not a conventional one, but a family. In this movie, according to Acevedo-Muñoz, "Almodóvar deals very directly with the theme of the difficulty of Spain's cultural transitions in the 1980s. ¡Atame! Has an unambiguously hopeful ending, with the trio of protagonists reconciled and driving into the sunset."[23] As we saw before in Almodóvar, melodrama gives way to parody, which in turn, takes us back to melodrama very swiftly. Something similar happens in Carne Trémula (Live Flesh, 1997), the only film that mentions Francoist Spain. But by far the most interesting and extreme of these movies is La Ley del Deseo, the story of a love that transcends all kinds of obstacles and that ends tragically. It is the love that a young man, Antonio (Antonio Banderas), feels for Pablo (Eusebio Poncela), an older, fairly successful film director. This love as we can deduce, is exaggerated and dramatic, but nonetheless remains pure and truthful. The film opens with the screening of one of Pablo's movies—in which a very attractive young man is sexually exciting himself in an empty room, while a male voice tells him what to do. Suddenly the shot opens and we see a recording studio where a couple of unglamorous, overweight, balding men are dubbing a movie. The effect is at once funny and disturbing, since we realize that this is a joke.

Immediately after that we see Antonio in a bathroom masturbating while repeating, "Fuck me! Fuck me!" which was the line of the character in the film. Since that moment on, it is clear that for Pablo films are a way to exercise some control over his chaotic life. Pablo does not believe that movies can teach us how to behave, but rather from his privileged position of making them, he tries to domesticate life by transferring many of its situations and characters to an artificial and controllable space, the screen. "I only make movies, but I cannot stand watching them," he answers to an admirer. The power that Pablo exercises over the audience is represented by the reaction of Antonio in the bathroom. Also symbolic of the control Pablo finds in performance is the staging of Jean Cocteau's *La Voix Humaine* (The Human Voice, 1959), a play that Pablo is directing and that will star his sister Tina (Carmen Maura), a transsexual whose life mimics the crisis of the character in the play. To emphasize even more the exaggeration of performance, this transsexual is in love with a woman, who is played by a real-life transsexual (Bibi Anderson). This theatricality in the film is a constant in Almodóvar's films as we can also see in the song "Teatro" ("Theater") sung by La Lupe in *Mujeres al Borde de un Ataque de Nervios* (Women on the Verge of a Nervous Breakdown, 1988). Clearly for Almodóvar, melodrama has in its exaggeration the seed of its own parody and deconstruction.

In the destructive effect he has on those who love him, Antonio represents the ironic reworking of the *femme fatale*, either because of natural wickedness or most likely because of the influence of his circumstances. He is a provincial young man who belongs to a religious and socially respectable family; because of that, he keeps his homosexuality a secret, and when he acts upon his desires, he goes to extremes. Although at first glance we could think that he is a confused young man, we soon realize he is playing a calculated game flirting with self-destruction. The theme of the destructive power of female love is clearly subverted here. In this way, Almodóvar is also incorporating his work into the rich tradition of Western culture, which according to Marcuse, is obsessed with tragic love. The frustration of the characters in this movie is resolved inevitably in violence and crime. Antonio, jealous of the boy whom Pablo really loves, seeks out the boy where he works. After trying to convince him to leave Pablo, Antonio attempts to rape him because he wants "to possess everything that is Pablo's." Because the boy rejects him, Antonio pushes him off a cliff and kills him. The destructive force of this passion is complicated by the police investigation and the car crash Pablo is involved in after visiting his dead love. The crash causes him to be amnesic, which in turn offers the opportunity for more exaggeration.

Here another farcical enactment is offered to the viewer through Pablo's amnesia, allowing Antonio to enter his life as his sister's lover. When Pablo finally recovers his memory, he realizes he cannot escape his destiny. Antonio has kidnapped Tina and threatens to kill her unless Antonio meets with him. Having no other choice, he accepts, and once alone with him in Tina's apartment the two men consummate for the last time the sexual act. The scene is one of the most intense in the film because we finally understand that Antonio has already accepted his passion as a tragic one. One cannot help thinking that this could have been prevented if he had accepted his homosexuality; however, we also realize that is easier said than done and see Antonio as a victim of a repressive society: "To love you like this is a crime, and I will pay for it. I suspected it would be a high price," says Antonio to Pablo before killing himself, moving him to tears. The movie tells a history of human passion, however, far from offering the traditional black and white, learn-from-other-people's-mistakes, or feel-good-at-the-end type of story. It has skillfully returned to the essence of melodrama; by making this a story about homosexual love, it has brought together two elements that supposedly exclude each other: melodrama, considered essentially feminine, and machismo, something that could be seen as extreme masculinity.

This use of melodrama illustrates the struggle between the needs of the individual expressed through sexual desire and the impossibility of these needs ever being fulfilled in a patriarchal society. Antonio, for example, always keeps the mask of a macho man by forcing Pablo to sign his letters with a girl's name. When they meet for the first time, he clarifies that usually he does not sleep with boys. This movie demonstrates how melodrama could go beyond a sentimental form of entertainment to become a mechanism of questioning collective aspirations and morals. What is more revealing is that by stretching the formula of melodrama to other levels, it reveals its farcical aspect and gives it a new dimension. Passion becomes suddenly neither a homosexual, nor a heterosexual experience, but a human one. Irony becomes also an instrument of reinterpretation, since irony has traditionally been the counterpart of melodrama, particularly because melodrama, far from being the immature expression of a culture, is an instrument that helps to interpret the world through exaggeration. As Vernon mentions referring to the final scene of *¿Qué He Hecho yo para Merecer Esto*, "Parody converges with genuine melodrama [. . .] Thus the ending represents not simply a self-conscious restatement of classic melodramatic closure but a more broadly self-reflexive gesture which Almodóvar uses to offer a slyly open conclusion."[24]

ALL ABOUT WOMEN

Like the films reviewed previously, a series of movies centered on women characters that focused on analyzing women's sensibility in contemporary Spain could be interpreted as subversive and as equally deconstructive. *Mujeres al Borde de un Ataque de Nervios* (1988) was perhaps the first international hit of Almodóvar that also caught the eye of Hollywood. The movie was nominated for the Oscar for best foreign film but lost to Bille August's *Pelle the Conqueror* (1987), a Danish-Swedish tale of immigration and discrimination within those Scandinavian countries. In a way, both movies could not be more opposite. *Mujeres* is a movie quintessentially Spanish if not *madrileño* that focuses on the life of Pepa (Carmen Maura) and other women from Spain's capital city who have to learn to rely on each other and let go of their past, including former lovers. In a way, we could say that the movie is about modern Spanish women moving beyond the traditional, patriarchal Spain of the past and idealization of country life with its traditions and religiosity and reinventing themselves in the big city. We can see them as a clear reaction to the provincial culture in which, particularly during the 1930s and 1940s, "a strongly folkloric cinema emerged that imaged a sanitized, provincial world of pure spiritual and moral value."[25]

The big modern city is a world away from the quintessential *femme fatale* in the context of Spanish culture, Carmen. If the movie apparently accepts the traditional idea of the hysterical woman who cannot go on with her life when she is abandoned and betrayed by the man she loves—the title itself seems to suggest that—it also follows the same pattern we observed before, that of alternating melodrama and the awareness of its exaggeration. For example, when Pepa finds out that Iván (Fernando Guillén) is leaving her, she burns her bed and tries to overdose with pills and gazpacho. But just when it seems that we are watching the same old story, the film turns to unexpected ways, via outrageous subplots, leaving the audience aware of its exaggeration. As Stephen Maddison observes, "If hysteria is a sign of the strain of maintaining the role of powerlessness, then I would suggest that *Women on the Verge of a Nervous Breakdown* eventually exploits the fault line such hysteria represents, fashioning it into a gender dissidence which attempts to refuse male control, male rationality. Yet even in *Women* the narrative and Pepa's emotional epiphany are both driven by the structuring absence of Iván. Pepa may transcend his cruelties,

but they define her actions, and those of the film."[26] That is precisely
the point, or rather the reason why Almodóvar's films manage to elude
classification, demanding to be put in a category of their own.

The complexity of absurd female characters is pushed a little further
in *Tacones Lejanos* (*High Heels*, 1991), a movie that tells the story of the
reunion of Rebeca (Victoria Abril) and her mother, Becky del Páramo
(Marisa Paredes), when she returns to Spain after living in Mexico for
several years working as an actress. Old wounds are open and what
seems already a bitter reunion between mother and daughter is complicated by rivalry since both women have shared lovers. The film
itself is complicated by the sexual ambiguities of many of the characters, including Letal (Migule Bosé), a drag queen who literally jumps
on Rebeca to make love to her while still in make up. Again, a movie
that seems to be pointing toward the old female universe, so typical
of the soap opera or of Hollywood movies of the 1950s, turns out to
have more twists and turns than expected. "Almodóvar's screenplay
is written like one of those soap operas in which the characters are
assembled in first one and then another combination until all of the
possibilities are exhausted," according to Roger Ebert, but presented
with "the eyes of a graphic artist" in bold, brilliant colors.[27]

Equally outrageous is *Kika* (1993), the story of a cosmetologist, the
Kika (Verónica Forqué) of the title, who gets involved emotionally
with the supposedly dead son of an expatriate American writer (Peter
Coyote), whom she was to prepare for his burial. But really Kika's plot
is the excuse to present the real theme of the film—the intrusion of the
media, particularly of talk and reality shows, in people's lives, presented with irony and very black humor that adds comedy to a rape
scene. Full of color and glossy images, sexuality, and chatty women
delivering, snappy, hilarious dialogues, supposedly spontaneously,
the movie seems a little repetitive—a summary, if you will, of the
director's career thus far. Or as the reviewer of the *Washington Post*
puts it, "Almodóvar has done this kind of thing before, and he's done
it better. In earlier works, such as 'Matador,' 'Dark Habits' and 'Law
of Desire,' Almodóvar laced his favorite obsessions—voyeurism, cruelty, rape and murder—with bold, satiric irony. Now, he's just
redressing the same stuff, as if his movies were mannequins in a window display. Something alarming has happened to Almodovar:
He has become commonplace and predictable."[28]

It is quite possible that because of that apparent exhaustion in *Kika*,
La Flor de Mi Secreto (*The Flower of My Secret*, 1995) feels like a cool
breeze and leaves the viewer with the feeling of having watched an

original film. Unlike most of his previous pictures, in this one Almodóvar presents no drag queens, no killer divas, sexually repressed homosexuals, or heroin-addicted nuns. The story is rather simple, which is another surprise—Leo (Marisa Paredes) is a middle-aged writer of romance novels who writes under the assumed name of Amanda Gris. Between books (her contract stipulates that she has to write several books with no political message a year) she has to deal with the indifference of her husband Paco (Imanol Arias) who obviously has stopped loving her. As Stephen Maddison mentioned before, here, too, the indifference of the male character motivates the entire plot and the actions of the female character; however, in this case that is not the end of the story, but a point of departure and the reason we find it interesting. The suffering of Leo is caused by the indifference and betrayal of her husband, but the secondary characters are very effective in supporting her and helping her to move on.

Of these characters, Ángel is the most important one, since he is clearly in love with Leo and offers his unconditional friendship to her, even when she rejects him. He is an editor, who offers Leo a job as a book reviewer and who for her first review assigns her, of course, her own book without knowing she was the author. Later he himself becomes Amanda Gris to save the career of his friend and to fulfill his own obsession with romance novels. Although they do not end up in a passionate relationship, by the time the movie is over they had become so comfortable with each other that we assume it is just a matter of time before she falls in love with him. Equally interesting are Leo's mother (the hilarious Chus Lampreave), who wants nothing but to return to her small village, and her sister Rosa (Rossy de Palma), who has to put up with the impertinent old woman. In a moment of weakness, Leo turns to her mother and together return to their village, but even these bits of local color seem tamed. There is a very nice scene where all the women of the village are in a patio sewing and singing traditional songs in a circle of feminine solidarity that provides Leo with the haven she needs to recover.

This nostalgic desire to return to the village as an ideal women's place is a recurrent theme in many of Almodóvar films, particularly as an aspiration of older characters that will become more important with time. In this movie we see a preview of that, since it anticipates the plot of his later film *Volver*, a film that appears very sympathetic of life in small towns. Frustrated by her love life, but also artistically, Leo has written a novel that deviates from the clauses stipulated in her contract by writing what seems a more personal book, only to have it rejected by her editor. That more personal novel is, judging by its description, an early version of the plot of *Volver*. *La Flor de Mi Secreto* develops almost like a soap opera that continues telling the same story; nonetheless, the film feels very fresh because it manages to find passion, drama, and human emotions in a universe that in itself defines the world by exaggerations and depends on teasing the female sensibility—the world of romance novels. And yet the film is one of the most measured and discreet to ever be advertised as a film by Almodóvar.

Perhaps what he does, when selecting the movies he wants to make, is the same thing he does with the stories he tells in them—he moves from genre to genre, theme to theme, and movie to movie with a very soft, almost imperceptible confidence and before we know it, we are already in the middle not of a movie, but of what Paul Julian Smith called "Planet Pedro." In the same tradition of an all-female ensemble, *Todo sobre Mi Madre* (*All about My Mother*, 1999) and *Volver* (*To Return*, 2006) are different from the previous movies in that they represent a more mature approach to the classic obsessions of the director. *All about My Mother* is an exquisitely wooden story of filial love, redemption, hope, and finding purpose in life. And even if there are in this film some of the traditionally shocking characters Almodóvar got us used to—a pregnant nun, a transvestite with AIDS, a theater diva whose life is equally theatrical—the sense of purpose and living for others that seems lacking in some of his previous pictures is not only present here, but it appears to be the reason of the story.

Like *Todo sobre Mi Madre*, *Volver* was unanimously received with praises by the critics. All the tricks, situations, exaggeration, sensibility, and even actresses and colors typical of the maestro were there, and yet there was also something unexpected and novel in these movies. *Volver* is a dark comedy that touches on patricide, sexual abuse, infidelity, and superstition, with characters who move through the screen with such grace and unaffectedness that it is a pleasure to watch them. Even the most absurd situations are easily and convincingly explained: "That is one of the advantages of living in a very superstitious town," tells Irene (Carmen Maura) to her daughter Raimunda (Penélope Cruz) when she realizes that Irene is not a ghost as the entire town believes. There is something very touching about the performance of Carmen Maura (a veteran of Almodóvar's films playing a provincial grandmother) and the excellent Blanca Portillo that exudes humanity and tenderness.

The same can be said of the performance of all the other main female characters of the film—the sweet Lola Dueñas, the amusing

Chus Lampreave, Yohana Cobo, and Penélope Cruz. Not surprisingly, they all received as a group the Best Actress Award at the 2006 Cannes Film Festival. This unusual homage could not have been more appropriate since the movie pays real homage to women and the solidarity with which they often support each other. "Those things have to be taken care of in private, among us, women," declares the cancer-stricken Agustina (Blanca Portillo) when she explains to Raimunda and Sole (Lola Dueñas) why she refused to talk about the affair of her mother and their father on national television, even if that meant not getting the money she was promised to go to Houston to get treated. The film is also a summary of a very Latin (not only Hispanic) or Mediterranean sensibility in which tragedy, faith, hope, death, comedy, and the supernatural mingle happily and with no contradictions—perhaps that is why the film resonated so loudly in many Latin American countries as well as in Italy and France. In the end, *Volver* is a rich film in which we find humor, tragedy, love, solidarity, and a bittersweet slice of life that leaves you happy and a bit sad, but never desperate or depressed.

Although most critics liked *Volver*, some pointed out that it did not have the brilliance or complexity of his most recent films, particularly of *Hable con Ella* (*Talk to Her*, 2002) or *La Mala Educación* (*The Bad Education*, 2004). In part, one can assume this is because it is a simple, happy story without much of the shocking early elements that made Almodóvar famous, and it ends on a happy, hopeful note. And this is true. What is not certain yet—and for that we will have to wait for his anticipated *Los Abrazos Rotos* (*Broken Embraces*, 2009) currently in postproduction—is if that optimism represents a radical shift in Almodóvar's career or just a trend. But particularly after *Hable con Ella* critics have noticed a change and maturity in Almodóvar's films compared with his previous pictures. *Hable con Ella* was certainly very different from many of his other films in that it was not centered on women or outrageous female impersonators, but on the male characters' love and obsession with women. The story follows two parallel narrations of love for a sick woman. One is centered on Benigno (Javier Cámara), who is fascinated by a ballerina, Alicia (Leonor Watling), and throws himself into taking care of her when she arrives brain-dead in the hospital where he works after a traffic accident. The other is about a journalist, Marco (Dario Grandinetti), who also dedicates himself entirely to taking care of the woman he loves despite barely knowing her. She happens to be a bullfighter named Lydia (Rosario Flores) who ends up in a coma and in the same hospital where Benigno works after being gored by a bull. Marco and Benigno become best friends in the process.

One of the first things we notice in the film is its complete disinterest in gender, rather than to denounce it or attack it. These men show characteristics traditionally considered to be feminine (taking care of someone, crying and being emotional, and carrying on endless chats about feelings and make-up), and in that respect they resemble many of the previous circles of women typical of Almodóvar's movies. However, the way it happens is so natural, that it never seems fake or preachy. If the story seems implausible, it is because it is implausible and so are the circumstances that surround it The narration is also implausible (the two men actually meet for the first time at a ballet recital where they are sitting next to each other, and one of them sees the other man cry; when they meet again in the hospital, they immediately become friends; the ballerina Alicia rehearses in a studio across the street from Benigno's house, and Alicia's father is Benigno's shrink, etc.). However, the emotions that the characters show are real, and we identify with their tender love and caring for these women. Both of them willingly give up their own personal interest to care for a woman who cannot love them back; although their love and dedication are real, so is the fact that their actions are a little selfish. After all, they are doing this because of the pleasure it gives them taking care of the women they love.

But this being an Almodóvar movie, it also shows how sexual—and therefore creepy—this devotion could be. This is perhaps the highest and most controversial point of the movie. As the spectator will find out at the end of the film, he or she would be struggling with serious moral issues because of the sympathy that he or she feels with the characters. As Marsha Kinder writes,

In *Hable con ella*, the nurturing interplay between physical gestures and words proves to have a transformative effect not only on the body of the dancer who is impregnated and revived, and on the writer who becomes bonded to the male nurse through identification and desire, but also on those of us in the audience whom this film manages to convince that every physical act (no matter how transgressive) can potentially be re-narrativized as an act of love.[29]

All in all, it is a wonderful movie that, like most of Almodóvar's films, is not afraid of confronting the audiences with serious, shocking issues, albeit always leaving us enlightened with a richer understanding of human nature and, why not?, sexuality.

Also sexuality and humanity (of a more twisted variety) are at the core of *La Mala Eduación*, a film that apparently takes on a hot issue—child sexual abuse by the clergy—but in reality is more concerned with human sexuality and its complexities in general. Above anything, the film is an exploration of the deceiving and elusive nature of sexuality and the performance of identity presented in such a way that sort of closes a circle with *La Ley del Deseo*. As in that previous film, in *La Mala Educación* nobody is what he or she seems or claims to be sexually or otherwise, and its tragic end is the result of a fundamental inability to connect with others and to exercise one's freedom and sexuality. To say it in the words of Geoff Pingree, "the movie is not just a story in which highly idiosyncratic characters transgress social boundaries at every level (something we have come to expect from Almodóvar), but also a world in which such characters are left to confront the inner conflicts that largely motivate their idiosyncrasies."[30] Sexuality in Almodóvar's film is a given, to agree with Roger Ebert, but also as the critic of the *Chicago Sun-Times* notes, "His movies are not about sex, but about consequences and emotions,"[31] and in this case, I would argue, about seeking redemption. As I mentioned, I see this film as closing a circle opened with *La Ley del Deseo*; it remains to be seen what course his career will take. No matter what, we can say that one way or another his films—and also Spanish cinema—cannot be the same after such *mala educación*.

NOTES

1. Paul Julian Smith, "The Curse of Almodovar," *Guardian*, June 17, 2008, http://film.guardian.co.uk/features/featurepages/0,,2286072,00.html#article_continue.

2. Ibid.

3. Jordi Minguell, "Almodóva: 'No Me Echéis la Cula,'" *El País*, June 24, 2008, http://www.elpais.com/articulo/cultura/Almodovar/echeis/culpa/elpepucul/20080624elpepucul_4/Tes.

4. Smith, "The Curse of Almodovar."

5. Fernando Méndez-Leite, "De Almodóvar a Amenábar," in *Las Generaciones del Cine Español*, ed. Juan Cobos (Madrid: España Nuevo Milenio, 2000), 100.

6. As a matter of fact, *El País* reports that Almodóvar was in the middle of filming his last picture when he decided to take a little break to write a letter to the *Guardian*. See Minguell, "Almodóva."

7. Marsha Kinder, "Reinventing the Motherland: Almodóvar's Brain-Dead Trilogy," *Film Quarterly* 58 (December 2004): 9.

8. Ibid., 10–11.

9. Ibid.

10. Ibid., 10.

11. David Denby, "In and Out of Love: The Films of Pedro Almodóvar," *The New Yorker* 80 (November 22, 2004): 85.

12. Ernesto Acevedo-Muñoz, *Pedro Almodeovar* (London: British Film Institute, 2007), 9.

13. Marvin D'Lugo, "Almodóvar's City of Desire," *Quarterly Review of Film and Video* 13 (1999): 52.

14. Mark Allinson, "The Construction of Youth in Spain in the 1980s and 1990s," in *Contemporary Spanish Cultural Studies*, ed. Barry Jordan and Rikki Morgan-Tamosunas (London: Arnold, 2000), 269.

15. D'Lugo, "Almodóvar's City of Desire," 51.

16. Kathleen M. Vernon, "Melodrama against Itself: Pedro Almodóvar's *What Have I Done to Deserve This?*," *Film Quarterly* 46 (Spring 1993): 28–29.

17. Ibid., 30.

18. Ibid.

19. Marsha Kinder, "Pleasure and the New Spanish Cinema: A Conversation with Pedro Almodóvar," *Film Quarterly* 41 (Autumn 1987): 37–38.

20. D'Lugo, "Almodóvar's City of Desire," 57.

21. Acevedo-Muñoz, *Pedro Almodóvar*, 78.

22. Rob Stone, "¡Victoria a Modern Magdalene?," 169.

23. Acevedo-Muñoz, *Pedro Almodóvar*, 133.

24. See Vernon, "Melodrama against Itself," 40.

25. D'Lugo, "Almodóvar's City of Desire," 47.

26. Stephen Maddison, "All about Women: Pedro Almodóvar and the Heterosocial Dynamic," *Textual Practice* 14 (2000): 272.

27. Roger Ebert, "High Heels," *Chicago Sun-Times*, December 20, 1991, http://rogerebert.suntimes.com/apps/pbcs.dll/article?AID=/19911220/REVIEWS/112200303/1023.

28. Desson Howe, "Kika," *Washington Post*, May 27, 1994, http://www.washingtonpost.com/wp-srv/style/longterm/movies/videos/kikanrhowe_a0b05d.htm.

29. Kinder, "Reinventing the Motherland," 22.

30. Geoff Pingree, "Pedro Almodóvar and the New Politics of Spain," *Cineaste* (Winter 2004): 6.

31. Roger Ebert, "Bad Education," *Chicago Sun-Times*, December 22, 2004, http://rogerebert.suntimes.com/apps/pbcs.dll/article?AID=/20041221/REVIEWS/41130003/1023.

CHAPTER 3

The Cinema of Mexico

THE DARLING OF LATIN AMERICAN CINEMA

In July 2007, the British Academy of Film and Television Arts (BAFTA) presented a unique retrospective of Mexican films, the first ever in BAFTA's history dedicated to a Latin American country. On that occasion, the United Kingdom and Mexico announced the opening of official conversations with the clear commitment on the part of both governments to "unite forces and work together" in the production of films, according to Clare Wise, director of the UK Film Council and Marina Stavenhagen, director of the Mexican Institute of Cinema (IMCINE).[1] At the closing of this retrospective, Rosa Bosch from Tequila Gang production company, who presided over a panel on Mexican film, spoke very favorably of the "gang" of recent Mexican filmmakers making noise all over the world, calling them affectionately a "mafia" and noting that at the beginning of the twenty-first century being a Mexican filmmaker was a hot thing. "Nowadays being Mexican in a film festival is like being Brazilian in a soccer team," she remarked jokingly.[2] Such exalted interest in Mexican cinema by the official British film community echoes no doubt a sentiment that has been prevalent all over the world, not only in international film festivals, but also in Hollywood as well as the American audience, one of the most reluctant to accept and recognize foreign films.

At the beginning of the twenty-first century, Mexican cinema was, apparently, one of the hottest cinemas around. The 79th Academy Awards in 2007 seemed only to confirm this. That year saw for the first time in history an avalanche of Mexican talent nominated for the Oscar in several categories, from best director (Alejandro González Iñárritu) and best foreign language film (*Pan's Labyrinth*, Guillermo del Toro, 2007), to best supporting actress (Adriana Barraza), best art direction (*Pan's Labyrinth*), best cinematography (Guillermo Navarro and Emmanuel Lubezki), best original screenplay (Guillermo del Toro and Guillermo Arriaga), best makeup (*Pan's Labyrinth*), and best original score (Gustavo Santaolalla). In the end, only best art direction, cinematography, makeup, and music were awarded to Mexicans, but nonetheless this represented an unparalleled event in the history of Mexican cinema and a rarity in the history of the Oscars. Mexican films had won awards in past decades from the more independent and regional festivals, such as San Sebastian, Sundance, Guadalajara, and Havana, to the newer ones, such as the international film festival Zerkalo or the Tribeca Film Festival, to the mama of all festivals, the Cannes International Film Festival. But they had never before won with such consistency and aplomb as at the beginning of the twenty-first century.

However, what seemed to many in the United States to be a sudden emergence of a film industry very few had ever heard of before was not really that unprecedented or new. Mexican films and filmmakers have always been around competing in festivals and circulating sometimes in peripheral theaters in the United States or in European Art Houses, not to mention cult movies shown on television all over the United States since the 1970s when K. Gordon Murray decided to import them and dubbed them into English. In addition, Mexican cinema has always had a prominent place in Mexico and other Latin countries, where for a long time they were the main attraction and the only rival of Hollywood. In fact, very few people realize that there has been a rich tradition of making films in Mexico that goes back to the turn of the century, with a period of consolidation around the 1930s and a golden age that covers part of the 1940s and 1950s, as well as the emergence of an independent cinema in the 1960s and 1970s. The problem with Mexican cinema, as with all Latin American cinemas, is that because of political and economic reasons it has not been able to maintain a constant production of films, not to mention films of any artistic and/or technological aspiration or merit. Added to that is the fact that during the last three decades of the twentieth century, Mexico suffered a series of economic catastrophes that coincided with the worst crisis of its cinema, a period of little official support and almost no private investment.

The rare instances in which private money was invested in the industry were more with the intention of producing easy, low-quality "movies" (called *churros* in Mexico) that could guarantee a fast, and lucrative, recovery of the investment, regardless of quality. Nonetheless, by the end of the twentieth century all that started to change rapidly. In 1985, a Mexican film, *Frida, Naturaleza Viva* (*Frida, Still Life*, Paul Leduc, 1985), surprised all by managing to bring back Mexican audiences to the theaters for the first time in decades to watch national movies. This triumph signaled a clear path to recovery that was confirmed in 1992 by the commercial success of *Like Water for Chocolate* (Alfonso Arau, 1992), a film that among other things was responsible for breaking all records at the American box office by becoming the longest-running foreign film ever in the United States; more surprisingly was the fact that the movies received praises by critics and audiences alike in Mexico and the rest of the world. By February 2002, this success was made official when *Screen International* called Mexico the "darling of Latin America," announcing that "Mexican cinema has indeed revived in all three areas of production (with market share rising from 3% to 20%), distribution (with local companies spending unprecedented sums on prints and advertisement), and exhibition (with old and unattractive theaters renewed for a wealthier and more educated audience)."[3]

If by the mid-1960s most Mexicans stopped watching Mexican films, their interest in national cinema did not die. As soon as there were any movies of significant cultural, artistic, or social interest, those very same audiences rushed to the theaters, demonstrating time and again that they were willing to give Mexican cinema a chance. *Frida, Naturaleza Viva*, a biographical picture that recalls the life of artist Frida Kahlo from her death bed, is a rather sophisticated exercise in narration told in a series of flashbacks and almost no dialogue; despite being a relatively difficult film, it became a turning point for contemporary Mexican cinema due to the crowds it managed to congregate for the first time in decades. There is no doubt, then, that Mexican cinema has become an important presence in the past couple of decades, but also it is important to remember that there has been a long tradition of making movies in that country and that, one way or another, new films and filmmakers feed from that tradition. It is true that Mexican audiences became with time more sophisticated and demanding in their cinematic taste, and this was beneficial for the industry; ironically by becoming more demanding, they were instrumental in the emergence of a new, exciting, more sophisticated cinema.

At the beginning of the new millennium, the result of an annual survey conducted by the European Audiovisual Observatory (*Focus 2000*), for example, offers some interesting statistics, in which Paul Julian Smith clearly sees that "Mexicans remain the keenest filmgoers in Latin America. Mexico also has the greatest number of screens in the continent, exceeding more populous Brazil by a considerable margin. Moreover attendance grew in Mexico by 7% compared with the previous year."[4] If the recent boom of Mexican cinema seems almost a product of spontaneous generation to many, all we need to do is look back to realize that it has always been around. Some talented Mexican filmmakers have emerged recently and have become very visible against all odds; some have moved to Hollywood and have risen to prominent places. (In April 2008 it was announced that Guillermo del Toro had been selected to direct the long awaited "The Hobbit," based on J. R. R. Tolkien's novel.) But many more have remained in Mexico struggling to continue with their successful careers there. They all, however, and regardless of where they are, will function as an arrowhead that will make way for Mexican cinema and force more people to pay attention to the films produced south of the American border. In a way, all, young and more established, directors are returning Mexican cinema to its place as one of the best and most diverse cinemas on the planet, according to Jason Word, director of City Screen, a chain of film theaters in London; he also reminds us that Mexico has one of the "longest [film] traditions in the world."[5]

THE NEW MILLENNIUM

The beginning of the new millennium as we said represents also the beginning of what is already called the revival of Mexican cinema or even its new golden age. The renaissance of Mexican cinema started with the rising of three directors—Alfonso Cuarón, Guillermo del Toro, and Alejandro González Iñarritu—who eventually moved to Hollywood, but particularly with the release of the widely popular pictures of two of them: *Amores Perros* (Alejandro González Iñárritu, 2000) and *Y Tu Mamá También* (Alfonso Cuarón, 2001). Even though these films were well received in Mexico and were a hit at the box office, their popularity remains striking outside of Mexico. One of the reasons is, no doubt, the frankness of their sexual scenes as well as the violence and the simplicity with which they mix humor, death, and love in a very matter of fact way, making them at once familiar in the international language of filmmaking and exotic with their local flavor. *Amores Perros* draws heavily on the fast editing so typical of music videos and commercial television advertisement and could be pinpointed as the film that inaugurated the episodic structure so popular in recent mainstream films (e.g., *Crash*, 2004, and *Babel*, 2007), even though a primitive version of that structure had already been used by Jorge Fons in *El Callejón de los Milagros* (*Midaq Alley*, 1995). *Amores Perros* also uses tricks generally associated with Hollywood—the main connector between the three stories of the movie, for example, is a car chase followed by a spectacular crash. However, some other elements remain alien to both Hollywood and music video traditions; if they cannot be called Mexican per se, they carry a foreignness that makes them believable—namely, the predominant presence of dogs in all three stories.

The film narration moves very rapidly from one story to the next following a couple of young men from a working-class neighborhood in Mexico City and their fighting dog; an ex-college professor turned revolutionary, turned killer for hire with a pack of stray dogs; and a supermodel with a noisy pooch, all of whom have a very close relationship with their dogs. Octavio (Gael García Bernal), one of the young working-class Mexicans, hopes to make enough money in the underworld of dogfights with his Rottweiler, Cofi, so he can run away with the wife of his bank-robbing brother. After a confrontation with some thugs who stabbed his dog when they lose a fight, he drives away speeding through the streets of Mexico City and crashes into the supermodel's vehicle (Goya Toledo), who happened to be driving to buy some wine for dinner to celebrate moving in with her lover. She ends up in the hospital with one leg amputated and is forced to revise her life and career. Witnessing the crash, the ex-college professor, and now a killer for hire, Chivo (Emilio Echevarría), steals Octavio's money and takes in the injured dog. Cofi later kills Chivo's pack of street dogs, forcing him to abandon his life of crime and to reconsider his future. He looks for his daughter, leaves a message on her answering machine asking for her forgiveness for having abandoned her as a child, shaves, showers, cuts his toenails, and walks toward the horizon with Cofi in search of a new life and, we assume, redemption.

Even though it sounds complicated, the plot moves smoothly between stories and the moment of the crash is exhilarating. What gives the movie its texture is the setting—Mexico City. This wonderful city appears at times as a nice, modern urban conglomerate of glass futuristic buildings and wide avenues, and at times as a labyrinth of poverty and violence out of a Buñuel movie. The omnipresence of dogs on the screen might surprise foreign audiences, but it surely looks natural to Mexicans and those who have spent some time in the country and have noticed dogs everywhere. They stroll through the movie, and by extension through Mexico, as symbols of love, violence, loyalty, hunger, cruelty, desire, and freedom—in other words, life. The decision to leave the original title in the version of the movie released in the United States is bold and symbolic as well —it proclaims, whether on purpose or not, that most Americans have grown so familiar with Mexican Spanish as not to be intimidated and chased away from the theaters by the foreign title (the same is true of *Y Tu Mamá También*, albeit in a different way). It is also a practical decision considering that it is virtually impossible to translate accurately *amores perros* into English. The international English title of the film (*Love's a Bitch*) is close, but still does not really capture the whole meaning and all the intricacies of the Spanish expression.

Similarly, *y tu mamá también* means many things in Spanish besides the literal "and your mama, too." The sexual implications in the allusion to the mother are clear and inevitable, and perhaps that is what makes this expression offensive beyond anything else in Mexico. That sexual implication is also evident in the film, which, following the tradition of the road movie, narrates the adventures, including the sexual adventures, of two friends from different backgrounds—in this case, during a trip to the beach with an older female, Luisa (Maribel Verdú), the unsatisfied wife of Tenoch's cousin, a yuppie wannabe writer. In fact, the title is revealed by Julio (Gael García Bernal) almost at the end of the movie when listing his sexual conquests to his friend Tenoch (Diego Luna), he tells the name of many women and adds at the end, "and your mama, too." Tenoch's reaction is that of disbelief, "Really? When?" he asks and then toasts to all the women his friend has had sex with, including, we assume, his own mother. All of a sudden we know we are in a different Mexico when this reference to one's own mother is cause for laughs and male bonding rather than a fight.

The originality of the film, however, is not in the subject matter, but in its treatment of it. Unlike a typical coming-of-age comedy from Hollywood, this Mexican film looks into the testosterone-ridden mind of young men with brutal and graphic honesty (there is, for example, a masturbation scene at a swimming pool shot beautifully that would make any spectator think twice before getting in the pool the next time he or she wants to go for a swim) and shows all the ups and downs, the glory, the cheating and lying, the abusing and using of people as well as the confusion and the innocence of the first sexual explorations. Luisa, who has accepted the invitation to travel with them to the beach and is aware of their "secret" plan to have sex with her, delights in teasing their desires and encouraging their silly rivalries, but she is also genuinely interested in knowing them a little better. She, as we learn at the end of the movie, has an ulterior motive for traveling with them, but that does not mean she is not honestly looking for herself or is not interested in the boys. However, after having sex with them, she realizes that their friendship has been broken.

Mexican critic Rafael Aviña has mentioned that in many ways these two characters are a modern version of the stereotypical Mexican macho from the golden age of Mexican cinema. He is right, particularly when he mentions *A Toda Máquina* (Ismael Rodríguez, 1951), another sort of road movie about two best friends who share an apartment, food, jobs, women, and even pajamas.[6] *A Toda Máquina* is the quintessential buddy movie that also serves as a parody of the homoeroticism latent in all male friendships in Mexico, something *A Toda Máquina* recognizes and exploits. Luis (Luis Aguilar) is a police officer who patrols the streets of Mexico City on his motorcycle. One day he runs into a hobo, Pedro (Pedro Infante), who claims to bring bad luck to anybody who loves him. Luis feels sorry for him and invites him to his place to have breakfast. Pedro eats everything, takes some of Luis's clothes, and never leaves the apartment. He also becomes a police officer, and he and Luis develop a manly friendship—which means they play tricks on each other and are always competing for the attention of the same women with comic consequences. There is even a vague recognition of the queerness of their friendship, something they both dismiss lightheartedly and use for laughs.

The difference between the two movies is 50 years and what they have done to Mexican society. If *A Toda Máquina* reveals a cheerful Mexico that wants to be modern, but is still divided between that desire and its beloved traditions, particularly when it comes to sexuality and family values, *Y Tu Mamá También* captures all the contradictions of a post-NAFTA (North American Free Trade Agreement) Mexico. In fact, one of the most intriguing aspects of Cuarón's film is its fragmented view of Mexico, of the urban, of the middle, and the upper-middle classes (even though Tenoch's father is a member of the government, he is a "subsecretario" of what seems a peripheral government agency; he is at the bottom of the upper-ranking government officials) and their interactions with the Mexico of the

poor and marginal, seen mainly through the windows of the dilapi-
dated car of the two "rich" kids. These two countries are by no means
credible to most Mexicans, and yet both seem oddly familiar, to the
point that according to Aviña, "the film is a faithful portrait of
the new Mexican adolescents, their foul language, their mediocrity,
their not giving a damn about social problems, and whose only goal
is self indulgence."[7]

However, *Y Tu Mamá También* is a fantasy about sexuality in a paradise more imagined than real: "You are very lucky to live in a country
so magical, so full of life," says Luisa to the two adolescents, and they
mockingly make a toast to "magical, musical Mexico," imitating a
radio announcer and repeating a media slogan popular in the 1970s
and 1980s. Yes, they are not buying it either, but paradoxically they
feel full of life. We are talking about a movie, so all pretense of realism
is either intentional or irrelevant. And in the case of this movie, as well
as in the case of *Amores Perros*, their beauty and their strength (according to most foreign audiences) as well as their weaknesses (according
to most Mexicans) reside in the fact that they are presenting so
convincingly a Mexico that looks and feels real, even though we all
know it is not. That in itself, I would argue, is a great accomplishment
and a political statement, albeit a meek one. But if the graphic and
unashamed sexuality and the hyperrealism of these two movies were
a revelation to filmgoers everywhere, the truth is that it is a characteristic not infrequent in Mexican, and even Latin American films,
perhaps since they first encountered Italian neorealism.

The third director who helped consolidate the renewal of Mexican
cinema is Guillermo del Toro. He is important because of his wonderful imagination, his cinematic technique, and for recovering a tradition that has also been part of the Mexican film industry—horror
movies. Del Toro has given a modern look and feeling to the traditional Mexican horror movie, starting with his acclaimed *Cronos* (*The
Cronos Device*, 1998), a movie that reworks in a very original way the
theme of the vampire. This vampire has a granddaughter and deterio-
rates physically with each incident to the point of the absurd (we see
the vampire at some point sewing his own mouth so he can keep it in
place). Unlike more metaphysical vampire stories, this one is more
about survival and the urge to keep feeding from others. After *Cronos*,
Del Toro left for Hollywood. Not always free and happy at first there,
he attempted new alliances and venues, working mostly with Spanish
co-producers willing to help him finance his movies. One of the
results of that was *El Espinazo del Diablo* (*The Devil's Backbone*, 1999),

which in a way anticipates his latest successful *El Laberinto del Fauno* (*Pan's Labyrinth*, 2006), before he became part of that gang of Mexican filmmakers mentioned by Rosa Bosch and acquired some power in the industry.

Set in Spain during the Civil War, these two movies revisit that "happy" time of childhood in an era of political and social violent crisis, something that both Mexican and Spanish societies can understand from their recent history. Reportedly, Del Toro wanted to set *El Espinazo del Diablo* in Mexico during the Revolution. That would have been an extraordinary film among other things because it would have given Del Toro the opportunity to revisit a moment of Mexican history so indispensable for its cinema. Given Del Toro's imagination, it is easy to imagine all the fun ways in which he could have subverted such a quintessentially Mexican genre. Unable to make the film in Mexico, he found the next best thing for this project in Spain and had to translate the story to the particular circumstances of the Spanish Civil War. Both movies are interesting, but the visual beauty and the daring way in which Del Toro takes a fairy tale and turns it into a political allegory without loosing its magic, as he does in *Pan's Labyrinth*, makes this film a true masterpiece of popular culture. Unlike self-referential and extremely self-conscious postmodern movies (e.g., the ones produced by Quentin Tarantino or Robert Rodriguez), Del Toro is willing to play the more traditional game—to keep a certain primordial, dilettante faith in the power of storytelling that seems more connected to literature than to an increasingly visual culture of virtual and immediate gratification. *Pan's Labyrinth* seems a very beautiful, old-fashioned fable, like the ones we used to read in textbooks, except for the digital era.

In contrast to the allegorical and "universal" political dimension of Del Toro's latest films and to the almost imperceptible political implications of the movies by Cuarón and González Iñarritu, a film produced with very little money and lots of heart and good intentions, *El Violín* (*The Violin*, Francisco Vargas, 2005), has forced Mexican audiences to look back into their recent past, specifically the peasant guerrilla wars of the 1970s, in what we can call in the most strict sense of the word, an example of revolutionary cinema. Shot in poetic black and white and with the visual texture of a documentary, *The Violin* tells the story of a group of peasants in some remote mountain village who revolt against the Mexican government and have to confront the army sent to contain them by any means possible. The plot gains in humanity by intertwining the lives of Don Plutarco (Ángel Tavira), his son

Genaro (Gerardo Taracena), and his grandson Lucio (Mario Gari-baldi). Don Plutarco, a quiet old man with a face wrinkled with suffer-ing and wisdom (we assume), earns a living playing the violin as an itinerant musician with his son, who plays the guitar, while his grand-son collects the money the passerbys give them. We soon learn that they are members of the insurrection, the army has occupied their village, and it has taken Genaro's wife and daughter prisoners.

The peasants who manage to get away run to the woods and hide while waiting for the opportunity to counterattack. When Gerardo learns that the army killed his wife and daughter, having very little to loose, he decides to attack with the other guerrilla leaders. With Gerardo occupied preparing the attack, Don Plutarco tries to help him to recover the arms and ammunition left hidden in the village. He gains the trust of the military with his peaceful appearance. The soldier in charge of the operation takes a liking to the old man and his music and allows him to move freely in and out of the occupied vil-lage with the request of returning every day to play the violin for him. The rest of the story is simple: Don Plutarco manages to take some of the ammunition and arms to the guerrilla fighters in his violin case under the unsuspecting eye of some military personnel and with the help of other soldiers who secretly give him pistols before he is discov-ered and his son is captured. With this turn of events, he knows every-thing is lost, so when he is asked sarcastically to play the violin while his son is being tortured, he only responds "music is over." The screen goes black and the audience's heart sinks in a hole as black as the screen imagining what is going to happen to them, particularly because the opening scene of the film is brutal in its realism and graphic violence mixed with sexuality. But unlike *Amores Perros* or *Y Tu Mamá También*, what we are witnessing here is torture in what could be some of the strongest scenes involving the Mexican Army ever seen on film.

Vargas is a unique case and so is his film, which already forms part, along with the films of Carlos Reygadas, Julián Hernández, and Fernando Eimbcke, of a different kind of cinema, an independent cin-ema or cinema of auteur. With only three films, Reygadas has already managed to capture national and international attention. His first fea-ture film, *Japón* (2002), marks one of the most unexpected beginnings in Mexican film history. The movie is as enigmatic as its title and feels equally remote (*Japón* in Spanish means Japan). It opens with a man in search of the perfect place to commit suicide and ends up in a forgot-ten, barren town, living with an old woman, whose silent and resigned presence makes him reconsider his plans. The story, however, is not a naïve and optimistic feel-good-about-living sort of tale, but is darker and richer; it is a more adult look at life, death, loneliness, and human solidarity (there are some graphic sexual scenes between a mature man and a very old woman). Many critics have been quick to point out the influence of Carl Theodor Dreyer or Andrei Tarkovsky and other European directors in Reygadas's films, and he himself has mentioned them as models. It is in his last film, *Stellet Licht* (*Silent Light*, 2007), however, where we can really see more clearly some of those influences. What is evident from the beginning is that he is a perfect cinephile. After he finished his career as an international lawyer, Reygadas decided to make movies, but with no formal training. He resolved to teach himself by watching the best movies he could find and reading a lot about film, according to his own account.

Stellet Licht is a beautiful film, a story about betrayal, love, forgiveness, and redemption amid the pastoral setting of a Mennonite community in northern Mexico. This religious sect, which has made a point of isolating itself from the rest of the world to the extent that the sect's members speak an ancient form of German and do not marry outside their group, is the perfect setting for this drama. Family man Johan (Cornelio Wall), who seems to have the perfect life, has an affair with another woman; because he is unable to stop, he causes infinite pain to his family, to himself, and to the community. "It is the work of the Enemy," says his father, a minister, when the tortured son confesses his sin. Confused and still unable to stop his affair, Johan represents a divided humanity whose existence is between heaven and earth; this existence is not without its moments of primordial joy and innocence (e.g., when he finds his children in a van watching old, full of life television performances, or when the family is swimming and washing in an Arcadian landscape). The end of the story is enigmatic, beautiful, and open-ended and has infuriated some spectators for its unrealistic and—according to some, pedantic—final sequences. At the end the film finishes with a very long take of a night getting darker and darker until there is nothing but the stars, dimmer and dimmer, and the sounds of the farm and the countryside. The beginning of the film is also a very long take of a starry sky that little by little turns into daybreak in front of our own eyes. Both sequences are a beautiful visual experience and frame this mystical story perfectly.

Batalla en el Cielo (*Battle in Heaven*, 2004), Reygadas's second film, is also a tale of redemption mediated by faith. Marcos is the chauffer of a rich businessman and his daughter Ana (Anapola Mushkadiz), who is a spoiled, rich brat of a girl with a secret. She prostitutes herself just for kicks, and Marcos is the only one who knows that. The movie starts with a very uncomfortable sexual scene—Ana performing fellatio on Marcos. The sequence is filmed with a crude realism more appropriate for hard-core pornography, which could make the whole experience more uncomfortable for some. This uneasiness is the result in part of the prejudices of our culture that teach us that only "beautiful," fit bodies (something Marcos is far from having) should be objects of desire. This same feeling is repeated when Marcos and his equally "ugly" and obese wife make love. But the sexuality in the movie is not the essence of the story; it is just part of life. The real battle in heaven is the fact that Marcos and his wife have secretly kidnapped a little boy from a friend and asked for a ransom. The boy dies under their care, and Marcos confesses this to Ana who realizes then that he is in love with her.

Ana rejects him kindly and he kills her. With the police following him closely, Marcos goes to the Basilica of Our Lady of Guadalupe in penance to ask for forgiveness in a scene that can symbolize the battle of the title; it is almost as if the entire movie has been an excuse for this moment. The Mexicanness of the movie, its national pathos and its connection with a very specific tradition, is given visually by the huge flag that is flown ceremoniously and then taken down every morning and evening at the main square in Mexico City. In the end, the movie is about faith as spectacle and as a practice of life, but also about the emptiness of civil rituals in a country such as Mexico that has failed to create the ideal conditions for a happy, prosperous existence and has left instead a fanatical sense of the divine and the ritualistic connection with the human.

As direct about love and human sexuality as Reygadas is, Julián Hernández is even more direct because his films are centered on the exploration of love in same-sex relationships. With his first film, *Mil Nubes de Paz Cercan el Cielo, Amor, Jamás Acabarás de Ser Amor* (*A Thousand Clouds of Peace Circle the Sky, Love, You Will Never Cease to Be Love,* 2003), a movie as long, beautiful, and lyrical as the title, taken from a poem by Pier Paolo Pasolini, the young director recovers the experimental type of cinema that had not been seen in Mexico in a long time. This cinema vaguely resembles attempts from the 1960s, such as those of Juan Ibáñez or the early works of Alejandro Jodorowsky, particularly *Fando y Lis* (*Fando and Lis,* 1968). *Mil Nubes* is a poetic look at first love with its pains and its small, but categorical triumphs. Gerardo is a young, handsome boy in love who goes in search of his elusive loved one through empty freeways, garages, empty lots, and other urban spaces. Filmed in black and white, with little dialogue, and without being afraid of feelings, the film seemed perfect for a close circuit of art, gay cinemas, and small gay festivals.

Fortunately that has not been the case, and the film has enjoyed well-deserved attention, although not always enthusiastic reviews. The *New York Village Voice*, for example, found the film a little exasperating, too long, and pointless, but could not say anything really bad about it. Even though the reviewer does not consider as flaws the director's "fussy affectations" or the cinematographer's "overly-precious" black and white, he concludes that "all the stylistic flourishes can't hide the lack of an actual plot, character development, or point," and like the main character, he adds, "we wait, hoping something will happen."[8] But this is a matter of perception and taste. In fact, then *Los Angeles Times* film critic Manohla Dargis considered the film the product of a "fine new talent and precocious aesthete" and proclaims that "the modest film provides further evidence of Mexico's recent cinematic renaissance." She also considers the film "a tribute to the glories of celluloid" and, most importantly, which is what many critics did not understand, "a pointed reminder that when it comes to most movies what happens inside a film frame is more important than how the plot unfolds."[9] Indeed, in the case of Hernández, as in Reygadas's case, it is the "lack" of plot—or of conventional plot to be more precise—that seems questionable to some critics, but as Dargis points out, sometimes movies are their own plot.

There are other young directors who have already received some attention nationally and internationally, promising a bright future for Mexican cinema. Among these new talents are Fernando Eimbcke whose first film, the excellent *Temporada de Patos* (*Duck Season*, 2004), is a sweet, subtle story about two friends, a pizza delivery man and a sexy neighbor, who unexpectedly find solidarity in what seems a world full of loneliness. What the movie teaches, besides a new way of pouring Coke, is that everything is part of life. Life sucks sometimes, yes; but pizza, brownies, and an unexpected friend sometimes can overcome reality. Eimbcke's second film, *¿Te Acuerdas de Lake Tahoe?* (*Lake Tahoe*, 2008), was received very favorably at the Berlin Film Festival and was mentioned even as one of the favorites for the Golden Bear. In the end the biggest prize went to Brazil's José Padilha with yet another tale of life in the slums of Rio de Janeiro, *Tropa de Elite* (*Elite Squad*, 2007) with México receiving the Jury Prize.

Other important young directors are Ernesto Contreras with *Párpados Azules* (*Blue Eyelids*, 2007) and Enrique Begne with *Dos Abrazos* (*Two Embraces*, 2007), both recent winners at international films festivals. Begne was the winner of the Best First Film at the Tribeca Film Festival, while Contreras won prizes and nominations at Sundance, Tokyo, San Sebastian, and Guadalajara film festivals, in addition to several Arieles (Academia Mexicana de Artes y Ciencias Cinematográficas awards). Also worth mentioning are Matías Meyer with *Wadley* (2008), Everardo González with *Los Ladrones Viejos* (*Old Thieves*, 2007), Daniel Gruener with *Morirse en Domingo* (*Never on Sunday*, 2006), Patricia Riggen with *La Misma Luna* (*Under the Same Moon*, 2007), Juan Carlos Rulfo with *En el Hoyo* (*In the Pit*, 2005), Gustavo Loza with *Al Otro Lado* (*On the Other Side*, 2004) and *Silencio Profundo* (*Deep Silence*, 2003), and Carlos Bolado with *Sólo Dios Sabe* (*Only God Knows*, 2004) and *Bajo California: El Límite del Tiempo* (*Under California: The Limit of Time*, 1998).

A CINEMA IN CRISIS

If the last few decades seem to many a new golden age of Mexican cinema, it is logical to assume that there was a previous golden age and that at some point it faded into oblivion. What happened in that period between the two so-called golden ages is perhaps one of the most interesting questions of Mexican cinema. The rest of this chapter will try to provide a comprehensive albeit brief answer to that question. Let us accept for now that there was a Golden Age of Mexican Cinema (something we discuss in more detail in the next chapter) and that around the early 1960s, it lost its connection with its audience. For decades, Mexicans, tired of the violence and the excesses of the Revolution (1910–1921) and with a genuine desire to find a happy formula that would lead them to peace and prosperity, accepted the new medium of film as a true representation of their lives and their culture, as well as an escape that offered them the possibility of returning, at least temporarily, to a better time, a time of simpler conduct codes and fewer moral dilemmas, a time where the good were good, the bad were bad, men worked, and women stayed at home. This was the beginning of the Mexican film industry.

With the massive arrival of industrialization in the 1940s and 1950s, Mexicans also sought the possibility of learning how to become more urban and modern in movies; simultaneously, movies also learned how to become more and more sophisticated in their techniques and subjects. Inevitably, however, with time these techniques and subjects became more and more conventional and the audiences more and more demanding. This industry, nonetheless, had become by 1947 the third largest national industry[10] and kept producing enough films not only for the national market, but also for the Spanish-speaking one, to the point that according to Seth Fein, "In the 1940s and 1950s, Mexico, the leading producer of Spanish-speaking movies, had one of the most important film industries in the world."[11] All through the 1940s, Mexico benefited from American assistance and support, particularly through the creation of the Office of the Coordinator for Inter-American Affairs, an office that saw in Mexican films and their popularity "a more authentic source of wartime propaganda for Latin American audiences. In addition, the United States allowed raw film stock—a commodity whose production it controlled in the Western Hemisphere and distributed through wartime quotas—to flow to Mexico and not to Argentina."[12]

The Mexican film industry, then, received preferential treatment from the United States, something that only helped the Mexicans to consolidate an already strong industry. The attitude of the United States, however, changed dramatically after World War II; in several reports to the U.S. Department of State from embassies all over Latin America, from Havana to Caracas, Lima, and Santiago de Chile, there was the same complaint: Mexican films seemed to be more and more popular in the region. As result of this, "Hollywood's international position and tactics, supported by the State Department, made it very difficult for Mexican producers to expand their exports."[13] All that favoritism shown by the United States had all but ended by the mid-1950s, and instead a diplomatic battle began between the two nations trying to protect their interests. "Given the credible threat by U.S. companies to boycott Mexico if protectionist measures of any kind were enacted, there was no way conceivable that reduction in film would not be dramatic."[14] The less friendly attitude toward Mexico was in part due to Mexico's international policies that would end with Mexico's support of the Cuban Revolution and its opposition to the American embargo in 1960.

This combination of increasing economic problems and the American pressure to the industry contributed to a dramatic decrease of film production in Mexico. At the same time, other national cinemas, particularly from Europe, began to be shown in Mexico and became very popular. French, Scandinavian, Russian, and even Japanese films soon became the favorites of the educated elite and of the middle classes who saw in them a possibility of being truly modern and in touch with the world. With an increase in the circulation of films from other traditions, besides Hollywood, and with an increase in the level of education and the urban population of Mexico, the themes and topics that had been so successful up to then suddenly seemed provincial, silly, and even embarrassing compared with the more sophisticated views of the world offered by foreign films, something more attune with the aspirations of the country to be a real player in the international scene, now that all the issues of the Revolution had been resolved. Because the film industry did not respond to that aspiration fast enough, it soon became synonymous with provincialism and backwardness.

Still all through the 1950s and 1960s movies were produced in Mexico, and some were of excellent quality and even presented original themes; some of them even kept a presence in international festivals. In 1968, however, things changed dramatically in Mexico. That year, while the country was getting ready to join triumphantly the international community by showcasing itself as a modern, democratic nation by hosting the Summer Olympic Games, the real social crisis of the country became evident. From the early months of that year, many groups of workers and students had been protesting against what they perceived as despotic attitudes of the government, which culminated with the occupation of the campus of the National Autonomous University of Mexico by the army. Students protested the invasion and started to demand more civil participation in the government's decisions. The expressions of discontent had been growing in numbers and intensity, including huge contingencies of the most important schools and universities from all over the country and of worker unions. On October 2, 1968, during a demonstration—and only 10 days before the inauguration of the Olympic Games—the army, with the excuse of crushing some internal disturbances, entered a square known as Plaza de las Tres Culturas in the centric neighborhood of Tlatelolco where the protesters had congregated and opened fire against the unarmed students, massacring dozens of them. "October 2, We Won't Forget" became the motto of successive generations of students and civil and political activists in Mexico until 1997 when the Mexican Congress established a National Committee to investigate the Tlatelolco Massacre, as it became infamously known.

Understandably, the massacre became taboo in most political and cultural circles. Even movies, a medium that decades earlier took advantage of historical events, such as the Revolution, remained silent about the event, with the exception of an obscure documentary and a movie that mentions the massacre in passing. But the crisis of Mexican cinema was already on its way in the 1960s. Soon after the student massacre, the government took control of many theater chains and created an institute to promote cinema, paradoxically contributing to the decline of the industry while trying to saving it. The 1960s also saw a new generation of critics that felt less compelled to defend a movie just because it was Mexican and became more and more preoccupied with pointing out the flaws of the films produced in the country and the need to recreate a more authentic cinema. Not less important in its contribution to the decline of cinema as the art of the people was the introduction of a new massive form of entertainment and communication in 1950—television.

Gradually television became the favorite form of entertainment of the people, and many of the films produced by the late 1950s and 1960s also showed that influence. Many of them either included television personalities or promoted their starts to become television personalities, such as the comedic couple Viruta and Capulina. But it was a bizarre subgenre of horror films that combined some absurd situations and simple plots with wrestlers as heroes that dominated the industry at its twilight. These B movies emerged at the end of the 1950s and developed a host of followers all over the world, becoming almost synonymous with Mexican cinema. It is ironic that after having had one of the most important film industries, Mexican films became better known in the United States by these wacky, charming, naïve movies, not always taken seriously, despite the fact that some of them were actually good recreations of gothic atmospheres adapted with success to the Mexican landscape and context.

It is this disinterest in political themes and the attempts, at times desperate, to keep an industry alive that mark the decline of Mexican cinema. It is important to mention, however, that even with all the difficulties facing the industry, it still managed to produce some outstanding films. Among the most significant are macabre comedies such as *El Esqueleto de la Señora Morales* (*The Skeleton of Mrs. Morales*, Rogelio A. González, 1959); metaphysical fables such as *Macario* (Roberto Gavaldón, 1959), the first Mexican film to be nominated for an Oscar; and political dramas about the Revolution such as *La Sombra del Caudillo* (*The Shadow of the Leader*, Julio Bracho, 1969), the only Mexican movie ever to be officially banned from exhibition for supposedly defaming the Mexican Army. The film was finally released in the 1990s.

A very interesting director who dominated the 1960s and whose films reflect the best attempts of the industry at that time is Roberto Gavaldón. Recognized as a master of the trade from his early works and then overlooked for being too much the perfectionist, Gavaldón is the last great director of the golden age. Such movies as *La Diosa Arrodillada* (*The Kneeled Goddess*, 1947), a beautiful thriller *noir* with diva María Félix; *La Barraca* (*The Hut*, 1944), a successful adaptation of the novel of Spanish writer Vicente Blasco Ibáñez; *La Otra* (*The Other Woman*, 1946), a suspense thriller of stolen identity with the impeccable Dolores del Río; *Rosauro Castro* (1950), an excellent example of the use of the possibilities of black and white in the narrative to explore power relations; *En la Palma de Tu Mano* (*In the Palm of Your Hand*, 1950) and *La Noche Avanza* (*The Night Falls*, 1951), very good examples of Mexican urban *noir*; and the country dramas of *El Rebozo de Soledad* (*Soledad's Shawl*, 1952) and *Flor de Mayo* (May Flower, 1957) belong to the rich tradition of the golden age.

While films such as *Miércoles de Ceniza* (*Ash Wednesday*, 1958), *Macario* (1969), *Rosa Blanca* (*White Rose*, 1961), *Días de Otoño* (*Autumn Days*, 1963), *El Gallo de Oro* (*The Golden Cockerel*, 1964), *La Vida Inútil de Pito Pérez* (*The Useless Life of Pito Perez*, 1969), *Doña Macabra* (*Ms. Macabre*, 1971), *Don Quijote Cabalga de Nuevo* (*Don Quixote Rides Again*, 1972), and *Las Cenizas del Diputado* (*The Congressman's Ashes*, 1976) came out when the splendor of the industry was fading away, yet they managed to keep the audience interested and compete with dignity in the international film scene. Worth noticing is *Macario*, a supernatural tale with hunger at its core. Macario (Ignacio López Tarso), a poor peasant in colonial Mexico, is so hungry that he swears never to eat again until he can have an entire turkey for himself without sharing it with anybody. His wife (Pina Pellicer), full of compassion and understanding, steals a turkey from the rich family where she works as a servant and cooks it for her husband. Macario, ready to fulfill his dream, goes to the mountain to work with his turkey. And just when he is ready to eat it, the Devil appears and asks him for a bite in exchange for riches.

Macario refuses and he moves to another part of the forest. Then God appears and asks him to share the turkey with him, but he refuses again. "You have everything, you are the creator of the universe; all I have is this. Why do you want to take it away from me?" Sad and disheartened, he moves farther into the woods, and then Death appears and promises to give Macario a magic water that would heal anybody, except if Death appears at the foot of their bed. Macario becomes rich and famous, but with richness and fame comes envy; he is accused before the Holy Inquisition of witchcraft and is found guilty; however, he is given the opportunity to save himself if he cures the son of the viceroy. Unfortunately, Death appears at the feet of the child. Macario runs away to the woods where he encounters Death in a cave full of candles. Death explains that those candles are the lives of humans and that the destiny of each human is already determined. He shows Macario the candle of the son of the viceroy about to be extinguished and then Macario's own candle, which is consuming fast. Macario takes his candle and runs out of the cave trying to protect it, only to die in the forest.

In his later films, Gavaldón continued to be an essential Mexican director. *Rosa Blanca* is perhaps his most political movie; it deals with a taboo subject in Mexican politics: the importance of the oil industry. Even though it denounces big American companies for being responsible for the dependency and economic backwardness of the country, the subject was still off-limits decades after the expropriation of that industry by the Mexican government; the film was finally released in 1972. *El Gallo de Oro* returns to the subject of power, mixing it with sexuality, politics, and corruption in a small town in Mexico. But *Días de Otoño*, a very interesting story about loneliness, is the one that better represents this new stage of the Mexican film industry. The story happens in Mexico City, in a modern bakery, and has no political implications of any kind; the film, also, presents very different characters from those that Mexican audiences were used to see during the 1940s and 1950s. Luisa (Pina Pellicer) is a young, independent woman who was left at the altar the day of her wedding who invents a pregnancy and a happy marriage for herself; Luisa's crisis is psychological, not social or political. The performance of actress Pina Pellicer is excellent and saves the film from becoming a melodramatic perorate, turning it instead into an introspective and ambiguous meditation on loneliness and hope.

Like *Macario* and *El Gallo de Oro*, *Tiburoneros* (*Shark Hunters*, 1963) and *Tlayucan* (*The Pearl of Tlayucan*, 1961), both films by Luis Alcoriza, explore life of the peasantry with an almost ethnographic attention. *Tlayucan* is the story of a poor villager who is desperate because he does not have the money to buy medications to cure the illness of his son; he steals the pearl of a sacred image from the town's church and is caught in the act by some tourists photographing the temple. *Tiburoneros*, a film that was nominated for an Oscar, is about a city man working in a fishing village as a shark hunter, but when he returns to the big city he is unable to adapt to life there and returns to a simple life as a *tiburonero*. At the same time, in contrast to these realistic films, there was a renewed interest in gothic and horror films. Carlos Enrique Taboada's *Hasta el Viento Tiene Miedo* (*Even the Wind Is Scared*, 1967) and *El Libro de Piedra* (*The Book of Stone*, 1968) are perfect examples of this style; both movies are exercises in style and psychological horror with an excellent understanding of how the genre works, something Taboada had already shown as a writer in *El Espejo de la Bruja* (*The Witch's Mirror*, Chano Urueta, 1959). These films continued the tradition that saw its best results with Fernando Méndez's *El Vampiro* (*The Vampire*, 1957) and *Ladrón de Cadáveres* (*The Body Snatcher*, 1956)

Hasta el Viento Tiene Miedo is the story of a boarding school for girls haunted by the spirit of a former student who committed suicide and now is trying to possess Claudia (Maricruz Olivier), one of the students, to avenge all the suffering caused to her by the cruel headmistress Bernarda (Marga López). The film offers all the expected elements of a psychological horror—sexual repression, female hysteria, and psychological cruelty, as well as a couple of twists that make this film very satisfying. *Hasta el Viento Tiene Miedo* was remade in 2007 by Gustavo Moheno with great public success, but bad reviews from the critics. *El Libro de Piedra*, on the other hand, is a Mexican version of *The Turn of the Screw*, or at least it is clearly inspired by the 1898 Henry James novel and its film version (*The Innocents*, Jack Clayton, 1961). It is the story of a little girl who "befriends" an ancient stone statue of a child named Hugo who is holding a book, which is standing in the garden of the family mansion; the statue supposedly comes alive and communicates with the little girl with destructive consequences for the little girl's stepmother, Mariana (Norma Lazareno) and her mistress, Julia (Marga López). As *Hasta el Viento* before it, *El Libro de Piedra* captures the atmosphere of the best gothic horror films, achieving some sequences of real psychological terror; it also became very popular, helped by television where it has been shown regularly earning it successive generations of fans.

Less memorable, but interesting in their own way, if only because they clearly show the modern aspirations of large urban sectors of Mexican society in a country still struggling with class and economic issues, are the films of actor Mauricio Garcés who developed one of the most memorable popular characters—the aging eternal bachelor who would stop at nothing to seduce women. These films that were often set in large department stores, boutiques, bachelor apartments, art galleries, or modern hotels became popular as a symbol of urban sophistication and a sign of the changing times. With his humor of sexual undertones and language of double meanings, including catchy and silly phrases (*"las traigo muerta*," "I'm killing them," or *"arroz!*," literally "rice!," which he popularized as an interjection that could mean anything), with his cynical exploitation of women for pleasure's sake, as well as his references to contemporary culture, Garcés's character pretended to represent the sexually liberated 1960s, Mexican style—that is without betraying the deeply patriarchal and conservative roots of a traditional Catholic society. Of these movies, perhaps *Modisto de Señoras* (*Fashion Designer for Ladies*, René Cardona Jr., 1969) is the most popular and representative, but the long list includes movies with such suggestive titles as *Don Juan 67* (Carlos Velo, 1966), *Click, Fotografo de Modelos* (*Click! Fashion Photographer*, 1967), *El Criado Malcriado* (*The Insolent Servant*, Francisco del Villar, 1968), *Departamento de Soltero* (*Bachelor's Apartment*, 1969), *Fray Don Juan* (*Brother Don Juan*, René Cardona Jr., 1970), and *El Sinvergüenza* (*The Shameless Man*, 1971).

We mentioned already the lack of political films during a time of social unrest and official repression, and the only exception was *El Grito* (*The Scream*, Leobardo López Aretche, 1968), a documentary on the student movement, which unfortunately was not shown or even well known. The most revolutionary aspect of the Mexican film industry during these years of crisis was personal enterprises by highly original mavericks. I am referring to some of the most interesting Mexican films by Luis Buñuel (a director I discuss in the next chapter) and of Alejandro Jodorowsky, as well as the first serious attempts to create a current of independent cinema by young filmmakers, such as Arturo Ripstein, Luis Alcoriza, and Juan Ibañez. *Los Caifanes* (Juan Ibañez, 1966) is the first effort to make a film that, although it seriously explores Mexican identity, goes beyond the pompous, folkloric early attempts. Liberated from any political or partisan affinities or commitments, and decades away from the Revolution of 1910, many intellectuals and artists finally felt free to explore with irreverence and a sense of humor its social consequences and the state of national identity. Juan Ibañez belongs to this generation.

His film *Los Caifanes* is a long voyage into the Mexican night. One evening, a couple of rich kids, Paloma (Julissa) and Jaime (Enrique Álvarez Félix), decide to leave a boring party early . At her insistence, they stop at a park to kiss, where a gang of lower-class thugs asks them to give them a lift. The couple and the five toughs then embark on a trip through the city that lasts all night and leads them to all kinds of adventures and characters, forcing them eventually to confront their own prejudices and class perceptions of each other. Clearly seduced by the vitality of the five men, Paloma accepts participating in all their innocent transgressions—they go to a funeral home and each one lies in a coffin; they put a skirt and a bra on a statue of Diana, the Hunter; they go to a bar and pick up an old, depressing whore; and they encounter a scary, drunken Santa Claus who cries, calling for his mom. Jaime, reluctant and clearly afraid of the thugs, tries to stop Paloma and to convince her that they are not like those losers and that they have status and names to protect. Overcharged with literal and visual references, the script tries to pass obvious references for world-liness and campy situations for a Felliniesque existential sense of the absurd. The movie is saved, however, by the acting, which is right on target. Not only is Julissa believable as a naïve, free-spirited girl, but Enrique Álvarez Félix (the son of the grand diva of Mexican cinema, María Félix) is excellent in a role that almost seems a parody of him-self; Óscar Chávez, a folk singer, is perfect as the handsome working-class man who catches Julissa's eye. Also good are Ernesto Gómez Cruz as Azteca, a lower-class young man proud of his Indian blood; Tamara Garina as the old, pathetic whore; and even writer Carlos Monsiváis who plays the drunk, mother-loving Santa Claus, in a performance that earned him an Ariel as best supporting actor.

In 1959 Alejandro Jodorowsky arrived in Mexico from his natal Chile, and he immediately joined the most avant-garde group of artists he could find. Interested in theater and avant-garde art, he joined a the-ater group commanded by writer Juan José Arreola and painter José Luis Cuevas. Soon after that, Jodorosky started making a series of bizarre, poetic, innovative movies that were like nothing else ever done in Mexico, not even by Buñuel. His first film *Fando y Lis* (1968) was a romantic fable in which a young couple goes in search of love and hap-piness in the mythical city of Tar only to fail in the end. *El Topo* (1969), his next film, is a metaphysical western with a hero that combines Zen Buddhism with hippie attitudes, psychedelic imagery, and a peculiar idea of justice to save a community terrorized by a lascivious villain. *La Montaña Sagrada* (*The Magic Mountain*, 1973) is also a psychological and physical trip by a Christ-like character in search of enlightenment. The film is full of religious images, sometimes shocking and sometimes ridiculous, and for moments it feels a little preachy and dogmatic.

Santa Sangre (*Holy Blood*, 1989), on the contrary, is one of those movies impossible to label. Filmed in Mexico with Mexican and

American actors and spoken in English, it is one of the most violent and realistic films by the Chilean filmmaker, which nonetheless includes religious fanatics, circus freaks, lots of blood, and a psycho-like relationship between an armless mother and a son. *Santa Sangre* happens in a circus, so it only makes sense that it is a story about the power of religion as spectacle. After that, Jodorowsky moved to France and made a couple of movies there; rumors of a sequel to *El Topo* (to be called "The Son of El Topo") starring Marilyn Manson have proven to be so far nothing but that. These maverick directors marked the beginning of a truly independent cinema that continued with directors such as Felipe Cazals, Jaime Humberto Hermosillo, Luis Alcoriza, Paul Leduc, and Arturo Ripstein, whose work coincided with the decline of the industry and the emergence of the New Latin American cinema.

Felipe Cazals produced some films worth mentioning such as *Mecánica Nacional* (*National Mechanics*, 1972), a mordant look at Mexican society and its idiosyncrasies; *Presagio* (*Omen*, 1974), a look at superstition and alienation; and *El Muro del Silencio* (*The Wall of Silence*, 1974) and *Lo Que Importa Es Vivir* (*What Matters Is Being Alive*, 1987), interesting stories of codependency and love that manifest in unexpected ways. Felipe Cazals created works of refinement rarely seen in Mexico after the golden age, and like Ripstein, kept working into the new millennium. Given such a long career and the changing social and economic circumstances of Mexico, Cazals's work is uneven, but some of his films are among the best produced during the most difficult years of the industry. These include such titles as *Su Alteza Serenísima* (*His Most Serene Highness*, 2000), a biography of General Santa Anna, of El Álamo fame; *La Leyenda del Padre Negro* (*Kino*, 1993), a biography of the missionary of California, the Franciscan Father Eusebio Kino; the entertaining *El Tres de Copas* (*The Card of Love, Luck, and Death*, 1986); *Los Motivos de Luz* (*Luz's Reasons*, 1985), a study of poverty and its extreme consequences for a poor, helpless mother who is accused of killing her children; and the effective thriller *Bajo la Metralla* (*At Machine Gun Point*, 1983).

However, three films are at the highest point of his career because they challenge traditional Mexican society and because of their quality and experimental technique. They are *El Apando* (*The Punishment Cell*, 1976), a movie about alienation, injustice, and power set in the microcosm of a Mexican jail; *Canoa* (1975), a film about hysteria, fear of otherness, and political manipulation by a priest that ends with the lynching of a group of young strangers; and *Las Poquianchis* (1976), a story taken from the pages of the sensationalistic press that, apparently, is just about a provincial brothel run by three church-going sisters, but ends up uncovering a whole universe of political and police corruption. Equally challenging was the work of Jaime Humberto Hermosillo, who produced one of the first films about homosexuality and did not feel compelled to either kill his character or make him a ridiculous clown—*Doña Herlina y Su Hijo* (*Doña Herlinda and Her Son*, 1984). This film also has the quality of being a sarcastic look at the relationship and alliances of mothers and sons, girlfriends and friends, and anybody who feels oppressed in a patriarchal society in order to live their lives and to keep appearances. Other significant Hermosillo films are *De Noche Vienes, Esmeralda* (*Come at Night, Esmeralda*, 1997), *La Tarea Prohibida* (*The Forbidden Homework*, 1992), *La Tarea* (*The Homework*, 1990), *María de Mi Corazón* (*Maria, My Dearest*, 1979), *Naufragio* (*Shipwreck*, 1977), *Amor Libre* (*Free Love*, 1978), *Matinée* (1976), and *La Pasión Según Berenice* (*The Passion According to Berenice*, 1975).

But perhaps no other director has represented the tradition of an independent cinema and its relationship with the main industry better than Arturo Ripstein, one of the best and most prolific independent directors. Ripstein started making movies in the 1960s, but it was in the following few decades that his style matured and defined itself and his films became recognized and respected not only in Mexico, but in other parts of the world. He has remained active at least into the first years of the twenty-first century. Some of his most representative titles are *El Carnaval de Sodoma* (*Sodom's Carnival*, 2006), *La Vírgen de la Lujuria* (*The Virgin of Lust*, 2002), *La Perdición de los Hombres* (*The Downfall of Men*, 2000), *El Coronel no Tiene Quien le Escriba* (*No One Writes to the Colonel*, 1999), *La Reina de la Noche* (*The Queen of the Night*, 1994), *Principio y Fin* (*The Beginning and the End*, 1993), *La Mujer del Puerto* (*Woman of the Port*, 1991), *Mentiras Piadosas* (*Love Lies*, 1987), *El Imperio de la Fortuna* (*The Realm of Fortune*, 1986), *La Ilegal* (*The Illegal Woman*, 1979), *La Tía Alejandra* (*Aunt Alejandra*, 1979), *El Santo Oficio* (*The Holy Inquisition*, 1974), *El Náufrago de la Calle Providencia* (*The Castaway on Providence Street*, 1971), *Los Recuerdos del Porvenir* (*Memories of the Yet to Come*, 1969), and *Juego Peligroso* (*Dangerous Game*, 1967).

Some of his best are *El Evangelio de las Maravillas* (*Divine*, 1998), the story of a millenarist cult in Mexico awaiting for the return of Jesus, with such screen icons as Kathy Jurado and Francisco Rabal as the spiritual leaders of the cult; *Profundo Carmesí* (*Deep Crimson*, 1996), the story of Coral Fabre (Regina Orozco), a fat, frustrated single mother in 1940s Mexico who meets a gigolo, Nicolás (Daniel Giménez Cacho), through a sentimental magazine and together start a chain of murders and robberies of rich, unhappy, frustrated women seduced by Nicolás. The film is cold and ironic and shows characters with no sense of right and wrong; *Cadena Perpetua* (*Life Sentence*, 1979), the life of Javier "Tarzán" Lira (Pedro Armendáriz Jr.), whose attempts to reform after a life of petty crimes and incarceration are systematically frustrated by a corrupt police system in modern Mexico; *El Lugar sin Límites* (*The Place without Limits*, 1978), an excellent study of desire, frustration, and latent homosexuality in Mexican machismo and the intolerance and violence that it provokes; and *El Castillo de la Pureza* (*The Castle of Purity*, 1973), a sober melodrama based on the true story of a man who, to preserve his family members from the evils of the world, kept them locked in his old mansion where his children run a small factory to produce rat poison to survive.

Paul Leduc marked with his *Frida: Naturaleza Viva*, as mentioned at the beginning of the chapter, the regaining of the national audience for Mexican cinema. Like Hermosillo, Alcoriza, or Cazals, his work started in the 1970s with *Reed, México Insurgente* (*Insurgent Mexico*, 1970), an objective account of the Mexican Revolution based on the writings of John Reed. Leduc has remained active, although not very consistently, turning to video and returning to film in his latest picture. Other films by Leduc are *¿Cómo Ves?* (*What's Up?*, 1985), *Barroco* (*Baroque*, 1989), and *El Cobrador* (*Cobrador: In God We Trust*, 2006), his latest film, which is an excellent adaptation of the stories of Brazilian writer Rubem Fonseca, where he explores globalization, injustice, and the relationship between capitalism and terrorism. Alberto Isaac is another director whose works have not been as abundant or consistent as the directors mentioned previously. His films include *Mariana, Mariana* (1985) and *Mujeres Insumisas* (*Untamed Women*, 1994), a rather naïve view of the relationships between men and women with an implausible ending in which these rebel women move to the United States to start new lives. His early films include *En Este Pueblo no Hay Ladrones* (*There Are No Thieves in This Town*, 1965), a film written by García Márquez and with a cameo appearance by Luis Buñuel; *El Rincón de las Vírgenes* (*The Corner of the Virgins*, 1972), a film with Emilio "Indio" Fernández as a cult leader; and *Cuartelazo* (*Surprise Attack to the Cuartel*, 1977), a film about an episode of the Mexican Revolution.

Along with these films, directors, and tendencies that tried to keep alive a respected Mexican cinema, both commercial and independent, there were a series of popular movies. Many of them were easy, cheap, and completely disinterested in film as a medium of expression, but with the clear objective of recovering fast cash by producing simple, inexpensive pictures, shot as fast as possible at the expense of story, plot, technique, acting, taste, or logic. Many more were produced with the intention of capturing the huge Mexican market in the United States, exploiting Mexicans' nostalgia for their country or their inability to speak English and therefore their likelihood to watch only films coming from Mexico. These films focused on themes important for the community of Mexicans living in the United States, such as drug abuse, drug trafficking, illegal workers, discrimination, and human trafficking. Other films were a little more "sophisticated" and looked into traditional forms of popular entertainment, but they were equally interested in fast money and in spending as little as necessary in production. All these films provided Mexican communities on both sides of the border with "national" films often using old formulas of burlesque and popular spectacles with poor taste, exuberant female dancers, and sexual jokes. Such names as Sasha Montenegro, Andrés García, Polo Ortín, Olga Breeskin, Alfonso Zayas, Fernando and Mario Almada, Maribel Guardia, Rosa Gloria Chagoyán, Ana Luisa Peluffo, Jorge Rivero, Lyn May, Rafael Inclán, and Lalo "El Mimo," to mention only a few, are forever synonymous with one of the most embarrassing chapters of Mexican cinema that lasted until the early 1990s.

NOTES

1. "Gran Bretaña y México Planean Coproducir Películas," *La Jornada*, August 2, 2007, http://www.jornada.unam.mx/2007/08/01/index.php?section =espectaculos&article=a09n2esp.

2. Ibid.

3. Paul Julian Smith, "Transatlantic Traffic in Recent Mexican Films," *Journal of Latin American Cultural Studies* 12 (2003): 394.

4. Ibid., 390.

5. "Gran Bretaña y México Planean Coproducir Películas."

6. Rafael Aviña, *Una Mirada Insólita. Temas y Géneros del Cine Mexicano* (Mexico City: Oceano/Conaculta/Cineteca, 2004), 43–44.

7. Ibid.

8. Jorge Morales, "Stormy Weather: Cloudy Skies, Murky Plot, Lots of Waiting," *New York Village Voice*, April 6, 2004, http://www.villagevoice .com/2004-04-06/film/stormy-weather-cloudy-skies-murky-plot-lots-of-waiting/1.

9. Manohla Dargis, "A Thousand Clouds of Peace," *Los Angeles Times*, April 16, 2004, http://www.calendarlive.com/movies/reviews/cl-et-clouds16apr16,2,2342216.story?coll=cl-mreview.

10. Seth Fein, "From Collaboration to Containment," in *Mexico's Cinema: A Century of Films and Filmmakers*, ed. Joanne Hershfield and David R. Maciel (Wilmington, DE: Scholarly Resources, 1999), 128.

11. Ibid.

12. Ibid., 129.

13. Ibid., 142.

14. Ibid., 154.

CHAPTER 4
Mexican Cinema of the Golden Age

THE GOLDEN AGE

The golden age of Mexican cinema includes roughly three decades and goes from the emergence of talking pictures in the early 1930s to the lack of interest of Mexican audiences in national themes and traditions, followed by an increasing interest in more cosmopolitan European films and the predominance of Hollywood. Most critics consider the 1940s and the 1950s the best decades for Mexican cinema, a period when according to film studies Professor Joanne Hershfield, "Despite the historical dominance of Hollywood, Mexican cinema was able to achieve a level of economic, artistic, and popular success [...] that was unprecedented in any other Latin American country."[1] Many critics think that these achievements were somehow related to the proximity of Mexico to Hollywood and to the favorable conditions and support that the United States, in general, offered to Mexico, its closest ally during World War II. Whatever the case, Mexico had already been able to develop and consolidate a national film industry even before the 1940s. Like Spain, Argentina, or Brazil, Mexico became fascinated with cinema soon after the medium was invented and in the late 1890s started producing films.

Mexico was able to maintain a constant production of movies and to develop a solid industry; it also was able to develop an authentic star system and a number of idiosyncratic genres. Even when Mexican cinema relied on foreign formulas and genres, those movies were presented, and accepted, as autochthonous both in Mexico as well as abroad. Mexican cultural critic Carlos Monsiváis believes that even though Mexican cinema imitated Hollywood, some genres such as Westerns or thrillers were simply impossible to translate to the Mexican experience since "there were no Mexican equivalents for specific US environments and moods."[2] Other films were so embedded in the Mexican culture that they could be possible only in that country, such as the cabaretera films or the wrestler horror flicks. Critics such as Hershfield consider that, "although the Mexican film industry may have imported technology; industrial structures of production, exhibition, and distribution; raw materials; and stylistic and narrative strategies [from Hollywood], Mexican filmmakers were able to forge a distinctive national cinema, one that finally gained international recognition during its Golden Age."[3] Perhaps one of the best assessments of Mexican cinema was offered recently by *New York Times* critic A. O. Scott while reviewing the retrospective of Mexican films presented at Film Forum in New York City during the summer of 2004 with the title "Cine México." Mexican cinema was for Scott a surprise, a "parallel universe" to American cinema—the revelation of an industry whose splendor "roughly coincided with that of the Hollywood studios."[4]

However, he sees fundamental differences between both cinematic traditions; one very important one is the "frankness" of Mexican cinema as well as its realism that is sometimes pure fatalism. The diversity of films offered in "Cine México" (a very carefully selected anthology of Mexican movies from the silent era to the 1990s), even though it includes comedies, abstract and political films, period pieces, and lots of tear-jerkers, is so full of death, pain, happiness, hope for the future, and a stoic view of the world, all combined, that it truly reveals something profound about Mexican culture to Scott. "There is nothing more alien to North American sensibilities," writes the *New York Times* critic, "than the idea of a popular culture rooted in tragedy." And for him, "one of the revelations of Cine México is that an essentially tragic sensibility can contain so much humor, so much variety, so much life."[5] It is that life evident in Mexican cinema that made its films so popular and in the end so enduring, even if sometimes they relied on formulas and foreign styles or if they endorsed official, demagogic, or reactionary political views. That is exactly what Scott means when he affirms that if one feels tempted to exclaim while watching Mexican films such as *Amores Perros* or *Y Tu Mamá También*, "this is the future of film," watching films from the golden age "after half a century you can still find yourself thinking: this is where movies are going. It turns out this is where they have always been."[6]

CINEMA AND THE REVOLUTION

The development of Mexican cinema is linked to the popular revolt against the dictatorship of Porfirio Díaz known as the Mexican Revolution (1910–1921). This is such an important moment in the history of modern Mexico that touches every aspect of its culture all through the twentieth century, among other things because it brought dramatic and abrupt changes to a traditional society that from that moment on struggled to transform itself into a modern, diverse, urban nation. The most evident and shocking of these changes were a fast and improvised industrialization; the return to a lay, civil government; the revalorization of ethnic and economic minorities; and the rethinking of gender roles provoked by the massive displacement of women who traditionally had been subordinated to a male figure. These changes were abrupt and they advanced faster than anybody anticipated, leaving a social void that many factions and political groups tried to exploit for their own ideological and political agendas. Not surprisingly, cinema became instrumental in such changes, while testifying to the confusion of the population at large.

Proof of the ambiguity with which Mexican society viewed these changes is the first Mexican talking picture, *Santa* (Antonio Moreno, 1931). This movie never mentions the Revolution at a time when that was the most important political and social issue; instead, it tells a sanitized version of the story of a deceived country girl who becomes a prostitute and dies of a horrible illness. Based on a novel of the same title written in 1903 by Federico Gamboa, *Santa* centers on a melodramatic contemplation of the fall of its heroine (Lupita Tovar), who is seduced, impregnated, and then abandoned by Marcelino (Donald Reed), a handsome and arrogant official of the Mexican Army. Something similar happens with *Allá en el Rancho Grande* (*Over There in Rancho Grande*, Fernando de Fuentes, 1936), the first Mexican cinema international hit, that tells the story of an idealized countryside where landowners, workers, peasants, and sweet provincial girls live in a pastoral background where the Revolution seems to be just a minor inconvenience, and where the real issue worth dying or killing for is the doubts of the virginity of beautiful, but innocent Cruz (Esther Fernández).

This movie immediately became a success in Mexico and other countries, including the United States, where it was projected with English subtitles, which means that it was intended for the public in general and not only for Spanish-speaking audiences. It was also the first one to be recognized in international festivals. After the Revolution, the confusion of a country that started a movement of redefinition "late enough in the nation's process of modernization to radically reconfigure the Mexican state, [but] too early in the history of state formation to forge a totalitarian or a regime,"[7] according to Claudio Lomnitz, required new ways of understanding nationalism and modernity. This favored the emergence of what has been called a "cultural revolution," in which radical, liberal ideologies such as anticlericalism and an education and art for the people were promoted through the modern ways of communication, including cinema and mass media, and mixed with "narrative and cultural forms that were in no sense revolutionary," such as a romanticized view of the indigenous populations and an overmelodramatic sensibility based on honor and traditional bourgeois values, so important for the previous generation.[8]

It is in this context that *Santa* and *Allá en el Rancho Grande* were successful while two quintessential films of the Mexican Revolution, also directed by de Fuentes, failed at the box office. These films were *El Compadre Mendoza* (*Godfather Mendoza*, 1933) and *Vámonos con Pancho Villa* (*Let's Go with Pancho Villa*, 1935). *El Compadre Mendoza* is an extraordinary example of narrative cinema that, unlike many of the films that became identified with Mexican melodramas, is sober and faithful to its own story, where the women are more realistically independent and complex characters. The story focuses on how rich landowner Rosalío Mendoza (Alfredo del Diestro) manages not only to survive the Revolution, but actually to benefit from it by supporting simultaneously the two opposite bands. "I am not fond of talking too much. Things must be done fast and well," he repeats constantly; Rosalio clearly represents a new opportunistic class ready to take over the new nation. *Vámonos con Pancho Villa*, on the other hand, focuses on the lives of five peasants, the Lions of San Marcos, who joined Pancho Villas's army because they had no other choice and who fought bravely to defend their right for a better life. However, one by one they died abandoned and ignored by Villa. "The life of one man means nothing if that means saving the life of many," barks the Villista official to the last survivor of the Lions when he orders him to burn the body of his friend who is dying of smallpox.

Very original—although it may seem dated to contemporary audiences of action movies—these films explore individuality and collective consciousness during a time of crisis with less than optimistic views. Along with these movies there is one often mentioned as part of a trilogy, *El Prisionero 13* (*Prisoner Number 13*, 1933), which is a very enjoyable morality tale about a drunken, abusive general who is abandoned by his wife and small son, and who years later, during the Revolution and due to some unexpected coincidences, condemns his own son to die by firing squad. Naïve and fresh, this movie along with the other two films added just the right dosage of humor, humanity, and skepticism to the exaggerated official discourse of hope and progress put forward by the post-Revolutionary government. All through the 1930s, the Revolution was the privileged subject of Mexican cinema with such films as *Rebelión* (*Revolt*, Manuel G. Gómez, 1934); *El Tesoro de Pancho Villa* (*The Treasure of Pancho Villa*, Arcady Boytler, 1935); *Con los Dorados de Villa* (*With Villa's Golden Squad*, Chano Urueta, 1939); and *La Adelita* (Guillermo Hernández Gómez and Mario de Lara, 1935) and *La Valentina* (Matín de Lucenay, 1938), two films about the famous *soldaderas* or women who fought side by side with their men. Important to mention is also *Los de Abajo* (*The Underdogs*, Chano Urueta, 1939), based on the novel by Mariano Azuela that inaugurated the literature of the Revolution.

However, by the 1940s, a realistic portrayal of the Revolution gave way to a more idealized, grandiloquent, and, occasionally, a frankly ridiculous view of that historical moment, with movies that rested heavily on the folkloric and on the picturesque, but that nonetheless forced Mexican cinema to develop more sophisticated narrative techniques and to pay more attention to detail—spectacular cinematography, careful editing, and authentic mise-en-scènes contributed to develop authentic visual aesthetics that became the most recognizable representation of Mexico. The cinematic images of the country—rough and beautiful, violent, and full of poetry with men on horseback and big sombreros galloping toward spectacular open skies—became one of the favorite images of national identity. It is perhaps the style of Emilio "Indio" Fernández and the photography of Gabriel Figueroa that best represents this Mexican aesthetics. The collaboration between these two artists will remain the most emblematic of Mexican cinema and the most recognized internationally.

If the Revolution was central for the narrative of many of Fernández's films, it often was nothing more than an epic background for torrid and passionate love affairs, as in the case of *Flor Silvestre* (*Wild Flower*, 1943), the story of a poor girl (Dolores del Río) in love with a rich rancher (Pedro Armendáriz) who joins the Revolution; *Las Abandonadas* (*The Abandoned Women*, 1944), which narrates the misfortunes of Margarita Pérez (Dolores del Río), a woman who has no choice but to become a prostitute when she is abandoned by the man she loves (Víctor Junco) and who is taken out of the brothel where she works by a revolutionary general (Pedro Armendáriz); or the excellent *Enamorada* (*Woman in Love*, 1946), which focuses on a love story that updates Shakespeare's *The Taming of the Shrew* in the middle of the Revolution. Beatriz Peñafiel (María Félix) is the beautiful and capricious daughter of a rich rancher who falls in love with a revolutionary general (Pedro Armendáriz) and leaves everything behind to follow him. Other films were not directly related to the Revolution, although they talk about the life of the peasantry before the Revolution. An example of this is *María Candelaria* (1943), perhaps the most famous of Fernández's films, that tells the tragic story of an Indian couple in love, again, that emblematic Mexican pair Dolores del Río and Pedro Armendáriz, who have to confront all the people against them.

La Perla (*The Pearl*, 1945) was a similar film in its approach and sensibility to *María Candelaria*, and it is important also because it cemented the international career of Fernández, who had adapted a novel by Nobel laureate John Steinbeck. In the same vein, *Maclovia* (1948), *Pueblerina* (1948), and *La Malquerida* (1949) explore the picturesque lives and dilemmas of Indians and poor peasants in spectacular settings with some hints of social consciousness, but without really crossing the real powers of the State, the army, and even the Church. Other movies were more political and directly supported the official attempts to educate the masses and to bring justice to all by promoting an end to centuries of servitude. The best example of this "social" cinema is *Río Escondido* (*Hidden River*, 1947), a didactic story about the mission and importance of educators in the new Mexico. Rosaura Salazar (María Félix), a beautiful and fragile schoolteacher, is sent by the president himself to reopen a school in a far, dusty village in the north part of the country. When she arrives, she has to confront the cacique of the town, a brutish man who runs the town and the lives of its inhabitants, and to fight centuries of tradition and indifference.

The films of Emilio Fernández are, regardless of all their flaws and virtues, marvelous examples of a national cinema happily and proudly embraced as such because of its sensibility. They also represent the happy marriage of a popular, if not populist, susceptibility and an official ideology that sought to summarize a concrete moment in the history and culture of the country. If early Mexican movies, such as *Santa* and *Allá en el Rancho Grande*, ignored the Revolution and

Emilio Fernández tried to place it at the core of popular culture, later movies of the 1950s took the subject to ridiculous extremes of grandiloquence and exaggeration, turning it into a spectacle where the ideas and the ideals were not important at all. It served as a bizarre excuse for ridiculous plots, such as the life of Pancho Villa narrated by his severed head. Some other examples are Ismael Rodriguez's *Así Era Pancho Villa* (*That Is How Pancho Villa Was*, 1957), *Pancho Villa y la Valentina* (*Pancho Villa and Valentina*, 1958), *La Cucaracha* (1958), and *Cuando ¡Viva Villa! Es la Muerte* (*Viva Villa! Means Death*, 1958).

CITY OF LIGHT, CITY OF SHADOWS

The Revolution, although concerned with the *problems* of rural life, started nonetheless a process of transformation that would eventually change urban existence, particularly affecting life in the capital. Mexico City, the center of cultural life and politics, became the ideal stage for intellectuals, artists, and filmmakers to explore the new ways of being Mexican and to question the postrevolutionary government's obsession with progress. Cinema found in urban comedies, and particularly in melodramas, the ideal vehicle for such explorations. The films of directors as different as Alejandro Galindo, Ismael Rodríguez, Julio Bracho, Juan Bustillo Oro, and Luis Buñuel, to name but a few, converged in a sort of social awareness evident above all in popular language and the use of urban spaces as the symbolic arena where the morals and virtues as well as perils of a new Mexican society were confronted. Cinema, an art associated with modernity and technology but with deep roots in popular culture, became the mediator between the illiterate masses and the citizens of the modern nation. According to Hershfield, Mexican cinema interprets modern culture for these people and "functions as an efficient 'structure of mediation' that works to legitimate unequal relations."[9]

Mexican melodramas and urban comedies of the 1940s and 1950s grew to reflect the city and mimic the speech and the way of life of the most diverse social groups as well as their social and political interactions. Typically, most urban comedies and melodramas began with a pan shot of the city, showing its streets, avenues, parks, markets, and buildings in order to physically locate the story as well as to demonstrate that Mexico City was, for better or for worse, just like any other big city in the world. Because of their popular appeal as a form of entertainment in a country of illiterate masses, movies were able to reach far beyond the possibilities of literature, confronting the most diverse sectors of society with issues such as modernization, class struggle, corruption, religion, sexuality, as well as the failure of the Revolution. Movies therefore allowed the public to participate in the social and cultural debates of the times, while provoking immediate (and often visceral) responses to the issues derived of such debates.

Big urban centers, but Mexico City in particular, became the point of junction of the two nations, the geographic one and the one built on studio sets. In the process, interesting hybrids were created to try to deal simultaneously with traditional values and the changing ones of the new times, particularly if they were politically and socially dangerous. *Dicen que Soy Comunista* (*They Say I Am a Communist*, Alejandro Galindo, 1951), for example, is a comedy centered on the naïveté of its main character who is seduced by false communist ideals, only to realize that he has been fooled by a group of corrupt gangsters taking advantage of innocent people who believed in the socialist rhetoric that abounded in Mexico after the Revolution. *Azahares para Tu Boda* (*Orange Blossoms for Your Wedding*, Julián Soler, 1950) is a melodrama that similarly opposes the traditional Mexico for the modernity the Revolution was bringing, particularly in new ideologies around the time of the Revolution. In this case, however, the film opposes communism to religious beliefs and a traditional way of life with a heavy dosage of tears.

If melodramas established a connection with the dreams and emotional needs of the public, the urban comedies mirrored, either voluntarily or involuntarily, the changing society at odds with itself that had created them. It is this complicity with the audience, above all, that makes movies of this period truly examples of what has been called a golden age. The highly critical nature of language and melodramatic exaggeration of Mexican movies had its roots in the political satires of the popular "carpas" or traditional tent shows that featured folkloric spectacles with vaudeville, burlesque, and flimflam artists, some of whom, including Mario Moreno, "Cantinflas," became movie stars. The early Cantinflas embodies the contradictions of the new society in which the new ruling class uses an empty and haughty speech that was full of promises but completely detached from the real needs of the people.

Other movies centered on different aspects of traditional Mexican culture such as death and sexuality. A curious, mildly funny example is *La Muerte Enamorada* (*Death Has Fallen in Love*, Ernesto Cortázar, 1950), a simple metaphysical fable about Death incarnated as a beautiful woman who falls in love with an unhappily married man only to help him and his wife fix their marital problems. If the film is really nothing out of the ordinary, with a predictable plot, undeveloped characters, and a sloppy mise-en-scene, the imposing beauty of Miroslava Stern who plays Death and a surreal scene of a dance of skeletons playing bone instruments (the xylophone is the carcass of an ox, the saxophone is an arm and a hand, and the trumpet is a femur) are reasons enough to watch the movie. *Locura Pasional* (*Madness of Passion*, Tulio Demicheli, 1956), on the other hand, is a loose adaptation of Leo Tolstoy's *The Kreutzer Sonata* (1889) that serves as an excuse to explore the culture of pornographic publications (or what seemed pornographic in the mid-1950s) and its dreadful implications for the new society in an exaggerated and sensationalistic way that neither inspires pity or sympathy for the main character, and in the end it fails to arouse audiences in any way.

More entertaining, but definitely less preoccupied with contemporary issues, were such movies as the light comedies *El Marido de Mi Novia* (*The Husband of My Girlfriend*, René Cardona Jr., 1951) or *Se Solicitan Modelos* (*Models Wanted*, Chano Urueta, 1954). Other films, particularly such melodramas as *Crepúsculo* (*Crepuscule*, Julio Bracho, 1944) or *Distinto Amanecer* (*A Different Dawn*, Julio Bracho, 1946), were more serious about the possibilities of the genre; in fact, Bracho is one of the first Mexican directors with the serious aspiration of auteurship who is among the best of the golden age and who really respected the intelligence of the audience. There is a scene in *Crepúsculo*, for example, where Arturo de Córdova's character, a rich doctor, gives a book also titled *Crepúsculo* to his butler. The book is the diary of a mentally ill person. When the butler, surprised by this action, asks his master if he thinks he will be able to understand such a complicated book, his master replies that he must, that everybody must. The movie begins then to tell (to illustrate) the story of that mentally ill person, who happens to be the famous doctor portrayed by de Córdova, who, in turn, happens to be the author of the book. This scene is a perfect metaphor of how melodramas function, interpreting things for the audience.

Distinto Amanecer, on the contrary, focuses on the story of a labor organizer who is trying to obtain some important documents. In the process he meets his college sweetheart and true love, who is now married to his college best friend who also used to share his ideals of social justice, but has since given up to disillusion. The film then focuses on the relationship of the three old friends in a *Casablanca*-like plot of politics and love, but with a few minor stories intertwined in the plot. The film is beautifully shot and makes excellent use of black and white, particularly of shadows, as well as the locations in Mexico City. Both Andrea Palma and Pedro Armendáriz gave some of their best performances. These two films opted for a more sophisticated way of interacting with the audience as the industry was developing. Another example of this complexity is *Una Familia de Tantas* (*A Family Like Many Others*, Alejandro Galindo, 1948), an intelligent tale of the clash between two of the most enduring symbols of Mexican society: the fragile maiden, Maru (Martha Roth) and the almighty patriarch, Rodrigo (Fernando Soler). The story revolves around Maru's struggle for independence from a tyrannical father and a traditional family so she can marry the man she loves and not the one her father had chosen for her.

The more sophisticated these movies became, the more they allowed the public to participate in the social and cultural debates of the times, while provoking immediate (and often visceral) responses to the issues derived of such debates. Some films that in one way or another challenged some traditional beliefs are Arcady Boytler's *La Mujer del Puerto* (*The Woman of the Port*, 1933), a film about accidental incest; Adela Sequeyro's *Más Allá de la Muerte* (*Beyond Death*, 1935) and *La Mujer de Nadie* (*Nobodies Woman*, 1937), two intelligent melodramas directed by a woman; Juan Bustillo Oro's *Dos Monjes*, (*Two Monks*, 1932), an experiment in expressionism, passion, and mental unbalance, and *Ahí Está el Detalle* (*That Is the Point*, 1940), a funny comedy that mocks an empty speech; Joaquín Pardavé's *El Baisano Jalil* (*My Countryman Jalil*, 1942), a film about Lebanese immigration to Mexico; and Alberto Gout's *Aventurera* (*Adventurous Woman*, 1949), an outrageous melodrama about a madam, her prostitution ring, her son, and the woman he loves.

No other cinematic genre is so identified as Mexican as the *cabaretera* films of the 1940s and 1950s; fewer films also are more intricately connected to the urban space and its underworld as these movies are about good girls gone bad and, sometimes, back again to being good. The reality of a country moving fast and chaotically away from a rural economy and without really being prepared for the challenges of an urban society did not go unnoticed by the people. Movies, being the modern form of art and entertainment, seemed like the natural medium of exploration of the contradictions that resulted from that modernization without modernity. In one way or another, this genre is a summary of the same dilemma lived by the nation as a whole: an innocent, naïve provincial girl taken away from what she knows, from the paternal household, and thrown into the underworld of sex and violence, has to utilize any possible means of survival, including crime and prostitution, but without ever loosing her righteous ways and her moral thirst for revenge.

The basic premise of all these films is the loss of innocence of the virgin maiden because she is deceived or betrayed by the man she loves or because society has turned into a jungle in which everybody has to kill or be killed to survive in the middle of complicated and passionate love triangles. Perhaps the best examples of this are Emilio "Indio" Fernández's *Salón México* (1948) and *Víctimas del Pecado* (*Victims of Sin*, 1950). In many urban melodramas and comedies, a preoccupation with popular culture is present; perhaps more than anything else it is the language that serves as the direct link between the public and the film. The assertiveness of Cantinflas, for example, derives from his mockery of official

language. The best example is *Ahí Está el Detalle*, in which a series of misunderstandings end up with Cantinflas in jail and on trial. During the process, his speech makes an already confusing situation even more confusing. And when everything seems lost for him, the real criminal appears, confesses, and Cantinflas is set free, to which he exclaims, "See it's just a matter of speaking clearly."

But what makes the movie subversive is that that is not the reason he is free and that at the end of the trial judges, defenders, lawyers, and all the representatives of law and order are talking like Cantinflas. That is also the case in Alejandro Galindo's *Campeón sin Corona* (*Champion without a Crown*, 1945), where language and popular realism are instruments stretched by Galindo to explore the inferiority complex of Mexicans. "Kid" Terranova (David Silva), a world boxing champion, is literally invincible in the ring until he has to fight the Chicano boxer Joe Ronda (Víctor Parra); he is clearly impressed by the fact that Ronda speaks English. Buñuel does something similar in *El Gran Calavera* (*The Great Madcap*, 1949), where the division of classes is marked by language. When two women from a poor neighborhood talk about the new neighbors (who are really rich people faking a bankruptcy), one of them says that she knows they were rich before. "Why?" asks her friend and she replies simply, "Because they talk funny." And when the rich woman addresses them in what she thinks is the way poor people talk, the poor women look at each other and smile sardonically.

Language clearly is identity. This issue of identity in language and cultural differences is also explored more directly in *Espaldas Mojadas*

(*Wetbacks*, Alejandro Galindo, 1950), a rare movie in the Mexico of the time that acknowledges and treats with respect and seriousness the issue of illegal immigration to the United States. Popular language and culture in the movies cannot be understood completely without understanding the space where they exist: the lower-class housing, or *vecindad*. The *vecindad* is the populist attempt to represent Mexican society at its best: poor, but honest, full of solidarity, honor, and a great capacity for suffering as best exemplified by *Nosotros los Pobres* (*We the Poor*, Ismael Rodríguez, 1948) and its sequel *Ustedes los Ricos* (*You the Rich*, Ismael Rodríguez, 1948), perhaps the most popular Mexican films ever. Unlike Italian neorealism, however, where social elements become a real issue through the testimonial aspects of documentary-like filming, Mexican urban films often treat all the characters more like types or even stereotypes, such as gangsters, *peladito* or street-wise guys, cabaret girls, prostitutes with a heart of gold, corrupt politicians, and phony labor leaders.

And yet, at the center of Mexican life, the city (the geographic one and the one built in studio sets) became the point of junction of the several Mexicos, where movies consistently functioned as the vehicle of their communication. If the struggle for modernization gave Mexican movies of the golden age the opportunity to connect with their audience, by the end of the 1950s, Mexican society was already on the fast track to become "modern" following an American model. Consequently, Mexico City started to be presented more and more as a cosmopolitan urban space. Now we see a city with an impressive university, with neatly rimmed parks, and the latest models of automobiles circulating through its streets. With the old city, much of the popular spirit that had made the work of Rodríguez and Galindo possible disappeared as well. It was also at this time that melodramas started to take seriously their roles as educators. The audience, too, had changed and rejected these simple, preachy new plots deprived of humor or irony. According to some critics, with the introduction of American and European sophisticated movies, Mexican middle classes came to detest machismo and the picturesque. And it is true up to a point because the truth is that by the end of the 1950s, Mexican cinema had already lost its connection with its once faithful audience. And this seemed to have been the case for decades, despite a period of relative revitalization both economically and artistically of the film industry during the administration of Luis Echeverría (1970–1976), one of the most populist presidents of modern Mexican history.

NOTES

1. Joanne Hershfield, *Mexican Cinema, Mexican Woman 1940–1950* (Tucson: University of Arizona Press, 1996), 4.

2. Carlos Monsiváis, "Mythologies," in *Mexican Cinema*, ed. Paulo Antonio Paraguana (London: British Film Institute/IMCINE, 1995), 117.

3. Hershfield, *Mexican Cinema, Mexican Woman*, 7.

4. A. O. Scott, "Film; A Different Mexican Revolution," *New York Times*, June 27, 2004, http://www.nytimes.com/2004/06/27/movies/film-a-different-mexican-revolution.html?sec=&spon=&&scp=1&sq=Cine%20México&st=cse.

5. Ibid.

6. Ibid.

7. Claudio Lomnitz, "What Was Mexico's Cultural Revolution?" in *The Eagle and the Virgen. Nation and Cultural Revolution in Mexico, 1920–1940*, ed. Mary Key Vaughan and Stephen E. Lewis (Durham, NC: Duke University Press, 2006), 335.

8. Ibid., 335.

9. Hershfield, *Mexican Cinema, Mexican Woman*, 5.

CHAPTER 5

The Cinema of Brazil

ELITE SQUAD

When José Padilha's *Tropa de Elite* (*Elite Squad*, 2007) won the Golden Bear at the 2008 Berlin International Film Festival, beating the other Latin American favorite, *Lake Tahoe* (2008) by Mexican Fernando Eimbcke, Brazilians knew that they had reached the point of validating talks of a renaissance of their cinema, particularly since that year the prize for best short film at the same festival also went to a Brazilian—Daniel Ribeiro for his *Café com Leite* (*Coffee with Milk*, 2007). Certainly this acknowledgment was not the first one Brazilian cinema had received recently. Only 10 years earlier the very same honor had gone to *Central do Brasil* (*Central Station*, Walter Salles, 1998), a movie that became an international hit, collected numerous prizes around the world, and was nominated for two Oscars. Nonetheless, the triumph of Padilha—whose film has also collected a considerable number of nominations and prizes worldwide—culminated a long process of recovery for Brazilian cinema that started in the last decade of the twentieth century, particularly in 1993, the year in which the support for film again became a priority for the Brazilian government with the creation of the so-called Audiovisual Law.

Even though the film has been shown, distributed, and honored, and even though Brazilian audiences look at it with pride as the newest accomplishment of their cinema, it somehow remains controversial among most critics and intellectual circles because of the violence, the coldness, and the ambiguity with which it treats the problematic relationship between the police and the population. Above all it has been accused of putting forward a reactionary view that portrays the police rather sympathetically, something most Brazilians have problems accepting. *Variety* in the United States went as far as to place this film, ideologically, on the extreme Right and even label it as fascist, something that prompted the director to react and defend his film. According to Padilha, the film was misunderstood by the critics, since his only intention was to "explain how the State corrupts the police and incites them to violence."[1] He had previously blamed Brazilian critics for having influenced the bad criticism the movie was receiving abroad, something he said did not bother him personally because, in his opinion, it was time to erase old distinctions between Left and Right. "Some people think we are intelligent and some people think we are fascist. I really do not care about that."[2] In reality this criticism to Padilha's film is somehow unfair if we consider the long tradition of this type of film and compare it with the reality of Brazil and, in fact, most Latin American societies.

Much less controversial and more audience-friendly for sure, particularly if we talk about foreign audiences, *Central do Brasil* also dealt with poverty and corruption, but instead of exploring social violence and injustice, it preferred to center on a personal trip of self-discovery. Both winners of the Golden Bear could not be more different, and yet they represent the two extremes of a film industry that, like the Mexican or the Spanish, went through cyclic periods of splendor, decadence, and recovery. When in 1993 the Brazilian government promulgated the new Audiovisual Law, "which adapted pre-exiting laws of fiscal incentive"[3] with the purpose of aiding and stimulating film production, it also placed the government in a central role—that of being the main support of cultural matters, something that a previous president, Fernando Collor de Mello, had considered unnecessary. With neoliberal ideas and old patterns of corruption, the short administration of Collor de Mello was one of the most devastating for the country and damaging for cultural affairs in general and for film in particular. His administration ended with his impeachment for corruption in 1992, only two and a half years after he was elected.

Soon after the new Audiovisual Law was restituted, the first signs of the recovery of the industry started to appear. In 1995 one of the strongest signs was produced by the release of Carla Camurati's *Carlota Joaquina, Princessa do Brasil* (*Carlota Joaquina, Princess of Brazil*), a film that looks back at the history of the country in search of new trends and ideas to understand the present. Perhaps that is why the film was a huge success to the point that it is considered the one that brought Brazilian audiences back to watch national films. However, it is important to mention that the disinterest in national films in Brazil, similarly to what happened in Mexico, was a long process that started much earlier. Unlike Mexico, though, Brazilian cinema had a great renaissance during the 1960s called *cinema novo* (new cinema), which we discuss in the next chapter. If *cinema novo* managed to convoke Brazilians around the screens to watch artistically complex films that explored the reality of the country, that was not the case during the following decades when political repression and censorship made it basically impossible for a cinema of quality to subsist.

In the words of Lúcia Nagib, "Brazilian cinema undergoes periodical births and rebirths and, after brief peaks, is afflicted by sudden deaths and prolonged silences."[4] The most recent, and most dramatic, rebirth is the one that resulted from the implementation of the Audiovisul Law, which came after the decline of the industry in the late 1970s, the 1980s, and the first years of the 1990s. This rebirth significantly included several women such as Carla Camurati, whose *Carlota Joaquina*, as we mentioned, "revealed that new directors and new themes could attract large audiences."[5] But between this resurgence and the *cinema novo*, there was a decline of the industry as the result of several factors. Many of them were shared by the whole hemisphere, such as the economic crisis of the 1980s and the consequent increase of production costs of filmmaking; the impoverishment of the majority of the population, particularly in large urban centers; the lack of class mobility; and problems of censorship, repression, and a lack of democracy. The decline of the industry came, ironically, just as the political establishment was crumbling with the end of the military dictatorship. Chaos followed, symbolically represented by the death of Tancredo Neves, the first elected president in more than 20 years, who died before he took office. His death shocked the nation. The last days of his life, spent in hospitals and operating rooms, were followed by the media; these events also became movie history when they were recreated in the film *Patria Amada* (*Beloved Homeland*, Tizuka Yamasaki, 1984).

Cinema novo, however, left a deep intellectual and artistic print on the national soul by creating a school that established, continued, and transformed themes and styles unique to the Brazilian idiosyncrasy. These unfortunately have not been matched by the *retomada do cinema brasileiro* (the reemergence of Brazilian cinema), as the new trend has been called, according to Carlos Diegues, one of the old masters of the movement. For Diegues, the crisis of the film industry is closely tied to the decline in attendance to movie theaters; he thinks it is a global trend, not just a Brazilian problem. Nonetheless, the problem is more evident in Latin America where people used to go to the movies with the illusion of seeing themselves projected on the screen. However, the constant economic crisis of many Latin American countries and the effects of globalization have only increased the numbers of people who can no longer afford going to the movies, while increasing the absurd illusion that those who can are more like the Americans they watch on the screen with the consequent loss of identity. "Having been transformed into a typical middle-class leisure activity, the cinematic spectacle has been subsumed into 'shopping centre' culture in Brazil. It is targeted precisely at the section of the population who, fueled by dreams and fantasies of a hypothetical 'first world,' refuse to recognize or take part in the realities of the country."[6]

In other words, it is not so much that people stopped watching Brazilian films, but that the interests and economic circumstances of the country changed in an increasingly globalized and free market. Whether we agree or not with Diegues, his assessment is provocative and suggestive because it is a direct response to the rhetoric of the big corporations and distributors of foreign films that argue that the government should stay out of the business of promoting or dictating what films should be seen. According to them, the public is the only one that should decide what to watch, or in the words of Arturo Neto, director of the biggest exhibition group in Brazil, "The public is the one who determines when a film is exhibited. None of us is so insensitive as to stop showing a movie that is getting a good audience."[7] And that is true, but as Cacilda M. Rêgo replies, it ignores the fact that in order for people to decide which movies to watch, they need to know at least what movies are being produced. Surely in a perfect world it would be people, not corporations, who decide what is shown; however, this is impossible if they do not know what is available.

THE *RETOMADA* OF BRAZILIAN CINEMA

It is undeniable that Brazilians have started to watch national films and that the quantity and quality of those films have been steadily increasing; furthermore, Brazil, along with Mexico and Spain, has been reaffirming its presence in the international market. The variety of themes and genres that has come out of the country in recent years is representative of the diversity and complexity of life in contemporary Brazil, but it is also an attempt to reconnect with themes traditionally privileged by Brazilian cinema. *Central do Brasil* is, for instance, a road movie that narrates the misadventures of Dora (the excellent Fernanda Montenegro), a disenchanted, selfish, indifferent woman who has to help a poor, motherless child travel through the country in search of his father; in the process she recovers her humanity. This film has many things in common with *Bye Bye Brasil* (Carlos Diegues, 1979) or even *O Pagador de Promessas* (*The Keeper of Promises*, Anselmo Duarte, 1962); therefore, we can say that it serves as a bridge between a new sensibility and the traditional themes of Brazilian cinema. The film, for example, begins in Rio de Janeiro, giving the audience a very good idea of the poverty and violent condition of life in the outskirts of the city; it also points toward the unhappiness that the city offers to its inhabitants, in opposition to life in an idealized countryside of which we get some glimpses in the film. The ending, however, unlike previous films that touch on similar subjects, is rather optimistic and romantic. The fact that the movie was the biggest hit of the 1990s suggests that something had changed in the audiences' preference, something movies had picked up on.

Nonetheless, *Central do Brasil* connects two recurrent themes in Brazilian cinema: the *favela* (shanty town) and the *sertão* (the countryside), particularly the arid impoverished regions of the Northeast. The *sertão* is important because it traditionally has been the setting of another important theme of Brazilian cinema, *cangaço* (banditry), a theme also recovered recently with great success in films such as *Guerra de Canudos* (*The Battle of Canudos*, Sérgio Rezende, 1997), *O Baile Perfumado* (*Perfumed Ball*, Paulo Caldas and Lírio Ferreira, 1996), and *Corisco e Dadá* (*Corisco and Dadá*, Rosemberg Cariry, 1996). *Guerra de Canudos* is an epic film and is perhaps the most expensive movie ever made in Brazil; it narrates the true story of a religious community in the state of Bahia that rebels against the republic instituted in 1889, which has shown a complete disregard toward the poorest of the poor. Guided by a charismatic religious leader, Antônio Conselheiro (José Wilker), the community confronts the Brazilian Army in the bloodiest civil battle ever to be fought in Brazil. The battle has been traditionally a source of inspiration for literature, especially in Euclides da Cunha's *Os Sertões* (1902), as well as popular culture, folklore, and film.

Guerra de Canudos is in the end a movie about a historical moment, and not exactly about banditry per se. *O Baile Perfumado* and *Corisco e*

Dadá, on the other hand, descend directly from the classic film *O Can-gaçeiro* (*The Bandit*, Lima Barreto, 1953). All three films deal with the lives of two famous bandits at the beginning of the twentieth century in northern Brazil, Lampião and Corisco, who became folk heroes because of their Robin Hood–like attitude toward the people and their constant defiance of the corrupt authorities who were more often than not at the service of the powerful landowners of the Northeast. *O Baile Perfumado* centers on the life of Lampião, using very ingenious techniques such as brilliant colors and folk music as well as the mixing of a fictionalized narrative with real footage of the bandit and his gang. *Corisco e Dadá* is perhaps less original, but it has the advantage of narrating the life of Corisco based on the actual recollections of his lover and partner in crime, Dadá, who died in the 1990s. Maybe the biggest difference between the *cangaço* films of the 1990s and the one from the 1950s is that, according to Stephanie Dennison, "the new films are concerned with revealing the more personal and intimate lives of the bandits, and in particular their relationship with colleagues, loved ones, and their surroundings."[8]

The other traditional theme of Brazilian film that is present in *Central do Brasil* is the violence of the city, particularly violence by and against children. This theme is pushed to its limits in *Cidade de Deus* (*City of God*, Fernando Meirelles and Kátia Lund, 2002), a film that was an international hit; through gorgeous cinematography, vibrant colors, and music, it brought the slums of Rio de Janeiro to the forefront of the cultural discussion all around the world at the beginning of the new millennium. The film registers some violent events that happened in a notorious *favela* between the 1960s and the 1980s; it opens with the fast-paced style we have come to associate with music videos, and then it changes to sepia tones to narrate the events of the late 1960s. The story fast-forwards to the 1970s in a transition that is marked by vibrant colors and the funky music of the time and ends in the Brazil of the 1980s. The plot is simple: a poor kid nicknamed Buscapé (Luis Otávio) dreams of a better life away from the violence of the neighborhood where he lives. In the process, he witnesses the change of power from the famous Trio Ternura, three small thieves who rob without killing, to Dadinho (Douglas Silva), a wannabe gangster with such a killer nature that he wants nothing but to be the city's biggest criminal. Desperate to escape, and eager to tell the world about the dangers of Cidade de Deus, Buscapé (now played by Alexandre Rodrigues) turns to photography as his only way out.

Also focusing on the *favelas*, but being somehow less successful than *Cidade de Deus*, we have another film about youth and poverty in Rio de Janeiro, *Cidade dos Homens* (*City of Men*, Paulo Morelli, 2007). The title obviously tries to respond to (or take advantage of the fame of) *Cidade de Deus*; it even uses some of the same actors. In this film we witness the friendship of Acerola (Douglas Silva) and Laranjinha (Darlan Cunha) and its ups and downs amid a war for control of the drug territories in the *favela*. A different movie that is far from the visual rush, the intensity, and the perfection of style, as well as the visual pyrotechnics of *Cidade de Deus*, and definitely more interesting than *Cidade dos Homens*, is *Como Nascem Os Anjos* (*How Angels Are Born*, Murillo Salles, 1996). Similarly, this film is about poor children from the *favela*, but in this case the story offers an ingenious switch—it moves the toughs to a rich neighborhood, more precisely to the house of an American ex-patriate (Larry Pine) and his daughter (Ryan Massey), to make the contrast between the two lifestyles more poignant. With this unexpected trick, the director manages effectively to comment on the painful disparities between a rich, privileged few and the majority living in infrahuman conditions, a contrast more bitter because the privileged are in this case foreigners.

Another recent trend in Brazilian cinema is a tradition of political films in the most literal sense, that is, movies about the political situation of the country, particularly, but not exclusively, during the more than 20 years of dictatorship. One of the most famous and accomplished of them (it was nominated for an Oscar) is *O Que É Isso, Companheiro?* (*Four Days in September*, Bruno Barreto, 1997), a recreation of the kidnapping of American ambassador Charles Burke Elbrick by a guerrilla group that opposed the military government on September 4, 1969. It is based on the book by the same title by Fernando Gabeira, a firsthand account of the event. Other movies recreate the political climate of the country and of the several guerrilla movements during the military dictatorship: for example, *O Ano em que Meus Pais Saíram de Férias* (*The Year My Parents Went on Vacation*, Cao Hamburger, 2006), the story of a boy left alone by revolutionary parents who dropped him off at his grandfather's house without knowing he had actually died. With a nostalgic aura, the movie is also an excuse to take a look at a Brazilian Jewish community during the 1970 World Cup competition in which Brazil became the world champion for the third time.

Similarly *Quase Dois Irmãos* (*Almost Brothers*, Lúcia Murat, 2004), a powerful look at class relations and political ideals admixed with samba, carnival, drug dealings, and the proverbial violence of the *favelas*, looks back at the years of the political prisoners. The film also puts race at the center of the inequality and the social struggles of the country and seems to suggest that there is no noble way out of prejudice. According to Stephen Holden of the *New York Times*,

> This bitter, hardheaded movie doesn't let us off easily. In the cruelest plot twist, Miguel's beautiful, insolent daughter, Juliana (Maria Flor), is having an affair with Deley (Renato de Souza), one of two warring gang leaders in Santa Marta. The film portrays the middle-class fascination with the lower depths (in Juliana's case, with hot outlaw sex) as a risky exercise in arrogant self-delusion. The despairing threads of the story twist into a tragic knot during the final scenes, in which Miguel drives through Carnival while the law of the street pays a visit to Jorge in prison. Every masked reveler leering into the windshield wears an expression of savage mockery.[9]

The involvement of the media conglomerate Globo in the film industry has been important in many ways and has also created some genres that cannot deny their close relationship with television format and conventions. If on the one hand Globo promoted the national film industry and secured distribution for many films either by buying them (*Guerra de Canudos*) or by creating a channel dedicated to Brazilian films, on the other hand it favored a film style that owes a lot to soap operas and even American television situation comedies. This perpetuates the illusion of a class that dreams about looking American and is completely indifferent to the reality of its nation. Some examples of this are *Como Ser Solteiro* (*How to Be Single in Rio*, Rosane Svartmann, 1998), a sort of battle of the sexes in a "real" Rio—that is a Rio without the superrich or the extremely poor; *Pequeno Dicionário Amoroso* (*Little Dictionary of Love*, Sandra Werneck, 1996), a conventional, if not cliché, story about love following the letters of the alphabet; *Amores Possíveis* (*Possible Loves*, Sandra Werneck, 2001), an equally conventional film, but with a better script; and *O Homem do Ano* (*The Man of the Year*, José Henrique Fonseca, 2003).

In the same vain, but clearly the work of a more mature and accomplished filmmaker, are *Deus É Brasileiro* (*God Is Brazilian*, Carlos Diegues, 2003), a road movie in which God travels through the Northeast of Brazil as a cranky, good-hearted old man, and *Bossa Nova* (Bruno Barreto, 2000), a sort of glossy excuse to showcase the director's two loves: his city, Rio de Janeiro, and his wife, Amy Irving.

Bossa Nova also points toward another distinctive characteristic of recent Brazilian cinema: an increase in the number of coproductions, not only with the United States, but also with Portugal, in movies such as *Terra Estrangeira* (*Foreign Land*, Walter Salles and Daniela Thomas, 1996) and *O Judeu* (*The Jew*, Jom Tob Azulay, 1996); Argentina, with *Anahy de Las Misiones* (Sérgio Silva, 1997); and even Paraguay, with *O Toque de Oboé* (*The Call of the Oboe*, Cláudio MacDowell, 1998). Recent movies have begun to pay attention to the experience of the different immigrant groups and their experiences in Brazil, particularly Italians—*Bela Donna* (Fábio Barreto, 1998), *Oriundi* (Ricardo Bravo, 1999), *O Quatrilhio* (Fábio Barreto, 1995)—and also Japanese, *Gaijin—Ama-Me Como Sou* (*Gaijing—Love Me the Way I Am*, Tizuka Yamasaki, 2005), a subject that had already been touched on in the 1980s. *Gaijin—Ama-Me Como Sou* is, in fact, a sequel to *Gaijin—Os Caminhos da Liberdade* (*Gaijin—Roads of Freedom*, Tizuka Yamasaki) from 1980.

These films contrast with the darker views of Brazilian society, particularly of the small middle class and its everyday negotiation with the lower classes, presented in the movie *Cronicamente Inviável* (*Chronically Unfeasible*, Sérgio Bianchi, 2000). The elements that make Bianchi's film so indispensable to understanding Brazil and Brazilian cinema in the new millennium are troubled race relations, a lack of class-consciousness, total disinterest in the situation of the country, a bourgeoisie that runs to New York whenever things become too dangerous at home, and the resentment of an underclass of millions who have neither the opportunity nor the hope for a better life. Narrated by a cynical intellectual, with what seems to be an honest meditation on the state of the nation, the story moves from the Northeast to the far South and then to São Paulo following the narrator and illustrating his story while emphasizing that he is talking about the entire country, not only to the "backward" Northeast or the marginal urban spaces. Perhaps the most disturbing element of the film is its complete lack of moral voices, since, for the most part, the audience is forced to listen and identify with the narrator. When he, at the end of the story, reveals the real reasons for his travels, he destroys any moral authority he could have had, therefore leaving the audience without any hope.

Bianchi has been recognized as one of the contemporary directors that most openly deals with social issues in a very critical way. Among his other films are *Romance* (*Romance*, 1988), *A Causa Secreta* (*The Secret Cause*, 1994), and *Quanto Vale ou É por Quilo?* (*How Much or Is by the Kilo?*, 2005). However, he is not the only one who makes films that

intend "to reveal a 'chronically unfeasible' country," in the words of
Lúcia Nagib,[10] who sees that as a clear trend of Brazilian cinema in
her essay about Beto Brant's *O Invasor* (*The Trespasser*, 2002). *O Invasor*
also deals with power relationships between people at opposite ends of
the economic ladder, except that it is the man from the *favela*, in this
case, who is the one who uses such relationships to advance economically and infiltrate the upper class. What is interesting about these
films is that they have been presented as reality, as a slice of real life.
This is something that has been encouraged by their marketing
strategies, as in the case of *Cidade de Deus*, a film said to be based on
a true story even though it is based on an autobiographical novel.
Nonetheless, as Nagib argues convincingly, these narrations are
fiction, even when based on reality—something that should not
diminish their value as social documents.

FROM *CINEMA NOVO* TO THE *RETOMADA* OF
BRAZILIAN CINEMA

We mentioned before that Brazilian cinema is constantly going
through ups and downs in its production, and yet it has managed to
maintain a continuous, although uneven, production of films. One of
the most interesting moments of this industry was the years after the
decline of the *cinema novo* in the 1970s. Even as the force of the previous films slowly faded away, the industry did not stop producing
movies despite the increasingly more difficult conditions and the less
successful attempts to conciliate popular taste with the national
production; this lasted until the 1990s. "With a few exceptions, notably Sérgio Toledo, Walter Hugo Khouri, Walter Salles Jr., and Hector Babenco, who turned to English-language co-productions,"
writes Cacilda M. Rêgo, "Brazilian film-makers found it difficult, if
not impossible, to make films in the absence of investments in production."[11] As the politics of the country changed and the society opened,
the situation became more favorable for cultural enterprises and manifestations that had been suppressed during the military government.
With the promise of democracy and the popular mobilization to
regain civil control of the country, a counterculture emerged that
was eager to record and be a part of the historical changes.

In a clearly political vein, but more concerned with political structures, not with politics in the wide Foucaouldian way, are the films
known as the films of the transition, particularly those that

documented the passing from a military dictatorship that lasted from 1964 to 1985 to a civil government under the pressure of the popular demand of *Diretas já!* (Direct elections now!). Besides the already mentioned *Patria Amada*—which ingeniously mixes real footage of the massive public protests calling for democracy with the fictional life of three friends covering the historical moment of the election of Tancredo Neves—we should mention *Céu Aberto* (*Open Sky*, João Batista de Andrade, 1985) and *Muda Brasil* (*Brazil, Change*, Oswaldo Cadeira, 1985). *Céu Aberto*, which also focuses on Neves's campaign, is "a requiem to the deceased president [and] a sort of timid welcome to the civil government that came finally with the presidency of José Sarney," in the words of Roberto Machado Jr.[12] Unlike the previous two films, *Muda Brasil* is not a fictional feature, but is a documentary concerned with the image of Neves, his figure as a public man, as a mediator, and his role as the father of democracy and the New Republic. The film ends with the victory of Tancredo Neves and makes no mention of his premature death.

But the 1980s as well as the second half of the 1970s experienced a crisis in the number of movie theaters that closed down in the country and the lack of intellectual and artistic ambitions in many directions. Film production did not stop because of that; on the contrary, as Robert Stam and Ismail Xavier point out, a "new generation" of filmmakers emerged in the 1980s, something that makes it easier to identify interesting trends in the film industry during those years. For them the first thing that is important to mention is the diversity of the films produced, which is "remarkable and quite unprecedented,"[13] and included films made by the old masters of *cinema novo* as well as by younger filmmakers associated with them, such as Tizuka Yamasaki, Jorge Bodansky, Fábio and Bruno Barreto, and Ana Carolina. Also important is a movement self-identified as underground (most notably Rogério Sganzerla), a group of young filmmakers from São Paulo, which includes Sérgio Bianchi and Carlos Reichenbach; and the revival of a typical Brazilian genre, the musical comedies called *chanchadas*, particularly mixed with sex called porno-*chanchada*.

In addition to the diversity of the films of the 1980s, Stam and Xavier observe an interest in what they identified as a "penchant for metacinema."[14] This self-reflexiveness of Brazilian cinema is observed primarily in such films as *Fulaninha* (*Jane Doe*, David Neves, 1986), *Sonho sem Fim* (*Endless Dream*, Lauro Escorel, 1986), *Brás Cubas* (Júlio Bressane, 1985), *Ópera do Malandro* (*Malandro*, Ruy Guerra, 1986), *O Beijo da Mulher Aranha* (*Kiss of the Spider Woman*, Hector Babenco,

1985), *O Cinema Falado* (*Talked Film*, Caetano Veloso, 1986), and *Cabra Marcado para Morrer* (*Twenty Years After*, Eduardo Coutinho, 1984), which refers to the time it took the director to finish his film interrupted by the military coup in 1964. All these films have cinema at their core and function both as films and as meditations on film. Some documentaries or pseudodocumentaries also belong to this cinematic tradition, such as Glauber Rocha's *Di* (1977), an excellent film about Brazilian painter Di Cavalacanti, and Artur Omar's *Triste Trópico* (1974). A curious manifestation of this metacinema mentioned by Stam and Xavier are spoof films, mostly parodies of Hollywood, made in Brazil in the 1970s, such as *Bacalhau* (*Codfish*, Adriano Stuart, 1976) or *Banana Mecânica* (*The Mechanical Banana*, Braz Chediak, 1973), parodies of Steven Spielberg's *Jaws* (1975) and Stanley Kubrick's *A Clockwork Orange* (1971), respectively.

Other movies from the same period returned to a more popular sensibility and took carnival, that quintessential Brazilian celebration, as their central theme and reelaborated the *chanchada*, clearly influenced by *cinema novo*'s and *tropicalismo*'s interest in erasing categories of high and low culture;[15] also there was a clear interest in a romanticized portrait of contemporary life and a softening of the harsh view of the *sertão* and the *favela* in an attempt to reconcile commercial possibilities with an artistic intention. Two films by Ivan Cardoso, *O Segredo da Múmia* (*Secret of the Mummy*, 1982) and *As Sete Vampiras* (*The Seven Female Vampires*, 1986), are representatives of a subgenre also popular at the time that makes a humorous pastiche of terror films, *chanchadas*, and sexy comedies called "terrir," a combination of terror and *rir* (to laugh in Portuguese). This happened simultaneously, however, with some milestone Brazilian films that never gave up, such as the excellent *Pixote: A Lei do Mais Fraco* (*Pixote, The Law of the Weakest*, Hector Babenco, 1981) and *A Hora da Estrela* (*The Hour of the Star*, Suzana Amaral, 1985). Other films of the period are *A Estrela Nua* (*Naked Star*, Ícaro Martins and José António Garcia, 1985), *Nem Tudo É Verdade* (*It's Not All True*, Rógerio Sganzerla, 1985), *Quando o Carnaval Chegar* (*When Carnival Arrives*, Carlos Diegues, 1972), *A Lira do Delírio* (*Lyre of Delirium*, Walter Lima Jr., 1978), *Samba da Criação do Mundo* (*Samba of the Creation of the World*, Vera de Figueiredo, 1979), and *A Idade da Terra* (*The Age of the Earth*, Glauber Rocha, 1980), the last film of this genial director who died suddenly at the age of 42 and for many the testament of *cinema novo*.

In addition to the films mentioned before, there was a series of movies with a more allegorical approach to their look into the social problems of their country. Some interesting examples of this are *Eles Não Usam Black-Tie* (*They Don't Wear Black Tie*, Leon Hirszman, 1981), a fine film about workers, union leaders, and family dramas coping with everyday life while on strike; *O Homem Que Virou Suco* (*The Man Who Turned into Juice*, João Batista de Andrade, 1980), a humorous story about a common worker and his literary aspirations; and *Memórias do Cárcere* (*Memories of Prison*, Nelson Pereira dos Santos, 1984), an adaptation of Graciliano Ramo's novel of the same title written decades earlier (published in 1953 after his death), about a school teacher in the Northeast who is put in jail when he is mistakenly implicated in a plot to overthrow the government. *Bye Bye Brasil* (Carlos Diegues, 1979), on the contrary, is a delightful road movie that follows an itinerant circus, "a Caravana Rolidei," with hints of surrealism and nods to Federico Fellini and Luis Buñuel (at some point the emcee makes fake snow fall over the amazed tropical audience members and asks them if they already feel as if they are in Scandinavia, Northern Europe, or any other snowy region of the First World). The film succeeds in giving audiences the opportunity to roam through the country and to glance into Brazilian everyday life in the late 1970s, as well as the dreams, frustrations, and triumphs of the people.

But perhaps the two major films of these two decades were the already mentioned *A Hora da Estrela* and *Pixote: A Lei do Mais Fraco*. These two movies can be placed on both extremes of the political scheme. *A Hora da Estrela* is the story of Macabéa (Marcélia Cartaxo), a stupid, ugly, orphan girl from the Northeast who struggles to adapt to the alien urban world of São Paulo, based on a novel by Clarice Lispector. The story is more about the human condition than national identity, and more about the individual than the masses—however, very ingeniously it uses Brazil's own idiosyncrasies (the dichotomy of North and South, *sertão* and *favela*, machismo, the alienation of the masses, the discrimination of the people from the Northeast in São Paulo, etc.) to illuminate this subject. Macabéa, ugly and dumb, has at least a "happy" ending when she is killed by a car while dreaming of her prince charming. In the last shot we see her, free at least, running toward the man of her dreams and then her lifeless body on the road, suggesting that it is her liberated spirit running to meet her love.

Pixote, on the contrary, is a harsh, crude look into misery and corruption and its devastating effects on the most vulnerable, the ubiquitous street children. *Pixote* is part "documentary" (the lead actor was one of those real street children who, years later, was killed by the police in a manner eerily reminiscent of the way he is killed in the movie) and part social drama with an incredible capacity for camera objectivity, which Babenco uses very convincingly to denounce injustice and reveal the humanity of the disposed. Pixote is a contemporary brother of the characters of Luis Buñuel's *Los Olvidados* (1950), as every single critic has mentioned before. However, Babenco looks at his characters with less detachment than Buñuel did with his Mexican street kids three decades earlier; it is almost as if he and the camera are one of them. Vincent Canby from the *New York Times* writes, "The movie that *Pixote* most quickly brings to mind is Luis Buñuel's classic *Los Olvidados*, though Mr. Babenco doesn't possess the dark Buñuel humor nor does he attempt to imitate Mr. Buñuel's air of detachment, which has the effect of making credible horrors that are beyond the ken of most of us."[16]

THE FIRST FILMS OF BRAZILIAN CINEMA

While *cinema novo* represents one of the highest points in Brazilian cinema, films in Brazil, as in most Latin countries, arrived early; in the case of this South American giant, it happened one year after the first projections of the Lumière brothers in Paris at the end of 1895. As in the rest of Latin America, some attempts began to adapt the new invention to the national culture, mostly by filming local scenes (the first images filmed in Brazil were of Guanabara Bay in Rio de Janeiro), apparently confirming what the brothers Lumière believed, that cinema had no future, since who would want to pay to see what they could see on the street for free. However, the invention caught on and in countries such as Spain, Argentina, Mexico, and, of course, Brazil, it developed early on into a national industry. In Brazil, early fictional films were made only after 1908, and the Portuguese Antônio Leal is considered the pioneer with his filmed version of one of the most important novels of the Romantic period in Brazil, José de Alencar's *O Guaraní* (1857). But his film *Os Estranguladores* (*The Stranglers*, 1908) is the one that inaugurated cinema in Brazil with a trend of medium-length films based on newspaper police stories. Actually the first Brazilian box office hit was one of them, *O Crime da Mala* (*The Crime of the Suitcase*, 1910) by Alberto Botelho.

Production and experimentation continued in many parts of the country, from Recife in the North to Porto Alegre in the South as well as São Paulo, Manaus, and Porto Alegre. However, the consolidation of the industry started with Mário Peixoto's genial *Limite* (*Limit*, 1930), but particularly with Humberto Mauro's films, such as *Na Primavera da Vida* (*Spring of Life*, 1926), *Tesouro Perdido* (*Lost Treasure*, 1927), *Sangue Mineiro* (*Blood from Minas*, 1929), *Labios sem Beijos* (*Lips without Kisses*, 1930), *Ganga Bruta* (*Brutal Gang*, 1933), *Favela Dos Meus Amores* (*My Lovely Shantytown*, 1935), and *O Descobrimento do Brasil* (*The Discovery of Brazil*, 1937). If Mauro represents the first professional filmmaker in Brazil, Peixoto is the *infant terrible*, the man of genius whose fame depends on only one picture, *Limite*. *Limite* is an experimental, beautiful film that could be called surrealist in as much as it does not really follow a traditional narrative line, but presents a gathering of images, "a series of shots or a series of visual poetic verses."[17] Full of poetry and imaginative images closer to photography than to narrative cinema, this film surely deserves to figure among the most innovative films ever produced. It is perhaps that preciousness that makes many critics and even directors of the *cinema novo* to compare it unfavorably to Mauro's *Ganga Bruta*.

CARMEN MIRANDA AND THE *CHANCHADAS*

In any case, both directors share the honor of being the founders of the national cinema. *Limite* is still a silent film, but soon after that Brazil started making talking pictures. Once the technology had been established in the country, the logical step was to take advantage of the rich tradition of popular music and folklore, and what better place to start that than with carnival, the national holiday. So in the 1930s the *chanchadas*, or musical comedies, appeared, a genre that would give the world, besides samba and batucadas, the unmistakable image of Carmen Miranda. The first successful talkie in Brazil was made by an American, Wallace Downey, ironically called *Coisas Nossas* (*Our Things*, 1931) and was greatly advertised as, finally, a film about "our customes, our music, our songs, our artists!"[18] These folkloric musicals were very successful in combining a popular sensibility with the need of self-representation on the screen, mostly through images of carnival. This happy formula resulted in the establishment of such studios as Cinédia, which produced *A Voz do Carnaval* (*The Voice of Carnival*, 1933), the film that really started Carmen Miranda's career.

After this film Cinédia and Waldow Filmes Studios teamed up to produce *Alô, alô, Brasil!* (*Hello, Hello, Brazil!*, João de Barro and Wallace Downey, 1935), a selection of scenes loosely connected that had the main purpose of parading popular singers, composers, and, above all, their rising star, Carmen Miranda. This movie was followed by *Alô, Alô Carnaval!* (*Hello, Hello, Carnival!*, Adhemar Gonzaga, 1936) and *Estudantes* (*Students*, Wallace Downey, 1935), in which Carmen Miranda played a promising radio star. Miranda's last film in Brazil, before she moved to Hollywood, was *Banana-da-Terra* (*Banana from the Land*, Ruy Costa, 1939). The popularity and light spirit of the *chanchada* contrasts dramatically with the political and social atmosphere of Brazil, since these are the years of the *Estado Novo*, a period marked by the authoritarian and populist government of Getúlio Vargas, who felt justified to take the federal government by force in the name of the people. *Estado Novo* lasted from 1937 to 1945, and for the first time the official governmental rhetoric included the indigenous populations as being important for the nation's identity. It also developed a project of modernization and urban planning on a scale never before seen in the country.

This political and social situation had an influence on a group of young men from Rio who at the beginning of the 1940s created a new production company, Atlântida, which had the noble intention of creating "a cinema capable of providing indispensable services to national greatness."[19] Its first films, *Moleque Tião* (*The Kid Tião*, José Carlos Burle, 1943), based on the life of comic actor Grande Otelo, had great success and was followed immediately by *É Proibido Sonhar* (*Dreaming Is Not Allowed*, Moacyr Fenelon, 1943); unfortunately this film was not able to attract the public or to appeal to the critics. Soon after this setback, Atlântida gave in to commercial pressure, lowered its standards, and became very successful when Grande Otelo teamed up with Oscarito, the most famous comedic couple of the classic *chanchadas*. These films strongly appealed to the masses, therefore creating an authentic popular cinema that declined only with the introduction of television. Some of the most popular films are *Tristezas Não Pagam Dívidas* (*Sadness Does Not Pay Your Debts*, José Carlos Burle, 1943), *Não Adianta Chorar* (*There Is No Point in Crying*, Watson Macedo, 1945), *Carnaval no Fogo* (*Carnival in the Fire*, Watson Macedo, 1946), and *Este Mundo É um Pandeiro* (*This World Is a Tambourine*, Watson Macedo, 1946).

Roughly at the same time the Companhia Cinematográfica Vera Cruz was being created in São Paulo with the intention of competing with Cinédia and Atlântida, both based in Rio. Vera Cruz continued the tradition of a popular cinema, but added melodramas that contrasted with the *chanchadas*. The first films were *Caiçara*

(Adolfo Celi, 1950), a melodrama about a simple girl (*caiçara* is the name given to the inhabitants of the costal villages of Rio de Janeiro and São Paulo) married to a drunken, older man and who uses macumba (black magic) to find love and happiness; and *Painel* (*Panel*, Lima Barreto, 1950), a short documentary about a panel painted by Cândido Portinari. Both movies were very successful. Other later films did not always succeed and often were too expensive, such as the most famous case *Tico-Tico no Fubá* (Adolfo Celi, 1952), a fictionalized biography of composer Zequinha de Abreu. The title refers to the song about a native Brazilian bird that he composed in the first decade of the twentieth century and that became famous all over the world in the 1940s thanks to Walt Disney and Carmen Miranda and in the 1980s thanks to Woody Allen's *Radio Days* (1987).

Other important Vera Cruz films are *Ângela* (Abílio Pereira de Almeida and Tom Payne, 1951), *Apassionata* (*Passionate*, Fernando de Barros, 1952), *Veneno* (*Poisson*, Gianni Pons, 1952), *Sai da Frente* (*Get Out of the Way*, Abílio Pereira de Almeida and Tom Payne, 1952), *Luz Apagada* (*Lights Off*, Carlos Thiré, 1953), *Na Senda do Crime* (*On the Road of Crime*, Flamínio Bollini Cerri, 1954), and *Floradas na Serra* (*Flowers in the Wild*, Luciano Salce, 1954). But by far the biggest accomplishment of Vera Cruz and one of the finest Brazilian films is the already-mentioned *O Cangaceiro*. *O Cangaceiro* is an epic film about a group of outlaws, commanded by Galindo Ferreira (Milton Ribeiro), who terrorize the Brazilian countryside and who are constantly battled by the police; in one of their attacks on a village of the Northeast, they kidnap the teacher of the town, Olívia (Marisa Prado). One of the bandits, Teodoro (Albert Ruschel), however, falls in love with her; he was a lad from a good family and joined the bandits only after he killed a man. He and Olívia escape and the movie then turns into a series of chases among the bandits, the fugitives, and the police.

When Vera Cruz finally ceased to exist in 1954, Atlântida seized the opportunity to monopolize the preference of the public with a project that had already started, projects with more ambition in scale if not in depth. Examples of this are *Amei um Bicheiro* (*I Loved a Lottery Ticket Seller*, Jorge Ileli and Paulo Wanderley, 1952), *Bernabé Tu És Meu* (*Bernabé, You Are Mine*, José Carlos Burle, 1952), *Nem Sansão Nem Dalila* (*Neither Samson, Nor Dalilah*, Carlos Manga, 1954), a parody of Cecil B. DeMille's *Samson and Dalilah*, *Colégio de Brotos* (*School of Youngsters*, Carlos Manga, 1956), and many more of Manga's films way into the 1960s. Many of these films were melodramas or comedies that still tried to keep the *chanchada* alive.

However, some of them also tried to be more serious and to adapt Italian neorrealism to the Brazilian context. None was so successful as the first film by Nelson Perira dos Santos, *Rio 40 Graus* (*Rio, 40 Degrees*, 1955), a documentary-like look at the people of Rio de Janeiro in which the camera challenges cinematic conventions by following for an entire day an array of characters. These scenes include some boys from the *favela* on their way to sell peanuts at different tourist spots of the city, a poor boy who finds happiness chasing a lizard at the zoo, a girl who fears her boyfriend will leave her when he finds out she is pregnant with his child, and an old soccer player who realizes his career is over when he is replaced by a younger man in the middle of an important match. Pereira dos Santos goes to the street and puts all his trust in the intuition of the people playing themselves to help him to produce a touching, vivid portrait of Rio and its inhabitants. This film, accepted by all, inaugurated what would become one of the most important and influential film movements in Latin America, *cinema novo*.

NOTES

1. "José Padilha Diz que 'Tropa de Elite' Foi Mal Interpretado Pelos Críticos," *Folha de São Paulo*, February 17, 2008, http://www1 .folha.uol.com.br/folha/ilustrada/ult90u373192.shtml.

2. "'Tropa de Elite' Conquista o Urso de Ouro do Festival de Berlim," *Folha de São Paulo*, February 16, 2008, http://www1.folha.uol.com.br/folha/ ilustrada/ult90u373056.shtml.

3. Lúcia Nagib, "Introduction," *The New Brazilian Cinema* (London: I. B. Tauris and Centre for Brazilian Studies, University of Oxford, 2003), xviii.

4. Lúcia Nagib, "Death on the Beach—the Recycled Utopia of *Midnight*," in *The New Brazilian Cinema* (London: I. B. Tauris and Centre for Brazilian Studies, University of Oxford, 2003), 157.

5. See Cacilda M. Rêgo, "Brazilian Cinema: Its Fall, Rise, and Renewal (1990–2003)," *New Cinemas: Journal of Contemporary Film* 3 (2005): 85–100.

6. Carlos Diegues, "The Cinema That Brazil Deserves," *The New Brazilian Cinema*, ed. Lúcia Nagib (London: I. B. Tauris and Centre for Brazilian Studies, University of Oxford, 2003), 25.

7. Cited by Cacilda M. Rêgo, "Brazilian Cinema," 92.

8. Stephanie Dennison, "A Meeting of Two Worlds: Recent Trends in Brazilian Cinema," *Journal of Latin American and Iberian Studies* 6 (May 2000): 131.

9. Stephen Holden, "Friendship as a Frail Bridge across the Chasm of Class," *New York Times*, July 1, 2005, http://www.nytimes.com/2005/07/

01/movies/01brot.html?_r=1&ex=1151726400&en=68a5b1a21239bbbe&ei =5083.

10. Lúcia Nagib, "Is This Really Brazil? The Dystopia City of the Trespasser," *New Cinemas: Journal of Contemporary Film* 2 (2004): 18.

11. Cited by Cacilda M. Rêgo, "Brazilian Cinema," 85.

12. Roberto Machado Jr., "Política e Cinema: Os Filmes da Transição," *Caderno de Crítica* 1 (1986): 22.

13. Robert Stam and Ismail Xavier, "Recent Brazilian Cinema: Allegory/ Metacinema/Carnival," *Film Quarterly* 41 (Spring 1988): 15.

14. Ibid., 16.

15. See Stam and Xavier, "Recent Brazilian Cinema" for a better description of the period.

16. Vincent Canby, "Babenco's 'Pixote' Show the Boys of Brazil," *New York Times* May 5, 1981, http://movies.nytimes.com/movie/review?res =9C0CE5DC103BF936A35756C0A967948260.

17. Jose Carlos Avellar, "Limite," in *The Cinema of Latin America*, ed. Alberto Elena and Marina Díaz López (London: Wallflower, 2003), 19.

18. Cited in Stephanie Dennison and Luisa Shaw, *Popular Cinema in Brazil, 1930–2001* (Manchester, UK: Manchester University Press, 2004), 35.

19. Ibid., 62.

CHAPTER 6
Brazilian Cinema Novo

With the success of *Rio 40 Graus*, Nelson Pereira dos Santos inaugurated a new way of making movies in Brazil, and if we cannot call it just yet *cinema novo*, it is clear that its narrative style, its flirtations with *chanchadas*, and, above all, its appropriation of Italian neorealist techniques were pointing toward a new cinema. However, the film that is considered by most critics as the inaugural film of *cinema novo* is Glauber Rocha's *Barravento* (*The Turning Wind*, 1962), a film that, like so many in a long tradition in Brazil as we have seen, centers on the Northeast region. Buraquinho is the fishing village in the state of Bahia to which Firmino (Antônio Sampaio) returns after being in the city to try to convince the fishermen that the conditions in which they work are not acceptable. But instead of acceptance, he has to struggle with ancient beliefs and traditions and with the lack of political interest. In the end, after a huge storm and because of all the complications associated with his being in the village, Firmino leaves the town again, this time forever. In this, his first film—although Rocha later said that it was not really his movie, alluding to the help he got from Luis Paulino and Nelson Pereira dos Santos in postproduction—the father of *cinema novo* mixes traditional Brazilian culture and folklore (which includes African, indigenous, and European myths, dances, rituals, and legends) with a stylized culture (for example, the music of Heitor Villa-Lobos and cordel literature) and a highly symbolic cinematic language.

Similarly to Pereira dos Santos, Rocha, and in general to all of the intellectuals of his generation, Ruy Guerra attempted to create an authentic national cinema that works with antithetical elements as an allegory of the country and its circumstances. Not only the characters, but also the traditional, cultural, and religious manifestations presented in his films were seen simultaneously as liberating and as a means of alienation. Also this style presents, on one hand, an almost ethnographic realism, and on the other, a lyrical tone that disarticulates all realism. "Stylistically, the realism achieved through the use of on-location shooting and non-professional actors, is counterpointed by the excesses of Eisensteinian montage and delirious camera movements,"[1] write Timothy Barnard and Peter Rist of *Barravento*, but the same can be said of most films of *cinema novo*. These contradictions are, as Randal Johnson has pointed out, the result of the close relationship between the directors and their own cultural circumstances, as we can observe in this quote: "Cinema novo is synonymous with Brazilian cinema and its contradictions are the contradictions of Brazilian cinema as a whole and Brazilian intellectuals in general."[2]

These contradictions also include the ambiguous relationship with the national bourgeoisie and its culture, particularly the film industry produced until then; but they also extend to the problematic relationship between *cinema novo* and the Brazilian government. The first phase of *cinema novo*, whose beginning is traditionally dated as 1960, developed under the administration of João Goulart, who succeeded Jânio Quadros in 1961, only seven years after the suicide of Getúlio Vargas who left a legacy of deep populism and nationalism that sometimes took the form of a rancid anti-imperialism. Its second phase goes roughly from 1964, the year Goulart was overthrown by the military, to 1968. These years, of course, were marked by a fierce political repression. While the films of the first phase of *cinema novo*, such as *Barravento*, for example, focus on the provinces, particularly the impoverished Northeast, the second phase turns its lenses to the urban spaces, not only the *favelas*, but also, and principally, the middle and upper-middle class neighborhoods. While in the first phase directors were preoccupied with exploring and recovering the essence of Brazilian culture by joining in the debate on the national question, in the second phase, "film-makers turned the cameras, so to speak, on themselves in an attempt to understand the failure of the Left in 1964."[3]

Among the most representative films of the first phase, besides *Barravento*, of course, are *Deus e o Diabo na Terra do Sol* (*Black God, White Devil*, Glauber Rocha, 1964) and two of the best movies ever made in Brazil, *Os Fuzis* (*The Guns*, Ruy Guerra, 1964) and *Vidas Secas* (*Barren Lives*, Nelson Pereira dos Santos, 1963). *Deus e o Diabo na Terra do Sol* (literally "God and the Devil in the Land of the Sun") is, like its title, a symbolic and at times contradictory, yet very original, revision of the essence of Brazilian culture and history. Like many other Brazilian films before it, *Deus e o Diabo* returns to the *cangaço* and its importance in Brazilian folklore and culture. In fact, the film is an imaginative retelling of the story of Corisco/Lampião (Othon Bastos) as well as the millenarian settlement of Canudos, guided in their rebellion against the government by the mystic Antônio "Conselheiro," who is called Black Sebastião (Lidio Silva) in the film. Fed up with these rebels, Colonel Moraes (Milton Roda), a local landowner, hires Antônio das Mortes (Maurício do Valle) to exterminate them. Detached and contradictory, the film is far from a simplistic look into Brazil's problems that would reduce them to a dualistic, good versus evil formula. In a particularly violent scene, Antônio das Mortes kills all the members of the mystic cult of Black Sebastião and slays the followers of Corisco/Lampião, all of whom are in reality hungry peasants.

Violence and hunger are, no doubt, the themes of the film. In fact, it came out a year after Rocha had published a very famous manifesto called "An Aesthetic of Hunger," in which he proclaimed that nothing would explain Brazil better than hunger and nothing would express hunger better than violence. And hunger is also the theme of *Vidas Secas*. Adapted from Graciliano Ramos's classic novel, *Vidas Secas* refers literally to the dry and arid lands of the Northeast, and metaphorically to the barren lives and future of the poor and dispossessed peasantry. As the film opens, we see Fabiano (Atila Iório) and his family—a wife, Sinhá Vitória (Maria Ribeiro); two children; and the faithful family dog, Baleia—on the road driven by hunger. Visually, the abundant white light of an overexposed camera is effective in transmitting to the spectator the heat, dryness of the land, and desperation of the people. Hunger is so important and is symbolically represented by the family eating its pet parrot to survive. The scene is chilling in its simplicity; however, more heartbreaking and effective in transmitting the desperation of poverty is the sequence in which Fabiano has to get rid of Baleia because they cannot afford to care for her anymore. Shot from the dog's point of view, the camera follows Fabiano as he chases Baleia, while the audience literally feels the dog's terror and desperation trying to flee to safety.

The scenes are so realistic that spectators in France were convinced the dog had been killed on film, and Pereira dos Santos had to bring the dog to Cannes to prove it was not true, without convincing all the skeptics. The sober narrative of the film and its faithfulness to the literary source is absolutely remarkable, and its black and white photography is so effective in conveying that quality of the precariousness of life in the Northeast of Brazil that it is truly a masterpiece not only of Brazilian film, but also of film in general. Even though dos Santos made a few films after *Rio 40 Graus*, *Vidas Secas* was the one that truly continued the tradition of *cinema novo*, including its contradictions, as can be seen in its somehow optimistic ending in which the family, still hungry, is again on the move in search of a better life. Similarly to *Vidas* (using also some of the same actors, for example, Atila Iório), *Os Fuzis* deals with hunger and with violence as the result of it. However, the dialectic approach to poverty and injustice demonstrates that Guerra possesses a more traditional style that in this case turns to be more appropriated for the subject. Like *Deus e o Diabo*, *Os Fuzis* is about injustice, poverty, exploitation, and religious fanaticism in the Northeast arid lands. At the beginning of the film, a mystic is preaching about hunger, animals looking for food, and God's anger, making it obvious that he is capable of convocation of great masses. The army meanwhile is sent to defend a cargo of food that has been sent somewhere else, and the authorities think that the people may steal it. The passivity of the population, alienated by religion, is contrasted with the anger of Gaúcho (Atila Iório), a truck driver who acquires some sort of class-consciousness when he sees a child die of hunger; full of holy wrath, he incites the population to revolt and steal the food, only to be massacred by the army.

Os Fuzis is less ambivalent in its political position than its predecessors, and perhaps that is part of the reason why some critics do not always consider Guerra a real *cinema novo* director. In fact, Guerra is an atypical case because he often was considered the foreigner of the group. He was born in Mozambique and moved to Brazil in his 20s after living in Europe for a few years. He is also the most international of all the *cinema novo* directors, having worked in Mexico, France, and Mozambique. Perhaps because of that he was not that eager to adopt the influence of Italian neorealism and instead uses a mix of styles from French new wave tendencies to some nods to Federico Fellini. Also, he seemed to gravitate toward a different atmosphere and scenarios; his previous, and first, Brazilian film, *Os Cafajestes* (*The Hustlers*, 1962), for example, is considered the inaugural film of *cinema novo* in Rio de Janeiro, an urban setting, using a style that juxtaposes documentary-like techniques with more traditional narrative formulas. Therefore it opposes the highly allegorical films of Guerra set in the Northeast.

The plot tells the story of a spoiled young man from an upper class family, Vavá (Daniel Filhio), and his friendship with the low-life Jandir (Jece Valadão) and a prostitute (Glauche Rocha). They plan to extort two older women and, in the process, they engage in many sexual scenes, including some containing full frontal nudity that provoked a scandal in Brazil and caused the movie to be banned temporarily, only to reopen to great success. The movie tries to offer a critical view of the middle and upper classes using the exclusive neighborhoods of Rio and the supposed lack of moral values of this class, as well as its inclination to sexual excess as background. Also from the same period, and with nothing in common with the traditional themes of the *cinema novo* was the first film by Carlos Dieuges, *Ganga Zumba* (1963), which is the first film to place the Afro-Brazilian experience at the center of the national cultural debate. Curiously enough, and even though traditionally Brazilians and non-Brazilians alike have long proclaimed that there is little or no racism in the country, the African experience had never been at the center of the national culture—not even with *cinema novo*, which in general proffered the symbolism of the peasantry or even the Indian and the dryness of the landscape of the Northeast as the true emblems of the nation. This will change as *cinema novo* develops, but it will fall short of really addressing the issue in all its complexities.

Ganga Zumba, then, is important in part because of that. The film for the most part centers on the young Antão (Antônio Sampaio), who learns of his royal blood as the descendants of African kings and becomes determined to end his servitude and run away to the *quilombo* of Palmares. *Quilombos* were the free communities of runaway slaves who managed to escape to the jungle. Even though the movie tells about the origins of Palmares, the most famous of them, through illustrations before the credits roll, and even though we constantly see the slaves talking, and dreaming, of freedom and planning to escape to the jungle to start a happy life, the *quilombo* remains elusive and acquires the dimension of a mythical land. Antão, aided by an elder, Arorobo (Eliezer Gomes), and in the company of a young woman, Cipriana (Léa Garcia), who will abandon him for another man, starts a journey that will be full of adventure and blood. Only at the end of the movie, and in the middle of a lush tropical paradise, does he seem about to be able to reach his goal of entering the *quilombo*, which is never shown but is implied. According to Vincent Canby, "*Quilombo* has something of the quality of fresco. It's colorful and deliberately idealized. Its characters are figures that have already passed into history. One watches it dutifully—with respect but with a certain amount of detachment."[4]

Very different in its treatment of the African experience in Brazil, *Orfeu Negro* (*Black Orpheus*, Marcel Camus, 1958) is a rarity, an exception to *cinema novo*. Technically it is not even Brazilian, but it is important because it is perhaps the most seen "Brazilian" film ever. Camus's film is set in contemporary Brazil, during carnival, and retells and updates the Greek myth of Orpheus and Eurydice. Orfeu (Breno Melo) is a worker and musician who lives in a *favela*; Eurídice (Marpessa Dawn) comes from the provinces to visit her cousin in the same *favela*. When they inevitably meet, they realize that they are destined for each other. Full of mystery, Eurídice is being chased by a strange man who appears to her the night of carnival dressed up as Death. He kills Eurídice and Orfeu falls to the bottom of a precipice while carrying the lifeless body of his beloved Eurídice. Orfeu was famous among the children of the *favela* because he could raise the sun with his guitar and his singing; so at the end of the movie one of the little boys is playing the guitar just as the sun rises, while his friend watches and a little girl dances to his music.

Beautiful and allegorical, with excellent performances and gorgeous music, this film has been criticized for its idealized portrait of Afro-Brazilians as a community of sweet, happy-in-their-poverty, music-loving people with no relationship to the harsh reality that surrounds them. The film is, as Dan Schneider writes, "an odd amalgam of modernity and the worst stereotypes about black culture worldwide. The whole film is practically one long festival of song and dance, which while apropos for the setting—Rio de Janeiro's Carnival, nonetheless kills off any hope for a real story."[5] In a way, the idealized view of the *favela* and its cast of all-black actors can be opposed symbolically to the *quilombo* evoked by Carlos Diegues; however, it can also be seen as the oversimplification with which many foreigners see the conditions of the impoverished citizens of Brazil, as well as other parts of the world, even fantasizing about their exotism. If not really offensive, the view of these characters is rather simplistic, although when the film gets to its climax it turns rather imaginative in its adaptation of an ancient myth to the contemporary world. The credit for this does not belong entirely to Camus since the film is based on a play by Vinícius de Moraes.

One of the most famous Brazilian films of the period, *O Pagador de Promessas* (*The Given Word*, Anselmo Duarte, 1962), is a film that was given the top prize at Cannes and was nominated for an Oscar and numerous other awards. It often is placed within the boundaries of *cinema novo*, a claim that is not without truth inasmuch as the poverty, the religious alienation, and the exploitation of the masses from, again, the Northeast are all present in the movie. But it really does not belong to the radical proposition of Rocha, dos Santos, or Guerra either ideologically or stylistically. It tells a story in the most traditional way, denouncing the isolation and desperate situation of the peasantry not only in Brazil, but in most of Latin America. Its style is conventional, yet effective in telling the story of a poor man, Zé (Leonardo Vilar), who made a promise to carry a cross to the Church of Santa Bárbara in the city of Salvador to thank God for having cured his donkey. He is prevented, however, from entering the church by the priest (Dionísio Azevedo), who considers this promise a disrespectful act. Moved by Zé's actions and determination, and aided by the press, the people rally around him. Zé is accused of being a communist agitator of the masses; when the police try to arrest him, a riot breaks out and he gets killed. The people, then, carry his body all the way to the altar, fulfilling his promise.

Closer to the classical "social" pictures of Hollywood, Brazil, and even Mexico, *O Pagador* is an interesting answer to the political and allegorical movies of *cinema novo* that focus on narrative, not allegory. Something similar can be said of another film that, like *Vidas Secas*, adapts a classic of Brazilian literature (*Menino de Engenho*, José Lins do Rego, 1932) to the screen—*Menino de Engenho* (*Plantation Boy*, Walter Lima Jr., 1965). *Menino* is a film that can be placed in between *Vidas* and *O Pagador*. Not entirely *cinema novo*, it shows more respect for traditional structure and narrative and a conscious lyricism that can sometimes be interpreted as allegorical; this film is a great example of literary adaptation. The story focuses on a boy, Carlinhos (Sávio Rolim), whose painful coming-of-age is full of social awareness, which leads him to reject his own class in what can be called a portrait of the new citizen as a young man. It is also a film that shows a distinction between *cinema novo* of the first phase, which centered on the Northeast and the exploration of alienation and injustice, and the second phase, which is more urban and self-referential. Randal Johnson described the latter as the directors "turning their cameras onto themselves."[6]

Another exception worth mentioning is *À Meia-Noite Levarei Sua Alma* (*At Midnight I Will Take Your Soul*, José Mojica Marins, 1963), if only because it shows that while *cinema novo* was emerging as the most representative cinema in Brazil and perhaps Latin America, there were other manifestations of the medium in the country, including independent and bizarre films. It is a horror film that feels dated and

shows all its tricks and shortcomings, sometimes in charming, sometimes in painful ways. But it manages to recover some of the magic,
mystery, and secret pleasures of cinema while being at the same time
"intellectual" and appealing to the masses. The intellectual aspect of
the film derived mainly from the contradictory nature of its main
character, Zé do Caixão (José Mojica Marins himself), known to
American audiences as Joe Coffin. Zé, with his tall hat, his cape, his
"blasphemous" attitude (he eats meat on Good Friday!), and his long,
curvy fingernails, is more appropriate for a hero from the turn of the
century than from 1960s Brazil. Also out of date, but somehow allur-
ing, is the reason for his evil ways—he wants to have a child, but is
married to a barren woman. This unfortunate situation drives him to
beat his wife, rape his best friend's girlfriend, kill his enlightened
doctor, and defy God to give him proof of the afterlife. In the end, at
midnight, the souls of those whom he harmed come to take him to
hell, we assume; to create a supernatural feeling, the director employs
a trick (using the negative of the film) that causes laughs more than
terror.

Since the first *cinema novo* films have the arid, poor, preindustrial,
quasifeudal areas of the Northeast as their setting, suggesting as Randal Johnson has observed that "[a]uthentic culture [...] comes, not
from the urban, industrialized Brazil, but rather from the more traditional areas of the country,"[7] it is almost logical that the second phase,
which happened just as the democratic government was ended by a
coup d'état, would focus on the urban centers where the middle classes
and the intelligentsia of the country were concentrated. These are the
same classes that, given the turn of political events, would be forced to
examine themselves in search of reasons why, as Johnson also suggested, the Left had failed. Those films are *O Desafio* (*The Dare*, Paulo
Cesar Saraceni, 1966), a film about a leftist intellectual and his love
affair with the wife of an industrialist who, after visiting the factory
of her husband, realizes the importance of her husband's function in
society. She also realizes that her young, intellectual lover is nothing
but a *petit bourgeois* who does nothing really to serve his country or
his class; all he does is complain and theorize about the situation of
the country without much action.

Very similar in its attack on the rhetoric and the empty messages of
some political discourses, *O Bravo Guerreiro* (*The Brave Warrior*,
Gustavo Dahl, 1969) tells the story of Miguel Horta (Paulo César Per-
éio), a young politician who, even though he represents the opposition
party in Congress, tries to play the political game of alliances, shifts,

and arrangements to advance his career and gain favor from those in power while still keeping the illusion of maintaining his leftist convictions. When his political tactics fail and he finds himself in a compromising position between the governing party and a worker's union, he attempts desperately to save himself by giving a speech that only reveals his ineptitude and dark intentions. Unmasked, he has to renounce his political career and return home to his wife, Clara (Maria Lúcia Dahl), who had pressured him to do that all along. Clara embodies that conformist middle-class ideal of tranquility found in political disinterest, while Miguel represents the failure of the political system that sooner or later corrupts everyone. The fact that Miguel believes, or depends, on political discourses to find his salvation is symbolic of a tendency in the region of pompous and empty political discourses. In a way, it also criticizes overly preachy political films. Love, politics, and empty discourses seem to be one of the most effective ways of exercising criticism of both one's own class and the state of the nation.

So *Fome de Amor* (*Hunger for Love*, Nelson Pereira dos Santos, 1968) makes this metaphor only more evident. The allegorical nature of the film is obvious from the very beginning. Alfredo (Paulo Porto), a blind, deaf, and, of course, mute ex-revolutionary lives with his younger wife, Ulla (Leila Deniz), on the island Angra dos Reis. When they are visited by expatriate and unsuccessful painter Felipe (Arduíno Colassanti) and his wife, Mariana (Irene Stefânia), a frustrated pianist and aspiring revolutionary, both couples see an opportunity to explore their relationships, and by extension social and human interactions. The two men, opposites in every way, end up swapping wives, while the four spend time philosophizing and having political discussions. Alfredo and Mariana realize that they can communicate, despite his handicap; Mariana also thinks that her husband is trying to kill her and Alfredo to keep her money. Alfredo represents the old left that has failed like an old patriarch; however, he can still can inspire rebellious feelings, and in the end, Mariana leaves him to join the revolution.

Perhaps the masterpiece of the period is Glauber Rocha's second film of his Northeast trilogy, *Terra em Transe* (*Land in Anguish*, 1967). This movie is the story of Eldorado, a fictitious Latin American country divided between two politicians and their obvious struggle for power—one, Porfirio Diaz (Paulo Autran), is a conservative, supported by revolutionary forces; the other, Felipe Vieira (José Lewgoy), is a populist. Both are equally corrupt. A journalist, Jardel Filhio

(Paulo Martins), is in the middle of this battle torn by the two ideologies and by the friendship he shared with both of them. Released in the United States to mixed reviews, the film became nonetheless a classic of Latin American cinema. Very revealing of the ambiguity with which most American critics received the film is the commentary of Roger Greenspun in the *New York Times*:

> To a degree, the failure of *Earth Entranced* results from its unwillingness to accept the fictional logic of its melodramatic plot. But to a greater degree, that failure rests in every scene, in the development of every idea, in every decision about placing and moving the camera and composing each individual shot. Where you can sense the movie going wrong most significantly is not so much in the gratuitous complexity of the larger moments (political campaigns, strategic crises, peasant protests, etc—including the lugubrious orgies), as in the rhetorical emptiness of the smaller moments. When the poet and his woman (Clauce Rocha) embrace, the result is not so much participation in a mood as the demonstration of a mood—exemplary and unreal.[8]

After 1968, the political crisis in Brazil become violent and repressive, and very intolerant of dissidence; artists in general had to be extremely careful to elude censorship, or even jail, torture, and death. Consequently, ways of saying things in hermetic and codified manners were necessary. "During this period of extremely harsh military rule [1968–1972], it was difficult for film-makers to express opinions directly, and allegory became the preferred mode of cinematic discourse of what is known as *Tropicalism* in Brazilian cinema."[9] *Tropicalism* was an artistic and cultural movement that manifested itself in, besides film, art, literature, and particularly music. The movement originated with the release of the album *Tropicália: Ou Panis et Circencis*, in which such Brazilian music giants as Caetano Veloso, Gal Costa, Nara Leão, and Gilberto Gil participated. Since the political climate required innovative ways of expression to elude censorship, *tropicalism* responded by creating a highly metaphorical language to talk about serious political and social issues. It is famous, for example, for Chico Buarque's song "Cálice" (chalice), which apparently is talking about human suffering in the figure of Jesus in Gethsemane right before his arrest, when an angel appears and offers him a cup (a *cálice*, chalice in Portuguese), while a chorus repeats the word "cálice," which is pronounced like the command *cale-se* (shut up).

Perhaps the most representative film of this movement is Joaquim Pedro de Andrade's *Macunaíma* (1968). An intentionally confusing, absurd, and carnivalesque film, *Macunaíma* tries to mimic the equally absurd reality of Brazil through the exploration of race issues as well as class, exploitation, political commitment, and the opposition between the jungle (barbarism) and the city (civilization). Macunaíma (Grande Otelo), the hero (or rather the antihero of the film), is born an adult black man from a white mother played by a man (Paulo José), who turns into a white man (played by Paulo José as well) when he bathes in a magic fountain. The film is based on the novel by the modernist writer Mário de Andrade, who subtitled his book "*A Hero without Any Character*." Andrade's text is rich and complex and is based on his ethnographic research about the Amazonian peoples of Brazil; in the novel he mixes myths, legends, and popular tales from different Indian tribes as well as from the Afro-Brazilian popular traditions and folklore. De Andrade clearly was making fun of the pretentiousness of the Euro-centered discussions on national identity of his time by creating a character that summarized the national spirit by taking elements from different peoples, both positive and negative, and even stereotypes (the famous phrase of Macunaima, for example, is *que pregiça*—what laziness!) with carnivalesque detachment. The film, in addition, shows a complexity of a different kind that aspires to take the novel as a perfect excuse to talk about the political situation of the country.

Another important example of the *Tropicalismo* movement is *Como Era Gostoso o Meu Francês* (*How Tasty Was My Little Frenchman*, Nelson Pereira dos Santos, 1971), a film that, like *Macunaíma*, shows its carnivalsque and revisionist intentions from the very beginning, starting with its title in fact. The comical title contrasts with the rather serious subject of the film and serves as its axis. A Frenchman (Arduíno Colassanti) is captured by the Portuguese, the enemies of the French in the race for the exploration and colonization of Brazil, and is about to be killed when a group of Tupinambá Indians attack their camp, taking as prisoners all the Portuguese, their enemies, including the Frenchman. The Tupinambás, who had made alliances with the French to protect them against the Portuguese, the allies of the Tupiniquins, their mortal enemies, kill most of the Portuguese and do not believe the Frenchman when he tries to convince them that he is their friend. Nonetheless, they decide to keep him alive as a slave. In a hilarious scene in which the Indians try to decide if the Frenchman is Portuguese or not, the Tupinambá chief asks him to say something and then asks the Portuguese cook to speak so he can compare their language. After listening to them carefully, he concludes that they both speak the same language, even though the Frenchman is speaking French and the cook is reciting a recipe in Portuguese.

The Indians incorporate the Frenchman into the tribal life and even give him a wife. However, it becomes clear to him that he has been kept alive by the Indians so they can eat him. In the end, he comes to terms with his fate and helps his captors win a battle against the Tupiniquins using gunpowder. On the eve of his sacrifice, he spends time with his wife who explains to him how he has to behave. What she describes is a very elaborate ceremony full of symbolism and even respect and admiration for the person that is about to be eaten; she, being the wife, will get to take the first bite from his body. The film ends with Seboipepe (Ana María Magalhães) eating her husband and smiling while looking straight into the camera. With this scene, we realize that the title is actually a phrase out of Seboipepe's mouth: she is the one expressing how delicious the Frenchman is.

The film is clearly a revision of Brazilian history. Actually it is one of the best movies ever made about the encounter of European and Native Americans. *Como Era Gostoso* is inspired by historical accounts of the exploration and colonization of South America, offering a more complex and complete interpretation of the event; also it presents Indians and Europeans as mirroring each other, and as being capable of doing the same things, socially and culturally speaking. Just as the French and the Portuguese hate and kill each other, for example, the Tupiniquins and the Tupinambás are enemies; just as the Portuguese ally with the Tupiniquins to fight the French and benefit from trading with them, the Tupinambás ally with the French who have the same purpose in mind. Language, or rather communication, is central to the movie since everything happens because of a linguistic misunderstanding or the inability to understand each other's language.

This complexity of the Indians also humanizes them. That humanization is emphasized by the ethnographic atmosphere of the movie. This is an interesting strategy used to present the Indians with as little interference from the "outside" world as possible, despite the fact that the movie is made in the twentieth century, that it depicts events from the sixteenth century, and that many of the "Indians" are actually actors playing Indians. The veracity of the movie is not compromised, however, since as Tzvetan Todorov affirms, we can interrogate historical documents and events "chiefly as actions, not as descriptions."[10] The speculative nature of the movie is strongly based on original documents from the time of the colonization of Brazil. The movie actually starts with a fragment from a letter of French admiral Nicolas Durand Villegaignon to Calvin written in 1557 where he describes the situation of the Antarctic France (the French domain in Brazil) clearly stating that the Indians are savages that make their exploration and exploitation of the new territories extremely difficult. However, immediately after that he adds that the Portuguese are an equal if not a bigger problem since being envious of the French, they had become their mortal enemies.

It is not accidental, considering these films, that Carlos Diegues decided to continue his exploration of the African experience in Brazil within the margins of *Tropicalismo* in his *Xica da Silva* (1976). Strictly speaking, this film does not belong to *cinema novo* and was criticized for reinforcing stereotypes about African slaves. But it is obvious that Diegues is using the same carnivalesque strategies that de Andrade and dos Santos use. Diegues is taking past history to comment on contemporary history in a moment when repression and censorship are still common practices in the country. While the subject is serious and the real historical records are more a tragedy than a comedy, Diegues pushes the anecdotic aspect of it to its most absurd limits with the intention of including in the national discourse a "people whose sensuality, exuberance, and creative imagination are capable of transforming reality in such an extravagant manner."[11] *Xica* is the story of a slave who manages to use her charm and, above all, her sexual powers to place herself in a prominent position within colonial society.

Historical revisionism was an important trend in Brazilian cinema at a time when the country was going through one of the biggest challenges to its democracy. Since the need to address the political and social issues of the nation under a fierce repressive regime helped *cinema novo* to develop a highly allegorical style, as we said, the decision to look for inspiration in historical documents and literary classics was a brilliant move that allowed the detractors to challenge a system that proclaimed to put the nation's interest first even if that meant civil repression and suspension of democratic principles. By focusing on the most subversive and critical aspects of such historical documents and literary texts, they also managed to elude censorship and to protect themselves. Two other excellent examples of this strategic cinema are Joaquim Pedro de Andrade's *Os Inconfidêntes* (*The Conspirators*, 1972) and *Azyllo Muito Louco* (*The Alienist*, 1970). *Os Inconfidentes* is considered an example of historical adaptation; it tells of a frustrated attempt to gain independence from Portugal, orchestrated by a group of enlightened Brazilian intellectuals from Minas Gerais, one of the richest colonial provinces.

The conspiracy was uncovered and the leader of the group, Tiradentes, was executed and his coconspirators were banished from the country or were committed to jail or asylums. Nonetheless, it is considered, officially, the first moment of a clear national consciousness and identity and, therefore, could not be censored. This was despite the obvious fact that what the conspirators did was to challenge the established order and that they paid with their lives and freedom for opposing a tyrannical, unjust government. The metaphor could not have been more obvious to Brazilian audiences and government, but the authorities could not do anything to suppress history, particularly the official version of it. The film was, therefore, seen by millions and became a huge success. Similarly, *Azyllo muito louco* (literally "the extremely crazy asylum") works as an allegory of the present, although it is based on a novella by nineteenth-century master Joaquim Maria Machado de Assis. The story is the typical opposition between sanity and insanity. More precisely, it is an attempt to define both terms and the catastrophic consequences that result from it, as well as the danger of any dogmatic truth even if proclaimed with the best of intentions.

Father Simão is a man of God with an inclination for the empirical aspect of science and who, upon arriving at his new church, and with the favor of an aristocratic lady who believes in him, decides to create an asylum to care for the neediest of the needy, the mentally insane. However, when the moment arrives to determine who is crazy and who is not, the priest keeps changing the definition in ever more bizarre ways until he ends up throwing half of the population in the asylum, with the other half wanting to go there for an easy life, which in itself qualifies them as "crazy" and therefore makes them eligible to be admitted. Soon everybody, even the aristocracy and the elite, are "committed" to the asylum, which becomes a microcosm of the country with its power struggles, revolutions, and political negotiations as well as repression, all done in the best interest of the people. As in the case of *Os Inconfidêntes*, *Azyllo* is based on an untouchable, the text of a canonical author that hardly could be called subversive, and yet through parody and absurd situations it is updated to comment on the contemporary situation of the country. It could have been virtually impossible for Brazilians not to draw similarities between the absurd asylum on the screen and the political situation of their country.

Simultaneously to *cinema novo* there was a film movement that rebelled against it because the directors had given into commercial interests and success by taming their subversive tactics to attract wider audiences; the leaders of this movement proposed instead an *estética do lixo* (aesthetics of garbage) that would later be called *cinema marginal* (marginal cinema). This cinema focused, obviously, on the marginal aspects of society and showed little or no interest in technical perfection; it was also known as underground or "undigrundi" (mimicking Brazilians' pronunciation of the English term), as Glauber Rocha called it sarcastically. Some of the most representative films of this movement are *O Bandido da Luz Vermelha* (*The Red Light Bandit*, Rogério Sganzerla, 1968), *Toda Nudez Será Castigada* (*All Nudity Shall Be Punished*, Arnaldo Jabor, 1973), and *Matou a Família e Foi ao Cinema* (*He Killed the Family and Went to the Movies*, Julio Bressane, 1969). A film such as *Rio Babilônia* (*Rio Babylon*, Neville d'Almeida, 1982) could very well be associated with the movement if only because of its frankness and determination to criticize the hypocrisy of the middle class.

The best example of this cinema, however, is *O Bandido*, which traces the life of a rising criminal, Jorge (Paulo Villaça), known as the Red Light Bandit because he had the habit of breaking into houses with a red flashlight since he operated mostly at night; he also had the habit of engaging in long conversations with his victims, whom he not only robs and rapes, but also sometimes kills. The indisputable king of the crime underworld of São Paulo, he boasts about his career of crime before he is chased by the police; when he finally finds himself trapped, he decides to take his own life. Trying to maintain an independent spirit and a critical and antibourgeois attitude, Rogério Sganzerla sprinkles his film with chunks of very dark humor and an apparent amoral detachment from the evils of his character, thus emphasizing even more the aesthetics of garbage. Sganzerla referred to *O Bandido* as a "film-summa."[12] Indicative of this sensibility is the pastiche of several genres including B movies from Brazil as well as from other cinemas, particularly Hollywood and the French *nouvelle vague* that he uses. In a way, it can be said that it anticipates the "pulp" cinema of Quentin Tarantino and Robert Rodriguez of the 1990s. Controversial when it was released and not very successful with the critics, the film today is considered an indispensable Brazilian film that inaugurates a movement, while still maintaining a dialectic relationship with *cinema novo*.

The other representative of this cinema is *Matou a Família e Foi ao Cinema*, a film with a provocative title that, like *Como Era Gostoso o Meu Francês*, seems more ironic and symbolic than serious. The story is fragmented and combines scenes of crude realism, eroticism, and movie-within-the-movie strategies to create a film that is a very personal commentary on society, media, violence, and alienation. One day, apparently annoyed by their arguing while he is watching TV, a man (Antero de Oliveira) stabs to death his elderly parents and then goes to the movies to watch a raunchy film that focuses on a lesbian relationship at a time when homosexuality was still taboo in Brazilian cinema. The movie then intertwines several unclear narratives, including a man being tortured, scenes from the lesbian film, violence, and apparently insignificant events (a woman working out or washing dishes). *Mato a Fámilia* is also a film with unconventional narrative and with techniques that emphasize the "garbage" of poor production, improvisation, a sordid (or at least shocking) subject, abrupt editing, and bad or badly recorded music that distinguished *cinema marginal*. However, it is important to take into consideration that this garbage is intentional. In an attempt to abandon all representation or allegory, *cinema marginal* relies on the images themselves to provoke a response that brings out only what it is already in the viewers themselves.

This is the main reason behind the accusation of being amoral that *cinema marginal* had to endure, particularly for not offering a clear-cut division between good and evil—that is between accepted and unaccepted bourgeois norms of conduct. However, it is clear that for these directors, cinema had to be about a ferocious attack on power and its alliance with those very same sectors of society that presented themselves as the moral and social engine of the country with a high degree of hypocrisy. Perhaps this criticism was more direct in Arnaldo Jabor's *Toda Nudez Será Castigada* because the film, unlike the two mentioned previously, is more "realistic," and therefore the situations work more effectively as social commentary. On the other hand, because of that, the film was also criticized for its apparently melodramatic tone. The story begins with Herculano (Paulo Porto) on his way to see his lover Geni (Darlene Glória). He is a pious, Catholic bourgeois who was mourning the death of his wife until he finally falls in love with Geni, who actually is a prostitute. When he arrives at her house, he finds her dead and a tape with an explanation; at this point the movie tells his story in flashbacks.

We learn that Herculano had promised his son Sérgio (Paulo Sacks) he would never sleep with any other woman after his wife had died; however, Herculano's brother Patrício (Paulo César), plotting to control his brother's life along with two old aunts, convinces him to see a prostitute (Geni). Herculano goes to see her and sleeps with her. At first he considers having slept with her a mistake, but he continues seeing Geni because he truly likes her and has feelings for her. However, rather than marry her, Heculano puts her in a house where he visits her regularly. When Sérgio finds out, he accuses his father of betraying his mother's memory; in a drunken stupor he attacks his father physically and is thrown in jail where he is raped by his cell mate. Plotting revenge, and encouraged by his uncle Patrício, Sérgio courts Geni; when she is in love with him, he abandons her and goes off to Europe with his ex-cell mate who has become his lover. Geni commits suicide and leaves a tape to Herculano confessing everything. It has been suggested by Stephanie Dennison and Lisa Shaw that Jabor "was not afraid to handle the depraved characters and situations [. . .] and [that] he was able to use shocking scenes of depravity to challenge bourgeois hypocrisy."[13] However, the melodramatic aspect of the film, as Randal Johnson has pointed out, is "melodrama taken to the second degree,"[14] that is, an exaggeration and therefore a parody of itself, and consequently not to be taken seriously as a sentimental mechanism.

This exaggeration is not that different from the carnivalization of *Tropicalismo* or the allegorization of the second phase of *cinema novo* or even of the occasional alliance between *cinema novo* and the traditional *chanchadas* in order to produce films that were popular, both in the number of people who watched them and in its use of themes that were appealing to the people. What this seems to suggest is that more than a movement in itself, *cinema marginal* is in many ways a continuation of *cinema novo* and that they, like *chanchadas*, belong to a larger tradition of Brazilian cinema. It is interesting, for example, to notice that when Leon Hirszman made *Eles Não Usam Black-Tie* (*They Do Not Wear Black-Tie*, 1981) in the early 1980s, people referred to it as *cinema novo de novo* or *cinema novo* again.[15] This is important to mention because Hirszman himself is considered a pioneer of "the second phase of cinema novo with *Garota de Ipanema* (*The Girl from Ipanema*, 1967)." Denisson and Shaw have argued that the 1960s and 1970s were not particularly remembered for the production of popular films, but rather for many boring and too intellectualized ones, except those that "incorporated the themes of the *chanchada* genre. Even the cinema novo auteurs, keen after 1964 to engage more productively with their target audiences, could not ignore the enormous impact that these popular comedies had on the public imaginary."[16]

NOTES

1. Timothy Barnard and Peter Rist, eds., *South American Cinema: A Critical Filmography, 1915–1994* (Austin: University of Texas Press, 1996), 127.

2. Randal Johnson, "Brazilian Cinema Novo," *Bulletin of Latin American Research* 3 (1984): 96.

3. Ibid., 98.

4. Vincent Canby, "Quilombo," *New York Times*, March 28, 1986, http://movies.nytimes.com/movie/review?res=9A0DE1DD1039F93BA1575 0C0A960948260.

5. Dan Schneider, "Black Orpheus," *Culturevulture.net*, http://www .culturevulture.net/Movies/blackorpheus.htm.

6. Johnson, "Brazilian Cinema Novo," 98.

7. Randal Johnson, *Cinema Novo X 5: Masters of Contemporary Brazilian Film* (Austin: University of Texas Press, 1984), 101.

8. Roger Greenspun, "Earth Entranced (1966). From Brazil Comes Film about Poet," *New York Times*, May 15, 1970, http://movies.nytimes.com/ movie/review?res=9D07EED81438EE34BC4D52DFB366838B669EDE.

9. Johnson, *Cinema Novo X 5*, 98.

10. Tzvetan Todorov, *The Conquest of America. The Question of the Other* (New York: Harper Perennial, 1982), 53.

11. Barnard and Rist, *South American Cinema*, 179.

12. Ibid., 152.

13. Stephanie Dennison and Lisa Shaw, *Popular Cinema in Brazil 1930– 2001* (Manchester, UK: Manchester University Press, 2004), 139.

14. Randal Johnson, "Nelson Rodrigues as Filmed by Arnaldo Jabor," *Latin American Theater Review* (Fall 1982): 27.

15. Cited by Randal Johnson, *Brazilian Cinema Novo*, 97.

16. Dennison and Shaw, *Popular Cinema in Brazil*, 145.

CHAPTER 7
The Cinema of Argentina

AN INDISPENSABLE CINEMA

With all the recent fuss about the excitement and novelty of Latin cinema, particularly with the films of Pedro Almodóvar or Alejandro Amenábar, Brazil's stylized visuals of poverty and graphic violence, or Mexico's "frijollywood" represented by the Three Amigos, Alfonso Cuarón, Guillermo del Toro, and González Iñarritu; people tend to forget that there is another great, vibrant, audacious Latin cinema, the cinema of Argentina. Argentina has had a continuous tradition of making films just as Brazil, Mexico, and Spain and like them has gone through periods of splendor and crisis. Argentina's film industry developed early, and for a while it competed fairly and strongly against Mexico and Spain, to mention only the traditions that share the same language. In the end Mexico was the country that dominated the Latin market during the 1940s and 1950s, but the Argentine film industry managed to maintain an uneven, if sometimes impressive, production of national films. Political, economic, and social problems, no doubt, contributed to its uneven production, but in recent decades Argentine cinema has given very strong signs of recovery and has circulated again a cinema as important and as rich as that of the other major Latin film traditions.

With a reputation for quality and vision and with a solid presence in international festivals, the cinema of Argentina has always been around and has proven many times that it is nothing but indispensable. Without it, our film traditions, and world cinema in general, would be a little poorer. Thankfully, the year 2008 confirmed that this cinema is as strong as ever. That year Argentina was the only Latin American country with a significant presence at the Cannes Film Festival with nine films being showcased, two in competition, and a warm reception for most of them. Even Mexican and Brazilian newspapers reported the good news, with the prestigious *Folha de São Paulo* being more than enthusiastic in declaring that this was a "clear demonstration of the vitality of that country's cinematographic industry,"[1] underlining also the participation in the festival of veteran Lucrecia Martel with her film *La Mujer sin Cabeza* (*The Headless Woman*, 2008). Martel had already participated in Cannes in 2004 with the excellent *La Niña Santa* (*The Holy Girl*, 2004). In 2009, however, the strongest film and one of the public's favorites was Pablo Trapero's *Leonera* (*The Lioness's Den*, 2008), a very powerful prison drama about Julia (Martina Gusman), a young, middle-class girl who, accused of killing her husband and a friend who could have been her husband's male lover, ends up in jail.

As it turns out, Julia is pregnant and does not know that at the time of her arrest, so when she finds out, she is determined to keep her baby and raise him in jail. Part of the film then follows the hard conditions Julia and her son have to endure. This apparently melodramatic plot is actually a powerful tragedy about life in an Argentine prison and the struggles of the protagonist to raise her son under those circumstances. Most importantly, the film raises two very important questions that would keep the audience thinking for a long, long time after watching the film—the two very basic rights, the right of a mother to be with her child and the right of a child to live a life of freedom in a healthy, normal, socially acceptable environment. The film is sure to be a favorite of art houses all over the world and to become an unavoidable reference for any discussion about contemporary Latin American societies, despite the commentaries of some Argentineans who praised Trapero for remaining authentic and faithful to his country's idiosyncrasy by creating "a national cinema, different from the cinema being done by Mexicans and Brazilians who are making films for a foreign market."[2]

This national spirit was evident in his previous films, such as the excellent *Familia Rodante* (*Rolling Family*, 2004), a hilarious road movie about a family who embarks on a two-day trip to the Misiones Province in a small motor home in which they manage to squeeze 13 people. Commanded by the matriarch Emilia (Graciana Chironi), the trip is full of adventures and misadventures, generational conflicts, and plenty of opportunities to examine the nation, and the human condition, through a microcosm with no air conditioner during a hot Argentine summer. Very idiosyncratic also is *El Bonaerense* (*The Man from Buenos Aires*, 2002), a movie about a provincial locksmith who is accused of robbing an office after he was sent there to open the safe. His uncle bails him out and sends him to Buenos Aires where he gets a job as a police officer and a second chance; quiet and well acted, the film is an excellent example of economic narrative. The same is true of *Nacido y Criado* (*Born and Raised*, 2006), a film about a man who sees his life transformed from a happy existence in the suburbs of Buenos Aires to a life of harshness in the Patagonian plains where he exiles himself after a car accident hoping that the wilderness will help him to exorcise his demons and get rid of his guilt. It can be said as well of his first movie, *Mundo Grúa* (*Crane World*, 1999), the movie that most openly shows a preference for the everyday folk and for nonprofessional actors. Here, too, as in all the movies mentioned before, Trapero focuses on the everyday existence of ordinary Argentineans with sympathy and enormous respect and with a wonderful understanding of the power of brevity in narration.

Ironically, considering this, *Leonera* seems more foreign-audience friendly than the other Argentine film in competition at Cannes, Martel's *La Mujer sin Cabeza*, which also deals with a traumatic event in a woman's life and the infinitely terrifying consequences of that event. Verónica (María Onetto) is driving home one day when she accidentally hits an animal, or so she tries to convince herself; however, she is not sure. Rather than stopping and finding out what it is that she killed, she decides to continue. From that moment on, she begins to lose her head. Nightmares, confusion, and a complete detachment from reality are masterfully captured by Martel's camera and brilliantly executed by the leading actress. The sensation of just existing, floating in a dream-like dimension, rather than living in the physical world is transmitted to the audience very effectively, making it feel Verónica's confusion after the accident. When she finally confesses to her family members that she may have killed someone, they convince her that she is imagining it and take her to where the accident happened only to find a dead dog. Even though it is never clear that she killed this dog, Verónica calms down and the world makes sense once more.

More extreme in its fragmented narrative and style than her previous films, *La Mujer sin Cabeza* confirms Martel's position simultaneously as the most prominent of the new Argentine directors and the most independent of them; in fact, she does not seem preoccupied at all with pleasing the audience in any way, while creating a cinematic language that is difficult and beautiful and seems destined to become a favorite of true cinephiles all over the world. In Martel's two previous films, we could already observe similar qualities. *La Ciénaga* (*The Swamp*, 2001), her first feature, for instance, is a ferocious look into the private world of Argentine middle classes, portraying them as hypocrite, racist, and irresponsible. Alcohol, rude remarks about the servants, and irresponsible behavior run freely in this film, and the accidents that come as a consequence of such behavior are inevitably present. Like *La Mujer sin Cabeza*, *LaCiénaga* uses private, almost intimate events in the interaction of a dysfunctional family to comment on the larger picture of the nation. It is not coincidental, for example, that in both films there is the catalyst of accidents with blood and shattered glass that brings to the surface all this ugliness, irresponsibility, and social conflict.

Also about hypocrisy and decadence of a different kind, according to Laura Sinagra in the *New York Village Voice*, *La Niña Santa* is a film that mixes sexuality and religion in the story of a Lolita-like girl with a religious "calling" to save the older doctor she perceives as a pervert.

> When a married doctor staying at the hotel flirts with Amalia's divorced mother, and later rubs against Amalia in a crowded street, she believes she hears God's call to save him. These developments unfold as less a plot than simply occasions to muse on the characters' private motivations. Martel insists she's not commenting on "teen sexuality," but rather investigating "the inability to translate experiences that occur in the space of loneliness, in solitude."[3]

The presence of Martel with *La Niña Santa* at Cannes was also a welcome event not only for Argentina, since it represents an international presence of its cinema, but also for cinephile audiences all over the world because of the artistic possibilities of the medium it revealed. Cannes—being the most famous film festival—is always a good indicator of the presence of a national cinema.

However, there are other important international festivals that are also important to consider to assess a cinema; in the case of Latin cultures, one of the most important of those festivals is the San Sebastián Film Festival in the northern Spanish city of the same name. And 2008 was a year also with a very distinguished presence of Argentine cinema in that festival, particularly with *El Nido Vacío* (*The Empty Nest*, 2008), the latest film by Daniel Burman, another director who is often mentioned in the international press as an example of the vitality of recent Argentine cinema. *El Nido Vacío* is a very different film from the ones that Burman has become famous for; it could even be seen as conventional in comparison, although perfectly executed and beautifully shot. His film tells the story of a mature couple that finds itself confused and in need of something else after their adult children leave the house. The mother, Martha (Cecilia Roth), is a housewife who decides to go back to college; the father, Leonardo (Óscar Martínez), is a playwright who is unable to write and seeks solace in an affair with a younger woman. More an exploration of the quotidian and the need for imagination and perhaps little transgressions to survive an ordinary life, the film is not so much a family drama as a look at a patriarchal society and a contemporary man's crisis.

A similar preoccupation with masculinity and success was already central in his previous *Derecho de Familia* (*Family Law*, 2006), a well-structured story about a handsome young lawyer, Ariel (Daniel Hendler), who apparently has everything to be happy, except that he tries to measure his life and success against those of his overachiever father. When he meets a woman, Sandra (Julieta Díaz), who is a physical trainer, he becomes infatuated with her to the point that he starts working out with her; soon they fall in love and get married. Even though the couple has a stable life, a nice place, and a sweet son, Gastón (Eloy Burman), we soon realize that there is trouble in Paradise and the couple has no more real reasons to stay together. The movie is very successful at following life as it happens, without any glorification or embellishment. The previously assertive Ariel is now a sad shadow of his father, and even his wife seems disinterested in him emotionally and otherwise. The center of the story, however, remains the relationship between father and son and the incapacity of Ariel to stand up for himself against his father's expectations and therefore his failure as a young man trying to claim his place in the world.

A relationship between father and son seems to be a theme central to Burman as we can also see it in the plot of *El Abrazo Partido* (*Broken Embrace*, 2004). Ariel (Daniel Hendler) has been living an ordinary life in Buenos Aires and making plans to acquire a passport that would allow him to flee to Europe, to the country of his Jewish ancestors who left Poland and settled in Argentina. Ariel is less moved by an urge to recover his identity than by a pragmatic desire to migrate to Europe in search of a better life. However, there is one thing that keeps him from realizing this desire: he wants to know why his father left his family to fight in Israel when he was born and never came back. The film pays rigorous attention to everyday life—as is typical of Burman's films—until Ariel's life takes a turn he was not expecting, reuniting him with his father and sharing, finally, an embrace with him. It is not a coincidence that the protagonist of most of Burman's films bears the same name, Ariel (and that he is played by the same actor), which means he is a sort of alter ego of the director, therefore expressing many of his obsessions.

It is in his second film, *Esperando al Mesías* (*Waiting for the Messiah*, 2000), where these obsessions appear for the first time as well as the character of Ariel. *Esperando al Mesías* talks about the life of a young man, Ariel (Daniel Hendler), and his relationship with his father, Simón (Héctor Alterio), in opposition to the relationship with a father-like figure, Santamaría (Enrique Piñeyro), a man who loses his job in a bank and ends up on the street surviving by helping people find their lost wallets and documents. Ariel lives his life struggling with his father's expectation—namely, that he could soon take over the family restaurant and marry a nice girl—and the life he dreams of. In direct opposition, the life of Santamaría is a life that wants to be free, but is not really convincing. He is supposed to be a sort of free-spirited bum who offers a contrast to the structured life Ariel is struggling to reject; however, he never really seems determined to embrace that happy wandering existence. These two men, and numerous other characters, cross paths at several points without really changing their lives. Not very original, the film is, nonetheless, interesting in its juxtaposition of the different lives that exist in the same world and the ways they sometimes touch each other.

Another film by Burman's that has had some success is *Todas las Azafatas Van al Cielo* (*Every Stewardess Goes to Heaven*, 2002), a romantic story about a stewardess, Teresa (Ingrid Rubio), who has a problematic love life and has given up hope of finding the love of her life until she meets Julián (Alfredo Casero), a man who has lost his wife and is transporting her ashes to her final resting place in Tierra del Fuego, where they meet. After failed attempts to commit suicide by letting themselves freeze to dead, they both decide to go on with their lives together. This is a little silly, but it is touching romantic comedy that reminds us of Alfonso Cuarón's similar film of the early 1990s, *Sólo con Tu Pareja* (*Love in Times of Hysteria*, 1991), in which a beautiful stewardess also frustrated with her love life decides to kill herself but instead falls in love with a man who is also trying to kill himself. According to the journalist Laura Gentile, Burman is identified in Spain with his films because Spaniards see their subject matter as a subject close to them, and therefore they do not see him as an "exotic Latin American product."[4] This is a curious assessment of the works of a director so preoccupied with issues of Jewish identity.

Fortunately, despite the erroneous misconceptions of some journalists, the diversity of the cinema of Argentina in the last two decades is evident and has already been established not only with Lucrecia Martel, Daniel Burman, and Pablo Trapero, but also with filmmakers who are not afraid of difficult subjects. One of the best examples of this is the debut of Lucía Puenzo—the daughter of veteran director Luis Puenzo—whose film *XXY* (2007) is an extraordinary story about hermaphrodites, perhaps one of the very few remaining taboos in contemporary Western societies. The film tells the story of Alex (Inés Efrón), a 15-year-old hermaphrodite who, confused and pressured by her parents to choose a gender, strikes up a friendship with Álvaro (Martín Piroyansky), the son of a family friend visiting them, only to add to her confusion. Lots of sexual experimentation and disorientation, mixed with pain, make this exploration of gender identity a little uncomfortable for most audiences. The subject is compelling and in Puenzo's hands it becomes strong and human, never sensationalistic or exploitative. There is enough light and compassion in this film to help us understand such a powerful issue and how it complicates the lives of already confused adolescents, forcing them to focus on the most delicate aspects of one's own identity at that age—gender. This movie was honored with the Cóndor de Plata for best film of the year in September 2008.[5]

Equally daring in its subject matter is the interesting *Un Año sin Amor* (*A Year without Love*, 2005) by Anahí Berneri, a film that touches on another contemporary taboo, homosexual sex and AIDS. The film is an excellent reflection on the nature of love, passion, and desire. Pablo (Juan Minujín) is a 30-something aspiring poet with AIDS who is desperately in search of love before he succumbs to the disease; one way of finding potential mates is through personal newspaper ads. These ads searching for Mr. Right do not produce, however, any appropriate, or otherwise, candidates for companionship; so, in desperation, Pablo decides to change his strategy. He then gets involved in a world of S&M (sadomasochism), leather, and sexual humiliation and finds in the pain of the whip and the humiliation of licking boots and wearing a dog collar the pleasure and the feeling of being alive he so desperately needed. Pablo's poetry is going nowhere, so again he decides to change gears and publish his diaries narrating in detail his sexual adventures. This material, of course, finds its way to the press, and to the family's library, which, ashamed of the cynicism of the prodigal son, shuts him from the clan forever. With no one to turn to, not even his hope-to-be master, Pablo sinks deeper and deeper in his sexual gratifications in search of that spark of love and the painful, confrontation of still being alive.

Both directors, Puenzo and Berneri, are young, and these two films represent each one's first feature; both are also women. This perhaps explains their courage and sensibility in treating sexual and gender identity so freely; after all, they have less invested in a patriarchal traditional society. Such brilliant débuts make audiences anxiously await their next films; nonetheless, they have already proven that Argentine cinema is as vibrant, audacious, and vital as ever. It is another woman who confirms this point—Mercedes García Guevara with her film *Río Escondido* (*Hidden River*, 1999). This picture is a more conventional story about a woman who suspects that her husband is keeping a second family in the far town of Río Escondido, near the Andes. Determined to find out the truth, she decides to investigate only to realize that the reality is very different from what she had suspected; in the process she starts questioning her own relationship. The film is not a masterpiece or very innovative in its narrative techniques; it does not deal with a controversial subject either, and it actually feels a little dated. Still, it manages to convey a personal worldview and to tell a story in the most traditional way with surprisingly entertaining and pleasing results, mainly due to its lack of pretentiousness. That ability to mold and adapt to many aspects of life is a quality that Argentine cinema has and often uses to its advantage, resulting in a rich diversity of styles and themes.

This diversity includes some of the most interesting films of recent years such as *La Rabia* (*The Rage*, Albertina Carri, 2008), an intense drama in the Argentine countryside; *Cordero de Dios* (*Lamb of God*, Lucía Cedrón, 2008), a political drama where old wounds from the time of the military dictatorship afflict a family after the kidnapping of the patriarch; and Pablo Fendrik's *El Asaltante* (*The Mugger*, 2007) and *La Sangre Brota* (*Blood Appears*, 2008), films about violence and crime in urban settings. There are also more conventional, and yet entertaining, films that prove that Argentine cinema, just as Mexican or Spanish, can also produce commercially successful pictures, such as *Un Novio para Mi Mujer* (*A Boyfriend for My Wife*, Juan Taratuto, 2008), the story of a man (Adrián Suar) who wants to separate from his whining wife, but does not know how to do it until a friend suggests that he hire a womanizer (Gabriel Goity) to seduce her so she decides to end the relationship herself, which results in, of course, not the desired consequences.

Also along this line is *Amorosa Soledad* (*Lovely Soledad*, Martín Carranza and Victoria Galardi, 2008), a romantic story about a girl (predictably named Soledad) who decides not to fall in love again after being dumped by her boyfriend and, in solitude, centers all her energies on her work. However, when she receives a phone call from her ex, she has to rethink her attitude. Similarly, *Motivos para No Enamorarse* (*Reasons Not to Fall in Love*, Mariano Mucci, 2008) narrates the story of Clara (Celeste Cid), an unlucky girl who spends her days dreaming of a different life, with an ideal man to fall in love with. After a frustrated relationship with Alex (Esteban Meloni), she ends up moving in with "Teo" (Jorge Marrale), an older man who agrees to let her stay in his house under the condition that they interact as little as possible and that they cannot fall in love with each other no matter what. Considering that neither one of them is really interested in or attracted to the other, this seems like a sensible possibility. But of course, little did they know, they start having problems with the arrangement and start to realize that perhaps they have more in common than they thought and that they could perhaps still have another chance to be happy.

Another interesting aspect of contemporary Argentine cinema is the presence of a director from an older generation as in the case of *Aniceto* (2008), a film by the veteran director Leonardo Favio. It is actually a remake of Favio's early *El Romance del Aniceto y la Francisca* (*The Romance of Aniceto and Francisca*, 1966), but unlike the earlier version, the director this time uses a more artistic approach to his "story of gaucho love."[6] The movie is reminiscent of Carlos Saura's dance films in its stylized view of tragic love rooted in folklore and popular culture as well as in his use of the dancer Hernán Paquín as the lead character —a handsome, sensuous force of a man who moves through the screen like moving through a dance stage. This film joins other local and international hits of the past 15 years such as the films of Adrián Caetano, whose *Pizza, Birra, Faso* (*Pizza, Beer, and Cigarettes*, 1998), a movie about disenchanted youths in Buenos Aires, opened the doors of festivals and art houses for him worldwide. While *Pizza, Birra, Faso* revealed an emerging talent, that talent was confirmed by *Bolivia* (2001), an excellent film about the discrimination endured by poor Bolivian immigrants in the capital of Argentina. Further confirmation was given by *Un Oso Rojo* (*A Red Bear*, 2002), a crime drama-thriller about a gentle giant, Oso (Julio Chávez), who returns to reunite with his family after spending time in jail for armed robbery and homicide.

Like Caetano, Marcelo Piñeyro has surprised audiences and critics alike with his style that mixes thriller and politics since his early films *Caballos Salvajes* (*Wild Horses*, 1995) and *Cenizas del Paraíso* (*Ashes of Paradise*, 1997), a murder mystery intertwined with politics; more recently, he has continued to impress with *Kamchatka* (2002), an interesting look at the 1970s, the years of the military dictatorship in Argentina, from the perspective of a middle-class family that moves around the country and assumes a different identity. The film manages to handle the subject of political repression and militant resistance without being preachy. This is true particularly of his homoerotic thriller *Plata Quemada* (*Burnt Money*, 2000). *Plata Quemada* was a huge international hit in part no doubt because of its subject matter, but also because of the excellent execution of the lead actors. The story is based on a novel by Ricardo Piglia that reconstructs some real event from the crime pages of the 1960s Argentine press. El Nene (Leonardo Sbaraglia) and Ángel (Eduardo Noriega) are two handsome, sexy criminals that from the moment they meet in the bathroom of a train station become inseparable both as lovers and accomplices. Dubbed the Twins by the police, the two men continue with a life of crime that forces them to move to Uruguay after a robbery goes wrong, only to end their lives in a bloody confrontation with the police in classical Butch Cassidy and the Sundance Kid style.

Other films that have contributed to the revival of Argentine cinema are *Nueve Reinas* (*Nine Queens*, 2000) and *El Aura* (*The Aura*, 2005), both films of Fabián Bielinsky. *Nueve Reinas*, particularly, is an excellent thriller about a con artist and his young apprentice, with a wonderful twist at the end that will surprise most viewers. The movie was later remade in Hollywood with John Rally and Mexican actor Diego Luna, but the original remains more entertaining and far more superior. Also of interest are *Cama Adentro* (*Live-in Maid*, Jorge Gaggero, 2004), an excellent story about power, appearances, and emotional dependency with the background of an impoverished Argentine middle class. When a wealthy woman, Beba (Norma Aleandro), suffers the effects of the economic crisis and can no longer afford to pay her live-in maid, or any of the other things she was used to, for that matter, she continues pretending she is the patrician lady of the house, bossing her maid around and doing everything in her power to keep the appearances. This film as well as *Valentín* (Alejandro Agresti, 2005), a sweet, although conventional, story about a little boy who, neglected by his parents, is raised by his grandmother and befriends his father's girlfriend, are the typical examples of art house cinema. In 1960s Buenos Aires, nine-year-old Valentín (Rodrigo Noya) dreams of reuniting with his mother who, after separating from his abusive father, left him living with his grandmother (Carmen Maura); with his charming personality and ingenuity, Valentín tries to solve other people's problems, including his dad's new girlfriend, Leticia (Julieta Cardinali), to whom he becomes close. When we review the number of films that have come out of Argentina in the past couple of decades, we can corroborate that it is true, as María Alejandra Gutiérrez has written, "If there is anything certain about the effervescence shaking up Argentina these days [it] is the great variety of cinematic themes and the legion of young, as well as not-so-young artists who have decided to bet on the movies as a way of life and expression."[7]

AFTER THE MILITARY REGIME

When María Luisa Bemberg premiered her film *Camila* in May 1984, the country had just returned to democracy, which was marked by the beginning of Raúl Alfonsín's presidency in December 1983. Nonetheless, the film had a huge impact on the public since it was a very powerful story of defiance to patriarchal tyranny and old values in the name of a love that went against everything: nation, society, morality, and even God. The film is the story of Camila O'Gorman (Susú Pecoraro), a rich girl in colonial Argentina who falls in love with her confessor, Father Ladislao Gutiérrez (Imanol Arias). Since he loves her, too, they decide to be together and run away so they can live the life that was denied them, even if it had to be as fugitives. The rest of the story is predictable: they are persecuted by civil and religious authorities, only to be executed in the end despite Camila's pregnancy. Many critics, and Bemberg herself, called this film the first one of the democracy, something that is very suggestive considering the subject matter. But that is not accurate since in reality the movie can be considered most precisely the last one of the dictatorship. Nonetheless, there is some truth in this assessment inasmuch as that even though *Camila* was already finished by 1983, that year represented a true renaissance of Argentine cinema. Among other things, it was the year of a presidential decree that guaranteed freedom of speech, as well as the year in which a considerable number of film projects were

encouraged by a more democratic government. Some of these projects
were *Noches sin Lunas ni Soles* (*Nights without Moons or Suns*, José A.
Martínez Suárez, 1984), *Pasajeros de una Pesadilla* (*Nightmare's Passen-
gers*, Fernando Ayala, 1984), and *Los Chicos de la Guerra* (*The Boys from
the War*, Bebe Kamin), an interesting film about the Falklands War
only a couple of years after the historical events that are depicted in
the film.

But this diversity of films and film projects that came with the return
to democracy was such that some critics called it *cinema manicomio*
(madhouse cinema).[8] Films such as Carlos Galettini's *Los Tigres de la
Memoria* (*The Tigers of Memory*, 1984), José María Paolantonio's *El Jug-
uete Rebioso* (*The Angry Toy*, 1984), Emilio Vieyra's *Todo o Nada* (*All or
Nothing*, 1984), David Lipszyc's *La Rosales* (*Battleship Rosales*, 1984),
and, of course, Luis Puenzo's *La Historia Oficial* (*The Official Story*,
1985), all made between 1984 and 1985, represent the beginning of this
trend. During the following years, other important films were made or
released, for example, *Tangos, el Exilio de Gardel* (*Tangos, The Exile of
Gardel*, Fernando Solanas, 1985), *Los Hijos de Fierro* (*The Children of
Fierro*, Fernando Solanas, 1972), *Gracias por el Fuego* (*Thanks for the Fire*,
Sergio Renán, 1984), *Los Insomnes* (*Insomniacs*, Carlos Orgambide,
1986), *Los Días de Junio* (*Days in June*, Alberto Fischerman, 1985), and
the excellent *Adiós, Roberto* (*Goodbye Roberto*, Enrique Dawi, 1985), a film
about a man who moves in with a gay friend when he has problems with
his wife; one night after heavy drinking, he has sex with his friend and is
forced to rethink his friendship as well as his sexual identity. Another
excellent film from this period is *La Película del Rey* (*A King and His
Movie*, Carlos Sorín, 1985).

La Película del Rey is, in the words of Ricardo García Oliveri, "one of
the best things that could have ever happened to Argentine cinema in
all its history."[9] The film is the story of the obsession a young film
director, David Vass (Julio Chávez), has with the life of an eccentric
French man, Orélie Antoine de Tounens, who in the nineteenth century declared himself the king of Araucania and Patagonia in a remote
part of South America. De Tounens had planned to establish a
democratic monarchy among the Araucanian Indians with the intention of helping them to become more civilized. This film-within-a-
film is a charming look into the comical results of that obsession and
the determination of David, who, against all odds and with numerous
troubles and desertions, continues with his plan of filming the story of
Orélie Antoine de Tounens even if in the end he has to do everything
himself, including the acting. The film manages successfully to mix

experimentation, lyricism (it contains some beautiful, haunting images of Patagonian phantasmagoric landscapes), and commercial ambition (for example, a logical, uncomplicated narrative and well-known actors) that in the end pays off in festivals first and then with the interest of the Argentine audiences.

The other important film of those years was *La Historia Oficial*, which won an Oscar for best foreign film—it became the first, and so far the only, Latin American film to receive this honor. This recognition—as well as the film's political content, presented with courage and sensibility, although in a very audience-friendly way that avoided large political questions and finger-pointing—made *La Historia Oficial* a huge commercial success all over the world. The story is actually very simple and could even be considered a "woman's picture," except for its political implications. Alicia (Norma Aleandro) is a middle-class history teacher who lives a comfortable life with her husband, Roberto (Héctor Alterio), who was raised in a working-class family and attained a prominent position in the military government, and her adopted daughter Gaby (Analia Castro). Disinterested in the political situation of the country more by conformity than indifference, Alicia is an exemplar mother, teacher, and citizen. However, the return of an old friend and the sudden appearance of a woman who claims to be Gaby's grandmother forces her to question for the first time her marriage, her husband's involvement in the dirty politics of the military, and her complicity with the regimen by remaining silent. These were years marked by the disappearance of thousands of civilians during the period of the worst repression against the dissidents and all who opposed the military that was leading the country.

While the movie touches on a very serious and difficult issue only a few years after the unfortunate events took place, it does so in a way that avoids openly denouncing the middle classes for their implicit complicity by allowing the reign of brutal repression by the military against the population. By doing this, Puenzo rids them of any guilt and portrays them as victims rather than accomplices, something some citizens saw as a problem. Very different is the case of *La Noche de los Lápices* (*Night of the Pencils*, Héctor Olivera, 1986), a film that very realistically depicts the disappearance, torturing, and killing of several high school students who had organized to demand a reduction in bus fares so they could go to school in a provincial city of Argentina in 1976. Equally brutal is *Garage Olimpo* (*Garage Olimpo*, Marcos Bechis, 1999), a film made a few years later about repression and torture during the hardest years of the *guerra sucia* (*dirty war*), as that period of extreme repression between 1976 and 1983 was known. Also of interest in its treatment of the *guerra sucia* is *Malayunta* (*Bad Company*, José Santiso, 1986), particularly because of its denunciation of the complicity of large sectors of the civil population with the military. The film was originally a play called *Pater Noster* staged by a theater workshop, Teatro Abierto, that actively questioned the system during all the years of the dictatorship. This film has been called "the most profound, disturbing, uncompromising, and novel of all the films of the new democratic period to examine the years of terror."[10]

With the return to democracy also came an interest in other topics considered taboo, such as homosexuality. We already mentioned Dawi's *Adiós, Roberto*, a film that, although it deals with a sexual encounter between two male friends, is not really a "homosexual" story. Such relationships are recurrent in the Latin American physique and popular culture as the novel *Kiss of the Spider Woman* (1978) by Argentine writer Manuel Puig demonstrates; this novel, which was later made into a film set in Brazil with William Holden and Raúl Julia (Hector Babenco, 1985), is about two male friends—one gay and one straight—who reach a point in their friendship at which they are capable of having a sexual relationship, without the straight one considering himself gay. Very different is the case of *Otra Historia de Amor* (*Another Kind of Love Story*, 1986), a film by Américo Ortiz de Zárate, which depicts with simplicity and on a very low key the subject of male homosexuality. This is an interesting film because it returns to a subject that basically disappeared during the dictatorship. Right before the coup, a film that treated the subject of gender and sexual identity with heavy social undertones was released and, amazingly, was not censored. The film, titled *La Raulito* (*Tomboy Paula*, Lautaro Murúa, 1975), was based on the real-life story of María Esther Duffau, who lived on the margins of society dressed as a man and survived by petty crime and doing odd jobs. She also was known for meeting and befriending famous people, including the boxer Gatica and later the producer of the film *La Raulito*, Armando Bo.

Even though there was a revival of Argentina cinema with the return to a democracy in the mid-1980s, the economic crisis plaguing the country since then has taken a toll on the industry. In 1987, for example, the only real box-office success was a film that had been made a year earlier, but had not succeeded in convincing the distributors of its potential because of its unusual topic. Marketed as a sci-fi picture that deals with extraterrestrials, not a very precise description, the film *Hombre Mirando al Sudeste* (*Man Facing Southeast*, Eliseo Subiela, 1986) was able to attract and thus disappoint many viewers expecting to see an intergalactic battle. But it also secured a huge court of followers because of its supposedly philosophical content. In reality, the movie was neither a sci-fi flick, nor a philosophical film, but a picture about a man, Rantes (Hugo Soto), who appears one day at a mental institution claiming he is from another planet. The movie also had the dubious honor of being remade by Hollywood starring Kevin Spacey and Jeff Bridges with the title *K-Pax* (Iain Softley, 2001).[11] While *Hombre Mirando al Sureste* and *La Clínica del Doctor Cureta* (*The Clinic of Doctor Cureta*, Alberto Fischerman, 1987), although to a lesser degree than *Hombre*, were box-office successes, the rest of the 1980s was less favorable for the industry, despite the fact that an Argentine film won the Golden Bear at the Berlin Film Festival in 1988.

This film, virtually an unknown picture to most Argentine citizens, was *La Deuda Interna* (Verónico Cruz, 1988). It contrasted dramatically with most of the important films of the industry that have been very successful in presenting themselves as the "legitimate" representatives of Argentine society. This film turns its camera to an excluded people—the indigenous communities—to address the discrimination they have suffered for centuries and to criticize the myth that a "European" minority from the capital is the only sector of the population that holds the key to a national identity. After that, the industry was virtually paralyzed; however, some films in the years between the mid-1980s and the reemergence of the cinema in the first decade of the twenty-first century are worth mentioning. Some of the most representative are *Nunca Estuve en Viena* (*I've Never Been to Vienna*, Antonio Larreta, 1989), a coproduction with the Netherlands; *Boda Secreta* (*Secret Wedding*, Alejandor Agresti, 1989); *Últimas Imágenes del Naufragio* (*Last Images of the Shipwreck*, Eliseo Subiela, 1989), a film that was not as successful as expected; *Las Tumbas* (*The Gravestones*, Javier Torre, 1990); *Un Lugar en el Mundo* (*A Place in the World*, Adolfo Aristarain, 1992); *El Lado Oscuro del Corazón* (*The Dark Side of the Heart*, Eliseo Subiela, 1992); *Siempre de Difícil Volver a Casa* (*It's Always Difficult to Start All Over Again*, Jorge Polaco, 1992); and *El Viaje* (*The Trip*, Fernando Solanas, 1992). But the best of the period was *Gatica, el Mono* (*Gatica*, Leonardo Favio, 1993), a film that won Best Picture at the San Sebastian Film Festival. It can be considered the last successful film of the cinema since the return to the democracy.

A GOLDEN AGE

After the return to democracy it was possible to talk of a new Argentine cinema only because there was an old tradition of making movies in the country that, as in the Mexican case, could be traced to the first decades of the twentieth century and even the last of the nineteenth century. Argentina, like most Latin American countries, received the new invention of moving pictures in 1896, soon after its invention in Paris and, as Brazil or Spain, started early with a considerable production of silent films. By the 1930s, it was ready to produce talking pictures. It was the year 1933 that saw the Argentine film industry, strictly speaking, take off with the first talkies, *Tango* and *Los Tres Berretines*. It is traditionally accepted, however, that *Tango* was the first sound film in Argentina. This film is rather conventional in its plot, which centers on the misfortunes of a young man left heartbroken by his girlfriend who abandons him for an older, rich man. This idea, of course, gives the director the excuse to intercalate several tangos in the overly sentimental story. So successful was *Tango* that afterward, Argentine cinema would return regularly to look for inspiration in the lyrics of the most famous tangos. As Timothy Barnard and Peter Rist mention, "The tango permeated Buenos Aires working-class culture of the first half of the century, and the history of tango and that of the cinema are closely intertwined."[12] Most of the early films in Argentina were permeated by popular culture mostly in the form of tango music, as well as the idealization of the countryside and the pampas that had captured the imagination of the country with their wilderness and rough, gaucho culture.

The importance of tango is evident in the first films of the industry, particularly in those that produced one of the first movie stars recognized in most Latin American countries and Spain, Libertad Lamarque. Libertad Lamarque was a tango singer whose most famous films are *El Alma de Bandoneón* (*The Soul of the Accordion*, Mario Soffici, 1935), a melodrama about poor people, tangos, and criticism about a traditional middle-class moral that does not accept tangos as a decent profession for their children to aspire to; as well as *Adios Argentina* (*Goodbye Argentina*, Mario Parpagnoli, 1930); *El Cantar de Mi Ciudad* (*The Song of My City*, José A. Ferreyra, 1930); *Dios y la Patria* (*God and Country*, Nelo Cosimi, 1931); and *Muñequitas Porteñas* (*Dolls from Buenos Aires*, José A. Ferreyra, 1931). Specially popular were the melodramas directed by José A. Ferreyra such as *Ayúdame a Vivir*

(*Help Me to Live*, 1936), a tearjerker in which Lamarque plays a woman who finds her husband in bed with his lover and is wrongly accused of killing her when the woman tries to flee and falls down the stairs; *La Ley que Olvidaron* (*The Law They Forgot*, 1938); and the popular *Besos Brujos* (*Bewitching Kisses*, 1937). Lamarque was perhaps the most famous actress from the classic era of Argentine cinema, although she remains less known than Mexican or Brazilian stars despite the fact that she moved to Mexico and worked there for several years during the Perón administration due to rivalries with Eva Perón, which made it practically impossible for her to work in Argentina.

Little by little movies became the favorite pastime of the urban middle classes during the first decades of the twentieth century, and more and more they tried to mimic, incorporate, and reflect their problems and lives. Buenos Aires became, then, the "almost exclusive center from which cinema radiated"[13] in two very specific ways: as a center of film production and as the idealized place where most of the action took place. An example of that is the work of Manuel Romero with *Noches de Buenos Aires* (*Buenos Aires Nights*, 1935), *La Vida Es un Tango* (*Life Is a Tango*, 1939), and *Casamiento en Buenos Aires* (*Marriage in Buenos Aires*, 1940). Other melodramas focusing on middle-class issues are *Con las Alas Rotas* (*With Broken Wings*, Orestes Caviglia, 1938), and *La Que no Perdonó* (*The Woman Who Did Not Lose*, José A. Ferreyra, 1939). But melodrama and tango pictures were not the only style. Other genres that were favored during those decades were the thriller, for example, *Fuera de la Ley* (*Outside of the Law*, Manuel Romero, 1937) and *Con el Dedo en el Gatillo* (*With the Finger on the Trigger*, Luis Moglia Barth, 1940); historic dramas such as *Fortín Alto* (*High Fort*, Luis Moglia Barth, 1941) and *El Cabo Rivero* (*Private Rivero*, Miguel Coronatto Paz, 1938); and comedies, a genre practiced particularly by Luis César Amadori with *Palabra de Honor* (*Given Word*, 1938) and *Hay que Educar a Niní* (*We Must Educate Niní*, 1940), as well as *Mujeres que Trabajan* (*Working Women*, Manuel Romero, 1938).

Among these directors we must underline the presence of Leopoldo Torres Ríos whose *La Vuelta al Nido* (*Return to the Nest*, 1938) is a very personal and understated look into the lives of the middle class that stands miles apart from the more conventional comedies and melodramas of the time. The plot is a very simple trick to set the film in motion, a film that was "a startling departure from the style of the melodramas, musicals, and comedies that dominated the period.

Described by a critic of the day as bearing a 'whiff of poetry,' it featured a lingering camera and remarkable attention to composition and detail."[14] Torres Ríos kept active until the 1950s and even codirected a couple of films with his son Leopoldo Torre Nilsson, who would become an important figure on his own account. Another exception to the more commercial films of the decade is the epic *La Guerra Gaucha* (*The Gaucho War*, Lucas Demare, 1942), a film about the war of independence from Spain. It is based on short stories written by Leopoldo Lugones, one of the most important Argentine writers, who at the end of his life confessed some fascist sympathies.

The film is faithful to the spirit of the original materials, even in the slightly reactionary views of Lugones. Although unconnected, the stories were woven into the coherent and fluid narrative of the battle between the gauchos led by a virile hero (Francisco Petrone) and the Spaniards commanded by a young lieutenant (Ángel Magaña). The lieutenant, injured in a duel, is nursed back to health by a loyal separatist (Amelia Bence) who converts him to the cause of independence. The film ends with the two men leading their troops to a final and triumphal, we imagine, battle against the Spanish forces. While *La Guerra Gaucha* is often considered one of the best films of the classic period of Argentine cinema, it has also been criticized for its extreme patriotic feeling that resulted in a less critical interpretation of the historical event it portrays. Independent of the ideological flaws, the film is an excellent epic that turns out to be very effective in its depictions of the Argentine landscape and the brutality of the war of independence, as well as of the heroism of the gauchos. However, toward the end of the 1940s there was an abundance of light comedies and heavy melodramas that can be seen as a decline in the diversity of this cinema. Claudio España has written that the themes treated in these films "were not liked that much"[15] by Argentine audiences.

César Maranghello considers this public disinterest in national films to be the result of the industry's desire to become more "international" by abandoning local and even folkloric themes in order to compete with Mexico, a country that had already established its primacy in the Hispanic market as the strongest industry.[16] Many critics agree that there was a decline of the cinema in the 1940s, but some excellent films and talented directors either emerged or kept working in less than favorable conditions. Worth mentioning are Hugo del Carril's *Historia del 900* (*Stories of the 1900s*, 1949); *Las Aguas Bajan Turbias* (*Muddy Waters*, 1952), perhaps his best film, and one of the best Argentine films of all time; and *Más Allá del Olvido*

(*Beyond Forgetting*, 1956). Also important are Fernando Ayala's *Ayer Fue Primavera* (*Yesterday Was Spring*, 1955) and *Los Tallos Amargos* (*Bitter Plants*, 1956), a film with an excellent track by musician Ástor Piazzolla; and the works of some veterans, such as Luis Saslavsky's *Historia de una Mala Mujer* (*Story of a Bad Woman*, 1948), Daniel Tinayre's *La Vendedora de Fantasías* (*The Fantasies Seller*, 1950), Lucas Demare's *Los Isleros* (*The Islanders*, 1950) and *El Último Perro* (*The Last Dog*, 1956), and Leopoldo Torres Rios's *Pelota de Trapo* (1948) and *Edad Difícil* (*Difficult Age*, 1956).

In 1957 there was a new law that was expected to promote the national film industry because it also promoted free speech, eliminated censorship, and established the Instituo Nacional de Cinematografía (National Institute of Cinema). However, the vacuum resulting from the nullification of the previous legislation and the slow pace with which the new law was being implemented dissolved the initial optimism of the resurgence of the industry and actually "crippled the industry." There was only one active studio producing a limited number of films. The following two decades were the difficult years, but it is worth mentioning some films, particularly those of Fernando Ayala, such as *El Jefe* (*The Boss*, 1958), *El Candidato* (*The Candidate*, 1959), *Sábado a la Noche, Cine* (*Movies on Saturday Night*, 1960), *Paula Cautiva* (*Captive Paula*, 1963), *Primero Yo* (*First Me*, 1963), *Con Gusto a Rabia* (*Tastes Like Rage*, 1964), and those of Leopoldo Torre Nilsson, such as *La Casa del Ángel* (*The House of the Angel*, 1957), *El Secuestrador* (*The Kidnapper*, 1958), *La Caída* (*The Fall*, 1959), *Fin de Fiesta* (*The End of the Party*, 1960), *Un Guapo del 900* (*A Handsome Man of 1900*, 1960), *La Piel del Verano* (*Summer Skin*, 1960), and particularly *La Mano en la Trampa* (*The Hand in the Tramp*, 1961).

Filmmaking did not stop in Argentina, of course. Decades later it would reemerge as an important cinema, but for those years it had to survive under less than ideal conditions. Nonetheless, it produced some of its best films, such as *Tiré Dié* (*Throw Me A Dime*, Fernando Birri, 1958), a short documentary about the children of the region of Santa Fe who would follow the train screaming *tire dié!* (throw me a dime!), asking for money—therefore the title; and particularly the excellent *Los Inundados* (*The Flooded Ones*, 1962). The film is the story of several families coping with life after their houses were flooded and the useless government and opportunistic opposition politicians who see an opportunity to gain the ignored people's favor and use the situation for their own purposes. Because of the possibly of being evicted from its temporary shelter, one family gets on a boxcar and is taken, literally, for a train ride that will not end until the bureaucracy works and does it justice.

NOTES

1. "Argentina Leva Nove Filmes a Cannes," *Folha de São Paulo*, May 15, 2008, http://www1.folha.uol.com.br/folha/ilustrada/ult90u402131.shtml.

2. Rodrigo Fonseca, " 'Leonera' Mostra Amadurecimento Artístico de Santoro," *O Globo*, May 15, 2008, http://oglobo.globo.com/blogs/cinema/default.asp?a=18&cod_blog=20&ch=n&palavra=&pagAtual=2&periodo =200805.

3. Laura Sinagra, "Hearing Voices," *New York Village Voice*, February 22, 2005, http://www.villagevoice.com/2005-02-22/film/hearing-voices/.

4. Laura Gentile, "Cine: Festival Internacional de San Sebastián. Momento de Decision," *El Clarín*, September 27, 2008, http://www .clarin.com/diario/2008/09/27/espectaculos/c-01211.htm.

5. This award is the most prestigious in Argentina, and it is given by the Argentine press. *La Nación*, September 16, 2008, http://www.lanacion.com .ar/nota.asp?nota_id=1050411.

6. "Se Presentó en San Sebastián el Film Argentino *El Nido Vació*," *La Nación*, September 26, 2008, http://www.lanacion.com.ar/nota.asp? nota_id=1053800.

7. María Alejandra Gutiérrez, "Bountiful Rebound of Argentine Cinema," http://findarticles.com/p/articles/mi_go2043/is_3_56/ai_n6292723.

8. Miguel Jorge Couselo, "Los Años de la Democracia," *Historia del Cine Argentino*, ed. Jorge Miguel Couselo et al. (Buenos Aires: Instituto Nacional de Cinematografía/Centro Editor de América Latina, 1992), 168.

9. Ibid., 172.

10. Timothy Barnard and Peter Rist, *South American Cinema: A Critical Filmography, 1915–1994* (Austin: University of Texas Press, 1996), 74.

11. The film *K-Pax* was actually based on a novel of the same title by Gene Brewer published in 1992. Even though it seems obvious that either the novel or the film were based on Subiela's film, Brewer assured me in an e-mail that he did not know the film when he wrote the novel.

12. Barnard and Rist, *South American Cinema*, 10.

13. Claudio España, "El Cine Sonoro y su Expansion," in *Historia del Cine Argentino*, ed. Jorge Miguel Couselo et al. (Buenos Aires: Instituto Nacional de Cinematografía/Centro Editor de América Latina, 1992), 58.

14. Barnard and Rist, *South American Cinema*, 14.

15. España, "El Cine Sonor," 82.

16. César Maranghello, "La Pantalla y el Estado," in *Historia del Cine Argentino*, ed. Jorge Miguel Couselo et al. (Buenos Aires: Instituto Nacional de Cinematografía/Centro Editor de América Latina, 1992), 89–108.

CHAPTER 8

The Cinema of Cuba

THE LAST FEW DECADES

A naïve, idealistic young man who happens to believe fervently in the Revolution and in the system, living in the Havana of the 1970s, is suddenly accosted by a flamboyant, cynical, contradictory homosexual who, despite the danger of being persecuted and incarcerated—if not sent to a concentration camp for sexual deviants—dares to live his life openly and indulges himself in some transgressions that include Santería and Catholic iconography; a passion for Cuban culture, particularly the poetry of Lezama Lima; and a weakness for bourgeois, decadent things such as whiskey or foreign literature without which he could not have been able to tolerate life in Cuba after the Revolution. This is the main premise of the Cuban film *Fresa y Chocolate* (*Strawberry and Chocolate*, Tomás Gutiérrez Alea and Juan Carlos Tabío, 1993) that in the 1990s brought the cinema of this Caribbean island back to the international screens. As the narrative takes off, the idealist man, David (Vladimir Cruz), is tricked into visiting Diego (Jorge Perugorría), the homosexual, in his little apartment, a sanctuary with the petite bourgeois idiosyncrasies most Westerners take for granted. Once in Diego's place, although he remains reluctant, David is obviously curious and fascinated with Diego's life and alternative sexuality, not so much because of it, but because of the freedoms he seems to encounter in it.

After that first visit, and the ineffectiveness of Diego's advances, the two men start to develop a friendship in which Diego becomes a mentor and a sort of a role model to David, as well as a means for him to find passion and perhaps love with Nancy, Diego's unstable neighbor and friend. At the same time, Diego is also instrumental in David's confirmation of his love for Cuba and his trust in a maybe imperfect, but still functioning, system despite its problems. Controversial for its subject, but also for its critical view of Cuba in the figure of the ambivalent outsider Diego, *Fresa y Chocolate* represents a new trend in Cuban cinema of the late twentieth century in which a significant number of films were produced and, most importantly, shown in and outside of Cuba to mostly positive reviews and great public interest. *Fresa y Chocolate* is also the first Cuban production to be nominated for an Oscar. Similarly, the last film made by Gutiérrez Alea, also in collaboration with Juan Carlos Tabío, *Guantanamera* (1996), was received with great reviews outside of Cuba. The film is a delicious comedy, a road movie about the absurd and stubborn bureaucracy in socialist Cuba, but also about the warmth and color of the island and its people.

While visiting her hometown, Gantánamo, an old, famous singer, Yoyita (Conchita Brando), dies; her niece Gina (Mirta Ibarra) and an old flame from Yoyita's youth, Candido (Raúl Eguren), decide to take her back to Havana. Along comes Adolfo (Carlos Cruz), Gina's husband, a bureaucrat with aspirations to move up in the system, who then takes control of the trip. Once on the road, they meet some truck drivers and engage in conversations with them about everyday life as well as philosophical discussions about God. One of them, the womanizer Mariano (Jorge Perugorría), it turns out had been Gina's student in college and has been in love with her since then. Before they reach their destination, Gina will have to make a decision between her husband and Mariano. This formula is, of course, the perfect excuse for a trip through the island and allows us to see the "real" Cuba with a mix of reality and fiction. Also typical of the director is a critical view of the system, contrasted with the vitality of the people and the determination of the individual, offered through a character that connects with the audience in the situation.

In this case Gina, for example, is a character that does not entirely belong to her environment, just like Diego in *Fresa y Chocolate*, and that helps us identify with her. She also presents some views and opinions that may be shared by the audience, providing some objectivity or a point of view that is different from the official one presented by other characters. Famous for his ambivalent position (he always declared his adherence to the system, but made films that criticized the government), Guitérrez Alea is perhaps the greatest Cuban film director so far; but most impressively, he is also one of the very few public figures that has been able to get away with open and well-intended criticism of the system. Allegedly, when Fidel Castro found out about *Guantanamera* he declared that the director was playing with fire, without knowing that the film had actually been made by Gutiérrez Alea.[1] But the movie is subversive only in that it makes fun of bureaucracy and extinguished idealism, as Roger Ebert interprets, in a very allegorical way. According to him, "Adolfo represents, perhaps, the crushing weight of the socialist bureaucracy. Mariano and Georgina, when they were younger, represented the hope of workers and intellectuals; now, in middle age, they wonder if they can recapture their exhausted idealism. On the road, they are surrounded by the vitality and humor of everyday Cuba."[2]

Another interesting film of the last decade is *Las Noches de Constantinopla* (*Nights of Constantinople*, Orlando Rojas, 2000), an allegorical comedy in which through humor and that very peculiar "Cuban way" (a mix of good humor, charm, and resilience), people manage to survive and to criticize the system. In this case, the film centers on the universal struggle of the new versus the old represented by a matriarch, Eugenia (Verónica Lynn). She is the force that holds together the most unusual and dysfunctional family, which includes her granddaughter Cristina (María Isabel Díaz), an aspiring singer; her eccentric uncle Jorge (Francisco Rabal) and Jorge's illegitimate son (Vladimir Villar); and, most importantly, Cristina's brother Hernán (Liberto Rabal), who is a writer of erotic fiction. When an opportunity arises for Cristina to sing in the city, Hernán fears that the excitement that comes with that kind of life may affect his grandmother's health. And, in fact, the old lady ends up in the hospital in a coma when she learns of the kind of writing her grandson does. The film is a very interesting look into a traditional family and the hypocrisy of the old ways; the fact that an aristocratic lady represents the traditional way of life suggests a time before the socialist revolution, although the contemporary setting and situations contradict this interpretation.

Similarly contemporary, at least in its proclamation that the dysfunctional family is not exclusive to the United States or the West, *Video de Familia* (*Family Video*, Humberto Padrón, 2001) is cleverly weaved around a family occasion, Raulito's birthday, and the videos the family has gathered to record with the intention of sending them to him to congratulate him and wish him happiness. Raulito (he never appears on camera) is one of the many Cubans who has left the island and found refuge in the United States, in his particular case motivated by his homosexuality. When Raulito's sister outs him accidentally while recording a video, the recording session turns into a series of reproaches, pleas, demand of explanations, and guilty mea culpas, only to end with the universal family snapshot in which all the members of the family gather around and smile for the lens to preserve the moment. As in many other previous films, scarcity is used to the film's advantage: not only the amateurish quality of the film, evident in the acting, but also the handheld, shaky camera, for example, adds realism (it is, after all, a family video), as well as the "epistolary" structure of the film divided into several 10-minute "videos." The opposition between the old and the new generations is evident also in the film and is often presented in terms of the opposition between socialism and capitalism (e.g., the father's reproach for having left Cuba, the assumption that Raulito's being gay is something "they" did to him in Miami, Raulito's sister's acceptance of his homosexuality, etc.). Sarcastically, the film is dedicated to Cuban families wherever they are.

Also of importance are the films of Juan Carlos Tabío. By the time Tabío started collaborating with Gutiérrez Alea, he already had a considerable career; after the death of Gutiérrez Alea, he continued making films alone, and his first film attempt after this collaboration with the master was *Lista de Espera* (*Waiting List*, 2000). It is a mildly entertaining comedy full of clichés (without the complexity and the subtle criticism to the system that we saw in Gutiérrez Alea's work) that revolves around a group of travelers stranded at a bus station unable to leave, a piece that brings to mind the theater of the absurd. Nonetheless, the film was successful and managed to be seen outside of Cuba and even to collect a couple of major nominations. In the end, the film's only intention seems to be to entertain; in that respect it does a decent job. The same is true of *Aunque Estés Lejos* (*So Far Away*, 2003) and particularly of *El Cuerno de la Abundancia* (*Horn of Plenty*, 2008), a similarly pseudocritical comedy with an even more absurd plot (and therefore more allegorical possibilities): in the eighteenth century a group of nuns deposited some money in a British bank and now, two centuries later, all of the descendants of the Castiñeiras family are entitled to a share of the money—now a fortune due to two centuries' worth of interest. The predictable unfolding of the story has to do with the failed attempts of a lot of people to get their hands on that money (in one scene, a man is told that although his last name is Castiñeiras, he spells it with a "y" and unfortunately the money is only for those who spell the name with an "i").

Tabío, although better known outside of Cuba for his collaborations with Gutiérrez Alea, started his career in the 1970s with shorts and documentaries; later he made feature-length films. In fact, some of the most interesting movies of the 1980s are two of his better known films, *Plaf* (*Plaff!*, 1988) and *Se Permuta* (*House for Swap*, 1984). *Plaf* is a funny and absurd comedy about a superstitious woman, Concha (Daisy Granados), who is trying to figure out who is throwing eggs at her (hence the title that is the onomatopoeic sound of the smashing eggs). As far as she is concerned, everybody is a suspect, including Tomás (Raúl Pomares), a taxi driver with whom she falls in love. The absurdity of this situation really allows Tabío to play more freely with the types (sometimes really stereotypes) and to direct more criticism on Cuban society. Concha dies in the end of a heart attack, somehow related to her obsession with the eggs thrown at her. This film is, in the words of Catherine Davis, both an homage and a parody of "imperfect cinema," a manifesto championed by Julio García Espinosa that, together with an aesthetic of hunger and cinema of garbage or *cinema novo* in Brazil, as well as the social-oriented cinema of Bolivia and Argentina, constituted the core of the so-called New Latin American Cinema of the 1970s.

Tabío uses in *Plaf*, for example, a series of alienation techniques that "include up-side-down shots, film rewound on the screen, actors missing their cues, the film-title featuring at the end, lost props, and the camera crew appearing on screen,"[3] which can easily be taken for "mistakes" by a spectator that is not familiar with the trends and experimentations of Latin American cinema of the period. *Se Permuta* is less absurd in its premise, and less political in its intentions, but equally interesting. Gloria (Rosita Fornés) needs a place to stay and she is counting on her daughter's sensible choice of life partner for that. When Yolanda (Isabel Santos), her daughter, meets a promising prospect, everything seems perfect, and Gloria makes arrangements to live in a suitable place. But when Yolanda puts her wedding plans on hold because she meets another man, Gloria has to start all over again making new living arrangements and so forth and so on due to her daughter's indecision. This film is also so effective in its usage of the limitations of the Cuban industry and employs similar alienation techniques, turning poverty of means into richness of meaning and into a weapon of social criticism. The idea for the movie is a good one, but the plot is not fully developed; in this case, unlike what happened with the previous film, this is a problem that interferes with the movie. However, as was the case with Brazilian *cinema do lixo* (garbage cinema), the intention of the director is to reject the perfectionism associated with Hollywood productions as a sort of Brechtian attempt to distance the spectator from the action.

Juan Carlos Tabío also directed *El Elefante y la Bicicleta* (*The Elephant and the Bicycle*, 1994) in between *Fresa y Chocolate* and *Guantanamera*. This film is an interesting look at the literal meaning of power to the people and a testimony to the importance of myth. In the story, an ex-con (Luis Alberto García) returns to his country (an island called symbolically La Fe) after being in jail, and among other things he brings with him an old film projector and a copy of a silent version of *Robin Hood*. After the man shows the film to the people several times, their amusement turns into interest and eventually moves them to action. Seeing a clear political allegory in the story of the thief of Sherwood, they start to plan to overthrow the dictator of La Fe (Raúl Pomares), who has ruled them with an iron fist. On the one hand, the film is a testimony of the power of images—at the beginning of the film we see a group of children watching clouds in the sky and trying to see what they look like: some see an elephant; others see a bicycle—but on the other hand, it is a proof to the power of interpretation. For the people of La Fe, Robin Hood is seen, as in most Latin American countries, as an invitation to start a revolution.

But despite the limitations of the economy and the inevitable political conflicts brought about by the changing times, the cinema of Cuba has managed to continue producing films, if not in great quantity, at least with a very steady pace and with a good degree of quality. The late 1990s and the first years of the new millennium saw one of its best moments in part, no doubt, because the films produced then reflected a new Cuba, a Cuba that is, or wants to appear, more open to external influences and to international collaboration, while exporting an image of tolerance and democracy more in sync with the new global scenario. Other important and representative films of the last decades are the films of Daniel Díaz Torres, particularly *Quiéreme y Verás* (*Love Me and You Will See*, 1994), a comedy about three old people recalling a bank robbery committed years earlier, and *Kleines Tropikana—Tropicanita* (*Little Tropikana*, 1997), an interesting comedy about an investigation into the death of a German tourist whose body appears one morning wearing wings and with an empty bottle in his hands. While everybody assumes that the man was just partying too hard and died as the result of it, Lorenzo Columbié (Vladimir Cruz), a young, provincial police officer recently transferred to Havana, suspects that there is something more to the death of the German

man and decides to find out. In the process of his investigation, he meets all kinds of colorful characters, therefore offering opportunities for an audience to contrast the foreign and the national with a critical and humorous result.

After *Tropicanita*, Díaz Torres directed *Hacerse el Sueco* (*Playing Swede*, 2001), another interesting crime comedy about a man that, in order to commit a spectacular robbery, pretends to be a Swedish literature professor visiting Cuba; unfortunately, he falls in love with the daughter of the man, an ex-police officer, nonetheless, who takes him into his house. Once he has accomplished his mission and is on his way to the airport with the police after him, he has to decide between the girl he loves and the jewels he has just stolen. But the movie that really secured Díaz Torres's reputation as an important filmmaker was *Alicia en el Pueblo de las Maravillas* (*Alice in Wondertown*, 1991). This movie is a satire about a cultural teacher who is sent to a town called Maravillas (Wonders) on a cultural mission only to encounter the most absurd situations and people who constantly interfere with her doing her job properly. Like Lewis Carroll's character, this Alicia confronts absurdity and is scorned for daring to point out the irrationality of the town's conduct. In the end, she realizes that most of the population of the town are fired bureaucrats that have been unable to find their way out of this bizarre town. The film also seems to be a metaphor for the "concentration" camps for undesirables—homosexuals, prostitutes, antisocial, etc.—that Castro's government allegedly promoted.

In the end, the allegorical nature of the film did not mask enough the fact that it was a very poignant criticism of Cuban government and society in the last decade of the twentieth century. This is also true of the films of another important figure, Gerardo Chijona, who has produced recently some very interesting films, such as *Adorables Mentiras* (*Lovely Lies*, 1991), a film about an aspiring screenwriter and an aspiring actress who, when they meet, pretend to be an established director and a famous actress; they start a relationship and never tell each other that they are married and have children and the real state of their careers, at least not until their lies are discovered. The film depends on the old Spanish formula of the *comedia de enredos* or comedy of misunderstandings as well as on never telling the truth, in this case to advance the plot. In this case the plot was inspired by an actual conversation Chijona heard when an extra tried to pick up a girl by telling her he was a member of the Instituto Cubano de Arte e Industria Cinematográficos (ICAIC), the most important film office in

Cuba.[4] The film is universal in its theme of frustrated ambitions and double lives; it is also, according to some, about Cuba and the lies people have to depend on to survive in that society. As Catherine Davis writes, it "is about broken dreams and lost illusions [therefore] it would cut deep with Cuban spectators who would recognize in these characters their own unfulfilled aspirations."[5] And although this is true, it applies to the human condition in general, not only to Cuban or socialist society exclusively.

The next film by Chijona, *Un Paraíso bajo las Estrellas* (*Paradise under the Stars*, 2000), is also a screwball comedy about an aspiring showgirl. Sissy (Thais Valdés) wants nothing more than to become a dancer at the famous Tropicana nightclub, Havana's hottest spot for the rich and famous visiting the island. Against her father's wishes, she gets a job working there under the supervision of her father's old rival Armando (Santiago Alfonso), who also courted Sissy's mother, an ex-dancer at the Tropicana. Things get even more complicated when Candido (Enrique Molina), Sissy's father, brings home a young biker he accidentally hit on the road. This man, Sergio (Vladimir Cruz), could actually be Candido's son, and therefore Sissy's brother, although this is not clear because the only proof of his identity is a mole the young man has on his buttocks, identical to the one Candido has on his. Unaware of their possible relationship, Sissy and Sergio fall, inevitably, in love, bringing to the plot not only social issues but also possible incest. This plot could also have been described by the title of Chijona's last film *Perfecto Amor Equivocado* (*Love by Mistake*, 2004), a title better translated as "Perfect, Mistaken Love." In this film, a man, also an aspiring writer, is conflicted among the love he feels for his wife, his mistress, and another woman; all this while his daughter's love for an older man mirrors that confusion.

Other films produced during the 1980s are—besides the already mentioned *Se Permuta* and *Plaf*—Gutiérrez Alea's *Hasta Cierto Punto* (*Up to a Point*, 1983) and Orlando Rojas *Papeles Secundarios* (*Secondary Roles*, 1989). *Hasta Cierto Punto* is a key film in the development of Cuban cinema and society because it tackles a very important issue, machismo, which was already at the core of the changing society after the Revolution, particularly with such films as *De Cierta Manera* (*One Way or Another*, Sara Gómez, 1977). *Hasta Cierto Punto* examines not so much machismo, but the possibility of a woman being truly independent even in a socialist culture. Lina (Mirta Ibarra) is a liberated single mother in a relationship with Óscar (Óscar Álvarez), a married film director. While he is doing nothing to change his situation, she is independent and determined enough to leave him and to live her life by herself. What is ironic, and therefore critical, is the fact that Óscar is not only educated and liberal, but is an intellectual working on a documentary about machismo in Cuba. The mirroring effect of the "true" life of the director and his film is a very clever way of commenting on the issue without having to sound preachy.

The fact that the film mixes fiction and documentaries with real footage Gutiérrez Alea actually shot years earlier for a documentary on the subject only adds to the blurring of genres. Even the title derives from this footage, from an interview he was conducting with an anonymous man for the documentary. Asked if he thought most Cuban men were okay with women's equality, the man answered, "sure, of course, well up to [a] point," turning what was supposed to be a joke into very poignant social commentary—all within the margin of a classic structure of a film within a film. *Papeles Secundarios* is considered one of the most important films of the 1980s and, as its title suggests, it is about a group of actors with secondary or supporting roles; the troupe is rehearsing a play, and the plot follows their lives on and off stage. The film is also important for focusing on the struggles of the individual rather than the collective, as one would expect from a dogmatic socialist system, in the dilemma of an older actress who has to come to terms with her decline, due to her age, and the pressure to clear the path for the younger generations. She, however, finds her salvation in the love of a younger, handsome actor.

Creative and curious, often working against less than ideal conditions, Cuba cinema turned out some delightful surprises from time to time. One of them is an interesting curiosity from the 1980s, Juan Padrón's animated film *Vampiros en la Habana* (*Vampires in Havana*, 1983). The film is charming, ingenious, and joyful, and it keeps enough allegorical elements in it to be read as criticism to war and international intolerance. The plot is simple and the animations are just perfect without looking too polished or too sloppy, while keeping some of the old charm of cartoons from the past. When the word gets out that a scientist has invented a formula that allows vampires to resist the sunlight and therefore to live a normal life during the day, a battle breaks out between the American (a mafia of vampires who want to destroy the formula so they can keep the monopoly of the artificial beaches) and the Eastern European vampires who want to make it into a commercial medication for all. What both groups really want is to seize control of the formula and therefore the power attached to it. In the end, Joseph Amadeus Drácula, the nephew of the inventor of the formula, who is a vampire without knowing it, decides to do the right thing and gives the formula free of charge to everybody who needs it.

AFTER THE REVOLUTION

Cuban cinema in the second half of the twentieth century has been one of the most interesting cinemas of Latin America, particularly after the Revolution that brought Fidel Castro to power. Practically nonexistent before it, a film industry developed rapidly after the rebel army took power. Cinema, and mass media in general, became, very early on, a priority for this government that saw in the medium an opportunity to reach the masses and to disseminate its message of social justice and socialism to an illiterate population; in fact, cinema was the second priority of the socialist government, just behind literacy. Many changes happened in Cuba during the years that followed the triumph of the Revolution in 1959, but because of the American embargo and the increasingly hostile policies that Washington directed toward the government that was seen as a threat and as a challenge to the U.S. monopoly in the country, most people were not aware of what went on in that Caribbean nation. This ignorance of the progress of socialist Cuba continued even when many well-to-do Cubans were exiled in the United States; many of them decided to abandon their country rather than remain in a nation ruled by a government that no longer represented their interests or respected and fought for their privileges.

In fact, many of these elite Cubans had an invested interest in demonstrating the failures of the new socialist administration in hopes that it would help them convince the international community to join the United States in condemning and punishing the new government. So when in 1973 Americans had a chance to see Cuban cinema of the 1960s and 1970s, it literally blew their minds away. One film, in particular, was received by the public and critics alike with the same enthusiasm it had already encountered in other countries of Europe and Latin America. This film, *Memorias del Subdesarrollo* (*Memories of the Underdevelopment*, Tomás Gutiérrez Alea, 1968), was called "a fascinating achievement [. . .] a film about alienation that is wise, sad and often funny,"[6] one of the best films of the year by the *New York Times*, "and [an] absolutely tremendous film" by the *Guardian* (Manchester).[7] The film was praised for its lucid, ironic, yet free tone; as a result, the

National Society of Film Critics gave an award to Gutiérrez Alea for his achievements. Unfortunately, the U.S. Department of State did not grant a visa to the director and threatened to prosecute anybody who would accept the award in his name, so Gutiérrrez Alea was not able to receive his prize.

This unfortunate event regrettably was not isolated, but it should not have surprised anybody, considering that a year earlier the U.S. Department of Treasury had canceled the First Festival of Cuban Cinema to be held in New York City. It is particularly hard for Cuban cinema to be appreciated in this country because, added to the economic pressures of the American government, there was a very hostile attitude toward Cuba in the general population fed by ignorance and fueled by the activism of right-wing Cuban Americans who remained very active in high circles of power with the clear objective of damaging the Castro administration. Determined to criticize anything that comes from the island, they have accused Gutiérrez Alea's films of being propaganda because they give the false impression that the Cuban government tolerates the freedom of constructive criticism. It is ironic in this context that more than 20 years after *Memorias del Subdesarrollo*, Gutiérrez Alea's *Fresa y Chocolate* was nominated for an Oscar.

This could be interpreted as the resilience of the Cuban people and Cuban artists who, against all odds, continue to produce a rich culture sometimes working in the most precarious conditions. *Memorias del Subdesarrollo* is a very interesting film in part because it summarizes these problems, attitudes, and contradictions. Unlike what most people expect from a socialist country, the film is neither propaganda nor a false praise of the system; it does not preach the aesthetic doctrine of socialist realism either. In fact, one of the things that surprises the most about the film is the freedom the main character enjoys. Sergio (Sergio Carmona Mendoyo), a bourgeois intellectual who at the beginning of the film goes to the airport to say goodbye to his parents and ex-wife, all of whom are departing for a life of exile in Miami, is so ambivalent about the revolution and his own role in the new order that it is not clear why he is not leaving the country with them. There is the possibility, of course, that he is more fascinated with the new society being built in front of his eyes than he admits, but also there is the possibility that he is just too lazy to move to a new country and start a new life in another language, with other people, at a distant place. This possibility is the one that seems more consistent with his "bourgeoisie," intellectual aspirations and the one that would immediately disqualify him for suitability in the new socialist order; Gutiérres Alea, however, is smart enough never to endorse or reject either point of view.

There is no condemnation of Sergio or his "antisocial" activities as intellectual, even though the film clearly makes a distinction between the negative recent past and the "now," or the era after the Revolution. If the past was unjust and easily manipulable by power, money, and class interests, the present wants to appear as clear and equal for all as possible, but it is not necessarily seen as more egalitarian or completely free of class bias, something particularly evident in the scene of Sergio's trial for seducing an underage, peasant girl and the reasons her parents want reparations and justice from the court. Sergio, as an intellectual who registers his impressions of the new system and his own personal conflicts in a diary, seems to be in direct contradiction with the supposedly collective aspirations of art and all human activities in a socialist country. Writing and thinking is a private activity contrary to the ideal of social betterment, but the movie seems to suggest that there is no way of controlling it, although there is always the possibility of trying to convince the masses of the futility of such a solitary, bourgeois activity opposed to the best interests of the collectivity.

The influence of Italian neorealism is evident in the film, but the director complements it with a dialectical opposition of fictional narration and real or documentary-like footage to contrast the point of view of Serigio and that of the camera—both of which do not always represent the point of view of the director. This mixing of fiction and real footages is a trick that Gutiérrez Alea uses to its maximum potential to make evident that he is not reproducing reality, but interacting with it, and therefore affecting it. Like Sergio, the film is very ambivalent, never being entirely a fictional narration or a documentary, and as Nancy Berthier has written, this "flirtation between reality and fiction produced breathtaking effects which refer the spectator[s] to themselves."[8] In the end, the film is not about Cuba or the Revolution, but about the role of the intellectual (and the individual) in history. The questions Sergio poses to himself are the questions we all confront at a time of crisis in which we have to oppose the personal to the collective. Those are also very specific questions raised during the Cuban Revolution by Cuban and other Western intellectuals, such as Jean-Paul Sartre and Simone de Beauvoir.

Memorias del Subdesarrollo represents one of the highest points in Cuban cinema, but it is only one of many interesting films worth mentioning. In fact, the decade of the 1960s, that is, the first years after the Revolution, is considered by many the golden decade of Cuban cinema because of the number of quality pictures produced during that time, but mostly because of the naïveté, ingenuity, and idealism of the directors committed to creating an industry out of nothing. Along with *Memorias del Subdesarrollo*, the other great film of the period is *Lucía* (Humberto Solás, 1968). *Lucía* is, after Gutiérrez Alea's film, the most commented on and respected movie of the young industry. But unlike *Memorias*, *Lucía* aspires to a greatness that can only be called epic. It is by all means a monumental film, including its length and its episodic structure that traces some 60 years of national history. The episodes tell the story of three different women named Lucía in three specific periods of the history of Cuba. Each episode follows the life of the protagonist and her relationship with the man she loves as well as her country. The first episode is set during the war of independence against Spain in the late nineteenth century; the second follows a Lucía who engages in a fight against dictator Gerardo Machado in the 1930s; the third one centers on a more ambiguous present that is at once the now and symbolically the future of the socialist country.

The first Lucía is an aristocratic lady (Raquel Revuelta) who has little interest in politics, although out of respect and love for her brother she relates to the clandestine separatist movement to which he belongs. Unfortunately, she is still a vulnerable woman who falls in love with the enemy and unwillingly reveals the plans of her brother's group, causing them to be massacred. The second Lucía (Eslinda Núñez) is a committed revolutionary involved in politics and actively working toward the overthrow of a dictator, even though she belongs to the bourgeoisie. While she and her lover Aldo (Ramón Brito) fight to liberate their country of oppression, their efforts do not necessarily succeed and in the end they seem frustrated when they realize that their attempt may not be that successful in changing the country, a realization that in turn prompts Aldo to participate in a suicide mission out of desperation. The third Lucía (Adela Legrá), logically, is an active supporter of the socialist revolution who manages to emancipate herself from her macho husband thanks to the Revolution and the efforts of the new government to educate the masses. This Lucía is less a fighter (there is no need to fight now that the Revolution has triumphed) and more a social restructurer and an organizer. The emancipation that the last Lucía obtains is the real freedom from exploitation and alienation.

More than a triumphal culmination of the historical process, the film suggests the Revolution as a work in progress—that of a society freeing itself from ancient prejudices, in which all ignorant, exploitative, and unjust practices will be eradicated. This is cleverly symbolized by the emancipation of women (which stands for all kinds of oppressed peoples, up to a point); particularly when we realize at the end of the film that the historical evolution we have witnessed is not necessarily toward a socialist society per se, but toward a society in which all, male and female (and by extension black and white, rich and poor, peasant and worker, intellectual and artisan), are equal. The only thing is that this, of course, can be attained only in a socialist society. Lucía symbolizes the struggle of all women in their transition from a patriarchal society to a free one, but also—because without it, it would not be possible—from a capitalist to a socialist system. "Lucía offers a specific image of Cuban social reality in a historical perspective. Making a woman the center figure allows Solás to illustrate the evolution of an oppressive system through its most oppressed elements,"[9] according to Julie Amiot.

INSTITUTO CUBANO DE ARTES E INDUSTRIAS CINEMATOGRÁFICAS

In 1962 Elizabeth Sutherland wrote about the situation of Cuban cinema only a few years after the Revolution had established the first socialist state in the Americas in a long reportage published in *Film Quarterly*. The first thing she noticed was the fact that in such a short period of time, "Cuba has built—almost from scratch—a film industry which is turning out work of striking quality."[10] This almost unprecedented phenomenon was, in her opinion, the result of a group of young, idealistic filmmakers and intellectuals, among whom she mentions Gutiérrez Alea, who had brought to the newborn film industry the same qualities of the Revolution, "youth, excitement, and self-confidence."[11] Also instrumental to the establishment of an industry where there had been none was the ICAIC. This institute would become fundamental in the development of the new Latin American cinema and in its support to revolutionary cinema everywhere. Founded in 1959, by the time Sutherland visited Cuba, "A huge new 'film city' was completed, worthy of Cecil B. DeMille: 600,000 square meters in size, with three shooting studios, sound studios, two lab buildings (one for color, one for black-and-white), office buildings for ICAIC personnel, employee housing, cafeteria, guest cottage for visiting foreign artists, library, artificial lakes, and so forth."[12]

This mega project was supposed to be the largest in Latin America and, more importantly, was supposed to turn out 10 feature films and 50 documentaries a year. Unfortunately, such an ambitious project was never quite as successful as originally planned, but still it is amazing to see that in only three years the ICAIC had established a serious film industry and produced some quality films. The importance of mass media was something the leaders of the new government, and Castro himself, always proclaimed. As a matter of fact, the decree that founded the ICAIC on March 24, 1959, is considered the first cultural act of the revolutionary government. "Alfredo Guevara, founding director of ICAIC insisted that film was in fact the second priority of the new government, preceding but subordinated in importance and in impact to the national literacy campaign of 1960–61."[13] Congress went even further and proclaimed cinema as the "art per excellence in our century."[14] This proclamation was very similar to the position taken by the governments of the Russian and the Mexican revolutions at the beginning of the twentieth century, confirming the prominence of film as the art of the people and of the century. Surely the popular and massive impact of film is something that has always been important for governments in general, including fascist and totalitarian governments, from Hitler, Franco and Mussolini, to Stalin to Pancho Villa, and Fidel Castro; they all saw film as an ideal way to get their messages to the people.

The ICAIC was always emphatic on its interests in film as a communication tool; the institute valued film for its power of communication and actually favored only the communicability of the medium, ignoring or disdaining such aspects as avant-garde experimentation or extremely allegorical works. It is not surprising then that many of the best films produced during the highest point of the ICAIC's existence were documentaries, such as *La Primera Carga al Machete* (*The First Charge of the Machete*, Manuel Octavio Gómez, 1969), *Girón* (*Bay of Pigs*, Manuel Herrera, 1974), or *¡Viva la República!* (*Long Live the Republic*, Pastor Vega, 1972), as well as movies that ingeniously mixed the techniques of both documentaries and fiction, such as *Memorias del Subdesarrollo*, *Lucía*, and *Hasta Cierto Punto*. Curiously enough this trend can still be seen in such contemporary films as *Los Dioses Rotos* (*Broken Gods*, Ernesto Daranas, 2008), an interesting picture that the ICAIC describes as a "thin line between reality and fiction,"[15] which tells the story of a Cuban Casanova assassinated by his French enemies who run a prostitution ring in Havana at the beginning of the twentieth century, and in *Kangamba* (Rogelio París, 2008), a film about the involvements of the Cuban Army in the Angola War of the 1970s that has already captivated audiences in other countries because of its realism, but also because of its quality and production.

This interest in communication is the result of the mission the ICAIC has set for itself—to educate the people. In few other Latin America countries has cinema been taken more seriously than by officials in Cuba. In fact, early on the ICAIC had groups of itinerant volunteers that would bring cinema to the farthest corners of the island called "mobile cinema." The ICAIC also sponsored television channels dedicated to educate people on the history of cinema as well as on its techniques and language, something no other government has done, as far as I know. Another important aspect of this mission of the ICAIC is its commitment to promote third-world cinemas, particularly the cinemas of other Latin American countries, which is the purpose of its International Festival of New Latin American Cinema, a festival held annually and that includes such personalities as Nobel laureate Gabriel García Márquez among its judges and supporters. This interest in education also explains the interest in historical films, particularly in dialectic history as a process toward socialism. Especially noticeable is the lack of allegory in Cuban historical films, all of which try to explain particular current problems as clearly as possible.

Perhaps it is not that surprising if we consider that this tactic was particularly important for Brazilian *cinema novo* when directors were trying to elude censorship and to practice a sort of "cinema of liberation" against the establishment, while in Cuba it is the establishment, that is, the revolutionary government, that controls the film industry. History, or the past, therefore, was subordinated to the present, although as Timothy Bernard says, the present is "submerged in the historical narrative."[16] Understandably, the present is always presented as positive or in progress, contrasting with the past, particularly the recent past when the system was not always trying to improve the lives of Cubans of all classes, races, or genders. Examples of films focusing on the recent past are *Ustedes Tienen la Palabra* (*It's Your Turn Now*, Manuel Octavio Gómez, 1974) and of course *Memorias del Subdesarrollo* and *Lucía*. But also there were some more difficult attempts to engage the colonial past in movies such as *Una Pelea Cubana contra los Demonios* (*A Cuban Fight against Demons*, Tomás Gutiérrez Alea, 1972) and *La Última Cena* (*The Last Supper*, 1976), also by Gutiérrez

Alea. Although apparently allegorical, the film is really a denunciation of the alliance of slavery and religion.

Interestingly enough, the only films openly presented as allegorical are a series of films that center on a feminine ethos, which represents both the Revolution and the nation through the struggles and triumphs of the female heroines. These movies include *La Bella de la Alhambra* (*The Beauty of the Alhambra*, Enrique Pineda Barnet, 1989), a film about Cuba in the 1920s and 1930s as seen through the eyes of a cabaret singer; *Cecilia* (Humberto Solás, 1982), a film about a woman who wants to climb the social ladder in colonial Cuba and who is willing to use unconventional methods, like Santeria, to make the son of a rich landowner fall in love with her at a time when Cuba is about to gain its independence; and even *Retrato de Teresa* (*Portrait of Teresa*, Pastor Vega, 1979). Teresa (Idalia Anreus) not only has to take care of her children and her responsibilities as a factory leader, she also has to deal with her husband's increasing requests for attention. Divided between her own freedom and the possibility of a family life, she leaves her husband.

The accomplishments of the ICAIC were certainly impressive the first several years, but in the end the effort remained too conservative and skeptical of experimental films, particularly of purely fictional films. Most of the efforts of the institute were then centered on documentary films with a production of more than 40 in the period between 1976 and 1977 and again between 1980 and 1981; unfortunately, the number of fiction films remained lower than anticipated. And since, as we said before, communicability was the quality most appreciated by the ICAIC, technique and plot were somehow less important than the message and considered just pyrotechnics. "Perfect" cinema was often synonymous with Hollywood cinema—a series of movies with a perfect technique but empty or, even worse, reactionary and corruptive. Perfect technique was always seen as reactionary, according to García Espinosa who called for an "imperfect cinema." "Imperfect cinema is no longer interested in quality or technique. It can be created equally well with a Mitchell or with an 8mm camera, in a studio or in a guerrilla camp in the middle of the jungle. Imperfect cinema is no longer interested in predetermined taste, and much less in good taste."[17]

Nonetheless, Hollywood remained as a reluctant model that could be useful because of its transparency and simplicity (as opposed to avant-garde or experimental films). This resulted in some attempts to use mostly as parodies some of the most popular Hollywood genres, such as the musical that many considered natural to the idio-syncratic culture of the island, and the fact that although documentary films are the most favored, fiction films are still considered superior, and the ones to which everybody aspires. In fact, many of the most important directors started as documentary filmmakers and managed to cross over to fiction, after they earned the right to do so. In the end, all these contradictions made it impossible for the ICAIC to deliver all that it had promised when it was created. Some people feel it failed because of the bureaucracy of a socialist government or because of its loyalty to the system that did not allow for any deviation from the norm. Others, such as Timothy Bernard, think the ICAIC declined because of its dependency on almost exclusively one genre, the historical film—when it was exhausted, so was the film industry. It is important not to forget that despite all of the ICAIC's praises, it has also been criticized because of its disinterest in favoring or promoting more aggressively women and Cubans of African ancestry. No matter what, the importance of the ICAIC will always be linked to the success of Cuban cinema.

NOTES

1. Nancy Berthier, "Memorias del Subdesarrollo," in *The Cinema of Latin America*, ed. Alberto Elena and Marina Díaz López (London and New York: Wallflower Press, 2003), 106.

2. Roger Ebert, "Guantanamera," *Chicago Sun-Times*, November 28, 1997, http://rogerebert.suntimes.com/apps/pbcs.dll/article?AID=/19971128/REVIEWS/711280301/1023.

3. Catherine Davis, "Recent Cuban Fiction Films: Identification, Inter-pretation, Disorder," *Bulletin of Latin American Research* 15 (1996): 187.

4. Ibid., 190.

5. Ibid., 182.

6. Vincent Canby, " 'Memories,' Cuban Film, Draws a Bead on Alienation," *New York Times*, May 18, 1973, http://movies.nytimes.com/movie/review?_r=2&res=9801E4D61330E63ABC4052DFB3668388669EDE.

7. Peter Bradshaw, "Memories of Underdevelopment," *Guardian* (Manchester), July 11, 2008, http://www.guardian.co.uk/culture/2008/jul/11/filmandmusic1.filmandmusic21.

8. Berthier, "Memorias del Subdesarrollo," 105.

9. Ibid., p. 116.

10. Elizabeth Sutherland, "Cinema of Revolution—90 Miles from Home," *Film Quarterly* 15 (Winter 1961): 42.

11. Ibid.

12. Ibid., 46.

13. Julianne Burton, "Film and Revolution in Cuba," in *The New Latin American Cinema*, ed. Michael T. Martin (Detroit: Wayne State University Press, 1997), 124.

14. Ibid.

15. *CubaCine*, http://www.cubacine.cu/losdiosesrotos/sinopsis.htm.

16. Timothy Bernard, "Death Is Not True: Form and History in Cuban Film," in *The New Latin American Cinema*, ed. Michael T. Martin (Detroit: Wayne State University Press, 1997), 149.

17. Julio García Espinosa, "For an Imperfect Cinema," in *The New Latin American Cinema*, ed. Michael T. Martin (Detroit: Wayne State University Press, 1997), 82.

CHAPTER 9

The Other Latin Cinemas

Even though not all Latin American countries have had a long and solid film tradition like Brazil's, Mexico's, Cuba's, or Argentina's, some of them have produced powerful and influential films of great beauty and quality. Some have maintained a constant, albeit extremely limited production of films; while others have managed to create, against all odds, sporadic stories full of life and heart about their own cultures and societies in a way that speaks not only to their national audiences, but that transcends their borders to enrich the human experience of nations in the most remote parts of the world. As we mentioned earlier, cinema arrived early in the Americas. Unlike what happened in Mexico, Brazil, and Argentina, however, in the other Latin American countries the exposure to the new technology did not result in the locals recording their everyday life or inventing stories with moving pictures. It was instead foreigners who decided to film the local scenes, and the local aristocracy, in order to increase the numbers of the curious willing to pay the rather expensive admission prices to watch these first films.[1]

This chapter focuses on reviewing some of the most important films of other Latin traditions that have not developed a consistent industry so far. In Costa Rica, for example, even though movies arrived in 1897, it was not until 1913 that some Costa Ricans began filming local scenes. Among the most important were the transferring of power between presidents Ricardo Jiménez Oreamuno and Alfredo González Flores, the operations performed by surgeon Ricardo Moreno Cañas, as well as popular events such as bullfights, carnivals, religious festivals, and civic parades. But the first documentaries filmed in Costa Rica were the Second Eucharistic Congress in 1913 filmed separately by Armando Céspedes Marín and Manuel Gómez Millares.[2]

Something similar happened in Colombia, where the first images projected on a screen were presented on April 12, 1897, in Colón, a port city in today's Panama, then part of Colombia.[3] However, by the next year projections were scheduled in almost all the big cities of the country as Edda Pilar Duque writes, "On November 1st, 1898 two wandering entrepreneurs, Wilson and Gaylord, gave the first cinematic show"[4] in Medellín with an Edison's Vitascope projector, "but the triumphal welcoming was reserved for the Lumière projector"[5] that popularized the cinema in the entire Colombian territory soon after.

The same year of 1897 was the year of the first projections in Venezuela, also with a Vitascope projector. Soon after that, some scenes were filmed by brothers Manuel and Guillermo Trujillo Durán. The scenes selected were, as in the case of Costa Rica, about the local landscape and what we can call scientific novelties, such as *Un Celebre Especialista Sacandomuelas en el Gran Hotel Europa* (*A Renowned Specialist Extracting a Tooth at the Gran Hotel Europa*) and *Muchachos Bañándose en la Laguna de Maracaibo* (*Boys Bathing in the Maracaibo Lagoon*). After that there was nothing until 1909 when the short *Carnaval en Caracas* was filmed by M. A. Gonhom and Augusto González Vidal.[6] This was also the year in which the first projections of moving pictures appeared in Peru, but it was not until 1911 that the first images were filmed in the country; the first short fiction movie, *Negocio al Agua* (*Business to the Water*), was made in 1913 by Federico Blume. None of these efforts, however, left a mark. The rest of the countries, except Uruguay, had to wait until the twentieth century to experience for the first time the magic of moving pictures and even longer for their first filmed images to appear.

In Chile in 1902 we have the first record of some images presented in Valparaíso: *Un Ejercicio General de Bomberos* (*A General Exercise of the Fire Department*) by an anonymous source, while in Bolivia in 1904 the first images were projected in the Teatro Municipal of La Paz. The rest of the continent has been less successful, in part due to the political and social problems all through the twentieth century, but also in maintaining a film tradition; not only did moving pictures arrive late, but serious attempts to produce some films were made only in the late 1970s, 1980s, and 1990s, as in the case of El Salvador and Nicaragua, where film schools and production were consolidated as the result of a revolution or an open confrontation with an oppressive military government and the need to open new venues of expression in the late twentieth century. In Nicaragua, for example, the first cinema in the capital city was in 1919, and in El Salvador the first narrative film was made in 1924, *Aguilas Civilizadas* (*Civilized Eagles*, Alfredo Massi), but then nothing was produced after that except some coproductions with Mexico.

Uruguay is a strange case, since movies arrived in this South American nation very early, earlier even by weeks than in Argentina or Mexico. In fact, it was the second Latin American country, after Brazil, to receive the marvelous new invention of moving pictures, the first of which were seen in Uruguay in 1896. The first images filmed in the country, a competition of cyclists, were realized in 1898 by a Spaniard, Félix Olivier. Even though there were some newsreels filmed during the first decades of the twentieth century in that country, there was never an attempt to develop a film industry. The proximity of the Argentinean capital and the economic and industrial development of this nation, as well as the advances it had already made in the establishment of a film culture and industry, made it even more difficult for Uruguayans to compete with their richer neighbor; in addition, the local talent began to move to that country because it offered more possibilities. We could say that the cultural and geographical proximity of these two nations made it "unnecessary" for Uruguayans to develop a film industry.

Other countries, such as Guatemala or the Republic of Panama, have only sporadically produced films; and we can surely say with certainty that they do not have a national film industry, despite laudable attempts such as *El Silencio de Neto* (*The Silence of Neto*, 1994) by Guatemalan filmmaker Luis Argueta, which is an excellent film about a well-to-do family coping with political problems, social issues, a political coup, and life in Guatemala in the second half of the twentieth century as seen though the eyes of a little boy. Many of these films are the direct result of the new Latin American cinema and of the interaction between cinema and the political situation of the nations that produced them, something that B. Ruby Rich considers

> very much the point through out the history of the New Latin American cinema movement [something that] continues to be today. Just as Latin American culture is a nexus between nationalism and regional coherence, and the New Latin American cinema a crossroads of aesthetic innovation and ideological motivation, so too have politically-committed filmmakers positioned themselves between individualism and identification with the popular sector.[7]

I will, therefore, offer in the following pages a general view of the accomplishments and the richness and diversity of those cinemas that were never able to establish an important industry, but that have, as Walter Salles has said, renewed our "faith in the narrative possibility of the cinema made here in our continent."[8]

COLOMBIA

After the success of the film *La Vírgen de Los Sicarios* (*Our Lady of Assassins*, Barbet Schroeder, 2000) in art houses around the world, people started to talk with excitement about the cinema produced in Colombia. It is a touching story about the love of an older man (Germán Jaramillo) for the handsome sixteen-year-old assassin Alexis (Anderson Ballesteros) amid drug cartels and rival gangs in the violent city of Medellín. When the star of *María Llena Eres de Gracia* (*Maria Full of Grace*, Joshua Marston, 2004) was nominated for an Oscar for best actress a few years later, turning the film into a hit worldwide, Colombian cinema was again in everybody's mouths, and many considered it a revelation. Ironically, however, this sudden interest in a national cinema was due to films that were not directed by Colombians and had been coproduced by the United States or Europe. As such they were considered hybrids; when Colombia presented *María Llena Eres de Gracia* as the official candidate for the Oscar for best foreign film, it was rejected for not being Colombian enough. The reality unknown to many of those praising Colombian cinema is that in the last decade the country has produced some very interesting films with a variety of themes: comedies to social dramas and thrillers, including, of course, movies that deal with the drug cartels and guerrillas, and also films that belong to a long tradition in Latin America of street children.

One of the best known directors from that South American country, for example, is Víctor Gavira who in 1989 surprised audiences with his *Rodrigo D.: No Hay Futuro* (*Rodrigo D: No Future*). This film is set in Medellín, as are many other Colombian films, where Rodrigo, a poor adolescent, cannot find work, love, or any hope for a better life. In a desperate situation, he tries to make some sense of his life with punk music. Like *Los Olvidados* (Luis Buñuel, 1950) and *Pixote* (Hector Babenco, 1981) before it, *Rodrigo D.* is a movie that attempts to portray the life of destitute youth. It takes the camera to the streets and tells the story in a realistic way that incorporates many of the techniques of the New Latin American Cinema, including nonprofessional actors and a documentary-like style. Very similar in its techniques and narrative, the next film directed by Gavira was *La Vendedora de Rosas* (*The Rose Seller*, 1998), a film also about desperate street children who, with no place to go, make the best of their situation in the streets of Medellín, surviving by selling whatever they can find as well as by petty crime. The film follows the life of Mónica, a little girl who survives by selling roses on the street, and Andrea, a runaway kid who cannot deal with abuse at home.

The latest Gavira film, *Sumas y Restas* (*Adding and Subtracting*, 2005), is also set in Medellín in the 1980s, but unlike his previous films, this one is more traditional in its narrative even though it maintains a realistic look. In *Sumas y Restas* we follow Santiago through the streets of a city controlled by drug cartels where the best way of making some fast cash is by joining them—drug trafficking—something Santiago does and then has to suffer the consequences for this regrettable decision. This provides the perfect excuse for a thrilling plot in which, nonetheless, we find some political overtones. This shift in style is representative of what has happened in Latin America in the past few decades, where the influence of Hollywood but also local traditions, such as Mexican melodramas as well as television, particularly soap operas and music videos, has somehow homogenized filmmaking, resulting in a cinema that is less "particular" and more mainstream, opening the possibility for wider audiences and a more global distribution. Gone are the years of the cinema of garbage or imperfect cinema, although some idiosyncrasies have remained; nonetheless, making films in contemporary Latin America means making pictures accessible to a universal audience, with just the right amount of local color to still make them look exotic.

That is the case of the film *Buscando a Miguel* (*Looking for Miguel*, Juan Fischer, 2007), a thriller about a young man who is left for dead and whose body was sold to a morgue so medical students could learn anatomy and practice on it. When the young man wakes up, just before he is about to be cut open, he runs away and has to keep running in order to stay alive; to complicate matters, he has lost his memory. For the rest of the movie he has to find out who he is and who is after him and why. Through flashbacks and conversations with others, he (as we do as well) learns that he was a promising politician who ended up in this mess after a wild night on the town. The film very effectively combines thrill and drama with black humor in a realistic style that, according to Fischer, wants to be cinema verité, "where one feels that the camera intrudes in the intimacy of the characters."[9] The film follows a polished script that results in a very enjoyable movie, one that can very easily travel from country to country and engage audiences, in part because the story resembles many they have seen before via Hollywood (*Memento*, Christopher, 2000, comes immediately to mind), but that still reflects national conflicts and identity. In fact, the movie puts identity at the core of its narration. As the tag of the movie suggests, one cannot find oneself until one looses oneself.

Similarly—although it deals more directly with a problem that has long been identified with Colombia, particularly after the recent rescue of kidnapped politician Íngrid Betancourt—*La Milagrosa* (*Miraculous*, Rafael Lara, 2008) tells the story of a well-to-do young man who is kidnapped by a guerilla group and has to fear for his life everyday, not only when dealing with the volatile guerrilleros who see in him an entire class they blame for their problems, but ironically when the rescue teams appear. Considering that these teams are made up of brutal military men, poorly trained and barbaric in their dismissal of human lives in pursuit of their objectives, he has a point. Most of the film is built around the chasing of the guerrilleros by the military and the conversations they have with their prisoners. The guerrilleros have to run from camp to camp taking their prisoners, some of whom have been captives for years, with them. In the moments they are not running, they spend their time arguing with the captives, which gives us the opportunity to hear their side of the story although mediated and sometimes distorted. An almost caricature view of the guerrilleros is evident particularly in their insistence on the futility of religious beliefs, which is ironic because, as an official in charge of the rescue says, only a miracle can save the young man. Meanwhile, he has to face his solitude and his demons to the point of madness, but he also confronts his own view of his country, his countrymen, and his life.

Other interesting films are *Perro Come Perro* (*Dog Eats Dog*, Carlos Moreno, 2008), an entertaining crime thriller about some dumb aspiring criminals and their adventures in their life of petty crime; *Esto Huele Mal* (*This Stinks*, Jorge Alí Triana, 2007), a dark comedy about a businessman who thinks he is on top of his game and can get away with everything until a bomb explodes at a restaurant where he was supposed to be having a business dinner. In reality he was with the woman he was having an affair with and now has to pretend he that he was injured at the explosion, survived it, and even helped other victims; *La Primera Noche* (*The First Night*, Luis Alberto Restrepo, 2003), the story of two peasants who move to the city in search of a better life only to be confronted with more injustice, violence, and discrimination; and *Dios los Junta y Ellos Se Separan* (*United by God, Separated by Choice*, Jairo Eduardo Carrillo, 2006), a family comedy with some dramatic subplots in which several situations, some comical, some not so much, revolve around a family and offer viewers the opportunity to look at contemporary society in Colombia. Also a comedy, although less ambitious, is *Muertos del Susto* (*Dead Scared*, Harold Trompetero and Jairo Eduardo Carrillo, 2007), a very silly, cheap comedy.

Much more ambitious are the films of Sergio Cabrera, for example, *Golpe de Estadio* (*Stadium Coup*, 1998), an entertaining comedy that takes soccer as a metaphor for Colombia's social and political condition coproduced with Europe. The film is funny and merciless in its sarcastic look at the nation. While the entire country is watching a game leading to the World Cup in 1994, a helicopter crashes against the oil tower owed by an American company and guarded by the army to protect it against terrorism. The incident causes chaos with political implications and lots of opportunities for black humor. A good idea and a well-executed plot cannot save the film, however, from some of the problems attached to an industry less experienced (the editing is somehow sloppy and the acting at times seems nonprofessional), but the film nonetheless became one of the most popular Colombian films of the past few decades. Other good examples are *Ilona Llega con la Lluvia* (*Ilona Arrives with the Rain*, 1996), a drama about the relationship of three friends, Marl (Humberto Dorado), Ilona (Margarita Rosa de Francisco), and Abdul (Imanol Arias), and the mysterious woman, Larissa (Paz Vega), that appears in their lives and alters their relationship forever; and *Las Águilas no Cazan Moscas* (*Eagles Don't Hunt Flies*, 1994), a drama about a young army cadet who returns to his hometown to unravel an old family mystery.

An industry that never really took off, Colombian cinema can be dated to 1915 with small news reels, but it is really not until the 1960s that we can talk of some consistency in filmmaking. According to Umberto Valverde, the years between 1929 and 1946 represent the first attempts with the arrival of talking pictures. And the years from 1947 to 1958 represent the period of the production of documentaries biggest crisis of Colombian cinema, while the years between 1959 and 1976 represent the period of documentaries. These frustrated attempts, he argues, failed because the local bourgeoisie has never seen film as an easy way of making money and the government has never been interested in developing a national film industry. The situation was so bad that up to 1960 a national "filmography did not surpass sixty titles."[10] In the 1960s a group of filmmakers who had studied in Rome, Paris, and the United States returned to the country to attempt once more to establish an industry, but they were not successful. This group (Guillermo Angulo, Jorge Pinto, Álvaro González, and Francisco Norden) is known ironically as "the masters." Carlos Álvarez writes sarcastically that "Colombia is the only country that without having ever produced a cinema, has already a generation of masters."[11]

Some recent Colombian films seen abroad and circulating in festival circuits are *El Rey* (*The King*, José Antonio Dorado, 2004), a quintessential Hollywood story—the rise and fall of a gangster—except that this is a drug lord in the Colombia of the 1970s, which adds a political dimension to the issue because of the involvement of the American government and the corruption of the Colombian political system; *Soñar no Cuesta Nada* (*A Ton of Luck*, Rodrigo Triana, 2007), a film about greed, another favorite theme of Hollywood, but from a very local perspective. When a group of soldiers chasing a guerrilla group find a stash of money in the jungle, knowing this is drug money, they decide to keep it. However, getting back to civilization and spending their money wisely will prove to be more of a challenge than they even thought; this gives the director the opportunity to explore a universal theme of greed and the relative dilemma of doing the "right" thing amid the most inhumane and corrupt conditions.

CHILE

Another Latin country that was not successful in establishing a film industry is Chile. This is a paradox because with fewer resources and even a less established cinematic tradition than Colombia, Chile has produced some directors that are among the best known outside of Latin America, particularly Alejandro Jodorosky, Raúl Ruiz, and Miguel Littin. Surely all of them have worked partially or completely outside of Chile, but still there they have maintained a relationship with their own nation. Particularly after the military regime and with a relatively more stable economy in the past decade, Chile has managed to present itself as a place where films are made. Perhaps Chile's biggest hit in recent years is *Machuca* (Andrés Wood, 2004), a wonderful coming-of-age story about two friends from different classes who meet in a private, all-English school where Pedro Machuca (Ariel Mateluna) has been accepted with a scholarship, despite his humble origins. There he meets Gonzalo, a rich kid, and they become best friends; through their friendship, the boys experience each other's worlds. The two boys and Pedro's friend Silvana (Manuela Martelli) experience life and the excitement, joys, and pains of growing up. As A. O. Scott writes in the *New York Times*, *Machuca* "is both sweet and stringent, attuned to the wonders of childhood as well as its cruelty and terror."[12] These particular youngsters have to experience it all in the middle of a violent political climate that would end with the repressive military coup that put General Augusto Pinochet in power in 1973.

The films produced in the first years of the new millennium that have had some success are very diverse and include comedies, dramas, and thrillers. An example is *Los Debutantes* (*The Debutantes*, Andrés Waissbluth, 2004), and intelligent thriller about two country boys' adventures in the big city that result in their loss of innocence. Silvio and Víctor are brothers from the provinces who move to Santiago and end up working for a mafia boss who is under the spell of an exuberant woman who complicates the men's relationships and lives. The story is presented in three sections ingeniously, although not originally narrated from different perspectives. After that film, Waissbluth made *199 Recetas para Ser Feliz* (*199 Receipts to Be Happy*, 2008), another story about three people—Tomás (Pablo Macaya) and Helena (Tamara Garea), a couple traveling through Barcelona to promote Tomás's book about how to be happy, and the girlfriend of Helena's dead brother, Sandra (Andrea García-Huidobro).

Rodrigo Marín explores the nature of female friendship and human relations in his film *Las Niñas* (*The Girls*, 2007); this is also a topic that interests José Luis Torres Leiva, particularly in his short *Obreras Saliendo de la Fábrica* (*Female Workers Leaving the Factory*, 2005), a film about the way in which friendship helps a group of women cope with routine, and in his first feature *El Cielo, la Tierra y la Lluvia* (*The Sky, the Earth, and the Rain*, 2008). *El Cielo, la Tierra y la Lluvia* is a beautiful and lyrical movie about everyday life on a remote island off the cost of Chile, where three women and a man live and interact with each other and with the rough, beautiful nature that surrounds them in an existence that is a silent search for love, affection, companionship, and ultimately of oneself. Equally lyrical and promising is *Play* (2005), the first feature film of Alicia Scherson, an urban story of young people in search of love: Cristina (Viviana Herrera), who roams the streets of Santiago playing games; Tristán (Andrés Ulloa), Cristinas's neighbor, who is in love with his ex-girlfriend Irene (Aline Küppenheim); and Manuel (Juan Pablo Quezada), who is in love with Cristina. All explore the marvels of the everyday contemporary urban existence and its simplicity and wonder, as well as the pains and glories of young love.

Very different are the cases of the comedies *Chile Puede* (*Chile Can*, Ricardo Larraín, 2008) and *Malta con Huevo* (*Scrambled Beer*, Cristobal Valderrama, 2007). *Chile Puede* is the humorous story of Guillermo's adventures as the first Chilean astronaut. Guillermo (Boris Quercia), a schoolteacher, is selected to be the first Chilean in space, but as soon as he is in orbit, mission control is dismantled and Guillermo gets stranded in space thanks to the newly created Chilean Aeronautics Office. The misadventure of this South American nation's dream of being in space turns into an international conflict when the United States, fearing a missile attack from its enemies, takes military action. The comedy transpires, of course, from the absurdity of the proposition of a space operation by a small, developing nation with a large part of its population living in poverty, but having dreams of modernity that cannot be sustained. Equally absurd, and entertaining, is *Malta con Huevo* (the title refers to a popular drink of beer mixed with raw eggs), a story about a slacker who moves in with his nerdy friend. He realizes that as a consequence of his drinking "malta con huevo," prepared and provided by his new roommate, he has been traveling back and forth in time.

The generosity of Jorge (Nicolás Saavedra), a neurotic and obsessed chemist, in allowing his irresponsible artist friend Vladimir (Diego Muñoz) to live with him, has, as it turns out, an ulterior motive—he wants to use him as a guinea pig for his secret murderous desires. The story is about the relationship of the two men and Jorge's girlfriend Rocío (Javiera Díaz de Valdés), who also moves in with them against Jorge's wishes. From this triangle and the expected disastrous results of three adults (a couple and the man's best friend) living together come the conflict needed for the development of the plot. According to writer Alberto Fuguet, who is a producer of the film with his production company CinéPata, *Malta con Huevo* is a crazy and delirious pop comedy, meaning that it is linked to graphic novels and comic books in its execution and premises. It is easy to see why Fuguet chose this project to be his first as producer; the film, in fact, looks and sounds a lot like Fuguet's own novels and short stories, all of them about Americanized, middle-class Chileans with a strong literacy in American pop culture.

As mentioned before, even though lately there has been a more constant production of films, it is the 1970s—in connection with the group of directors associated with the New Latin American cinema —that had a more systematic Chilean cinema. Miguel Littin, one of those directors, surprised everybody with his first feature, *El Chacal de Nahueltoro* (*Jackal of Nahueltoro*, 1969), a story inspired by real events. It is not only one of the most viewed films from Chile, but according to many, its best. The film tells the story of a mass murderer, José or Jorge (he went by several names), a poor man who killed his lover Rosa and her five children, with a shocking realism and with a documentary-like style, including many shaky shots done with a hand-held camera. The purpose of the film is not so much to tell the story of the crimes or even to try to analyze them from a psychological or sociological perspective, but to show how crime and violence can also be the result of marginalization and of exploitation. José, the Jackal, is portrayed in the movie as a man who all through his life has been exploited by the system, society, and the military, even the Catholic Church. As Timothy Barnard and Peter Rist have written, this film "constructs the argument that to be a marginalized person is to be ignorant of, and deprived of, all that it takes to be a complete person."[13] And consequently, it is a highly political and subversive film.

After *El Chacal*, Littin did what would become the most important film of the Allende administration. Littin, in fact, was the director of the official institution in charge of promoting cinema, Chile Films, during the presidency of Salvador Allende (1970–1973), the leftist president that was killed during the military coupe that brought Augusto Pinochet to power. This film is called *La Tierra Prometida* (*The Promised Land*, 1973) and is based on the attempts to establish the first socialist republic of the Americas in Chile. When a group of peasants in search of a place to live settle on some public lands, encouraged by the proclamation of a socialist state by Marmaduke Grove Vallejo, they become a threat to the rich landowners and the establishment of the provincial capital. José Durán (Nelson Villagra), the natural leader of the peasants, names himself the new governor; when he is told that the socialist government has been overthrown, he runs to the mountains with his men, only to be killed. During the filming of this movie, Allende was also overthrown, and Littin managed to escape to Mexico where he produced other films such as the Oscar-nominated *Actas de Marucia* (*Letters from Marucia*, 1976), *El Recurso del Método* (*The Recourse of the Method*, 1978), and *La Viuda de Montiel* (*The Widow of Montiel*, 1979).

He produced other films and documentaries in Mexico and collabo-
rated closely with Cuba and other countries such as Nicaragua. In fact,
he produced the first film of that country during the Sandinista
administration (1979–1990), *Alsino y el Cóndor* (*Alsino and the Condor*,
1982), a film that was nominated for an Oscar and is today one of
the most successful films from Central America. Also in Nicaragua
he made *Sandino* (1990), a film with a multinational cast about the
revolutionary Augusto César Sandino with, among others, Kris
Kristofferson as Tom Holte and Joaquim de Almeida as Sandino.
Twenty years after his exile, he returned to Chile to film *Los Náufragos*
(*The Shipwrecked*, 1994), a film about a man who returns to Chile after
20 years of exile in search of answers and of himself—the story actually
sounds very much autobiographical. That movie was followed by
Aventureros del Fin del Mundo (*Adventurers to the End of the World*,
1998), *Tierra del Fuego* (2000), as well as some films in Palestine, such
as *Crónica Palestina* (*Palestinian Chronicle*, 2001) and *La Última Luna*
(*The Last Moon*, 2005), about two friends in 1914, one Jewish and
one Arab, who have to struggle with prejudices and cultural differences in a place that does not seem that different from contemporary
Palestine.

If Miguel Littin is the director of the opening of Latin America, as
Jacqueline Mouesca describes him, then Raúl Ruiz is the director of
a cinema without borders.[14] Of all the directors from the generation
of the 1960s, the one who gave prestige to Chilean cinema is Raúl
Ruiz, who became more experimental and who finally found a place
in European cinema, particularly in France. His first film, *Tres Tristes
Tigres* (*Three Trapped Tigers*, 1968), is about a subject he has explored
all through his career, the opposition between the bourgeoisie and
the lower classes and their particular idiosyncrasies, something he
knows how to do always with "a great sense of humor and an eye for
detail,"[15] according to Peter B. Schumann. His second film,
La Colonia Penal (*The Penal Colony*, 1970), was left unfinished when
he departed from Chile. It tells the story of an island nation that is
an ex-penal colony, which after gaining its independence, becomes a
militarized country (all the inhabitants, for example, are in uniform
and carry weapons). Obviously, this can be seen as an allegory of Chile
and so many other Latin American countries with a military
government. In his native country Ruiz also made *Nadie Dijo Nada*
(*Nobody Said Anything*, 1971) and *La Expropiación* (*The Expropiation*,
1971), where his experimental style became more evident, including
the mixing of popular and high cultures without making any

distinction. After that, he moved permanently to France where he has continued producing films until now, combining all kinds of styles, from avant-garde experimentation to B movies, including adaptations of literary classics such as Robert Lewis Stevenson's *Treasure Island* (1985), Shakespeare's *Richard III* (1986), and Camilo Castelo Branco's *Mistérios de Lisboa* (*Mysteries of Lisbon*, in postproduction).

Many other directors went to exile, such as Patricio Guzmán, whose *La Batalla de Chile* (*The Battle of Chile*, 1974–1979) has been compared to Gillo Pontecorvo's *La Battaglia di Algeri* (*The Battle of Algiers*, 1966). This seminal film of Latin American revolutionary cinema is an almost five-hour epic documentary about the government of Salvador Allende, which took years to complete and that was finished thanks to the help of the Instituto Cubano de Arte e Industria Cinematográficos, the Cuban Institute of Cinema, the country where Guzmán went into exile. The film is divided into three parts, the first, "Insurrection of the Bourgeoisie," is about the people who voted against Allende; the second, "Coupe d'Etat," is about the coup that ended with the death of Allende; and the third, "The Popular Power," is about worker unions and Popular Unity. This film has been mentioned by many critics as one of the best political films ever and has been awarded numerous prizes worldwide. This film also marks the renaissance of the documentary as a powerful tool of social activism particularly during the years of Allende's presidency or of Popular Unity (1970–1973), some of the most productive years in the history of Chilean cinema until the new millennium. During those years there were several centers of film culture, such as Chile Films, Instituto Fílmico, Cine Experimental, and the Cinema School of Viña del Mar, plus a couple of film centers supported by worker unions.

All of these were dismantled during the years of the dictatorship. After the coup, as mentioned, many film professionals left the country. Many others were repressed, tortured, or killed, for example, Eduardo Paredes, the last director of Chile Films; Jorge Müller, the cameraman of *La Batalla de Chile*; and Carmen Bueno, an actress in *La Tierra Prometida*. The military also destroyed many of the archives and film materials of Chile Films and turned it into a "producer of publicitary films."[16] Many filmmakers tried to continue making films in the country, but most did only publicitary shorts or nonpolitical documentaries such as Carlos Flores's *Pepe Donoso* (1977) about the novelist José Donoso. Other very interesting attempts were Christina Sánchez's *Vías Paralelas* (*Parallel Tracks*, 1975), *El Zapato Chino* (*The Chinese Shoe*, 1979), and *Los Deseos Concebidos* (*Conceived Desires*, 1982). Along with her, only Silvio Caiozzi managed to make some interesting films, such as *A la Sombra del Sol* (*Under the Shadow of the Sun*, with Pablo Perlman, 1974) and *Julio Comienza en Julio* (*July Begins in July*, 1979).

It is interesting to mention as well Sergio Bravo-Ramos's *No Eran Nadie* (*They Were Nobody*, 1982) and *El Último Grumete* (*The Last Marine*, 1984), a film backed by Chile Films, now under the direction of a major in the Chilean Army, about the war among Chile, Peru, and Bolivia that was an "idealized view of war and the military; a nationalist and militarist spectacle."[17] A year later a film appeared that was a sign of the changing times, *Hijos de la Guerra Fría* (*Children of the Cold War*, Gonzalo Justiniano, 1985), a film about a middle-class couple who, ignoring the signs of the economic disaster that was approaching, buy a car they can barely afford and go on a trip. When the economic crisis hits them, they go around committing petty crimes in a sort of rebelliousness against a system that no longer works for them. Filmed around the same time, in fact, only two years later, but not released until 1990, *Imagen Latente* (*Latent Image*, Pablo Perelman) is the first film dealing seriously with the dictatorship of Pinochet: Pedro (Bastián Bodenhöfer) is a photographer with no particular interest in politics, until a relative disappears; then he begins to realize little by little all the atrocities of the Pinochet regime and therefore acquires a social consciousness. The film was forbidden at its premier, but became very popular and acclaimed in international festivals.

Some other recent Chilean films include the first feature of writer Alberto Fuguet as a director, *Se Arrienda* (*For Rent*, 2005), a very conventional story about the anxiety of an uncertain future in Latin America and the power of imagination; *Mi Mejor Enemigo* (*My Best Enemy*, Alex Bowen, 2004), a humanist look at international conflicts and how people are always more important than any ideals; *Sábado* (*Saturday*, Matías Bize, 2003); *Gringuito* (*Little Gringo*, Sergio M. Castilla, 1998), the touching story of a boy who has to confront his identity as Chilean when he and his family return to their country of origin after years of living in New York; *El Chacotero Sentimental* (*The Sentimental Teaser*, Cristián Galaz, 1999), the story of a radio talk show and its host who offers sentimental advice to the callers and strikes a chord with his listeners all over the country; *Coronación* (*Coronation*, Silvio Caiozzi, 2000), an excellent adaptation of José Donoso's novel by the same title; *El Leyton* (*Leyton*, Gonzalo Justiniano, 2002), a story of passion, friendship, love, solitude, and life in a small Chilean fishing town as background; and *La Fiebre del Loco* (*El Loco Fever*, Andrés Wood, 2001), a surreal comedy about the harvesting of a fish, "el loco," that has a reputation as an aphrodisiac and the consequences for two con men trying to buy the entire catch.

BOLIVIA

This South American country did not have a cinema until the appearance of Jorge Sanjinés in the 1960s. However, this director was a major force behind the new Latin American cinema; not only has he dominated the national production with such films as *Yawar Malku* (*Blood of the Condor*, 1969), but his film *El Coraje del Pueblo* (*The Courage of the People*, 1971) is a classic of revolutionary cinema and caused him to be exiled. He returned to his country only in 1980 to film *La Nación Clandestina* (*The Clandestine Nation*, 1989). His career started in 1960 when he went back to Bolivia after studying philosophy in Santiago de Chile. At first, he worked in commercial publicity while trying to explore his social interests; then in 1964 the civil government of Paz Estenssoro was overthrown by the military, and he took charge of the Instituto Cinematográfico of Bolivia. A few years later his *Yawar Mallku* came out right after the death of Che Guevara, and its popularity was fed by the paranoid anti-American atmosphere in Bolivia at the time. The plot focuses on the Progress Corps, a Peace Corps–like American group that, with the excuse of providing assistance to indigenous communities, sterilizes their women without them knowing it. When they realize it, an angry mob attacks the Americans while the indigenous leader Mallku is accused and hurt in a dispute with the police. Mallku is taken to the capital, La Paz, where he suffers racism and discrimination and is unable to get the medical attention he desperately needs. Despite all the efforts of his family, he dies as a result of his injuries. The film is an allegory of the dreadful consequences of American colonialist power and its intervention in the region, even in its most benevolent manifestations. The film was censored the same day of its exhibition for offending a powerful ally.

El Coraje del Pueblo two years later resulted from the period of a relatively democratic opening of the military government; it was a period of popular mobilization with Asamblea Popular (Popular Assembly), and the film attempted to show the "incredible capacity of resistance of Bolivian workers,"[18] who despite the abuses and repression they have always suffered continue their fight for justice and better conditions. The plot about the attempts of a group of miners to unionize themselves because of the repression they suffer is a subject that has been present in many cinematographies, including American independent films (for example, *Matewan*, John Sayles, 1987). In this case, the action happens the night of San Juan, a traditional festive night in many Latin countries associated with fire; in 1967, on the night of San Juan, the army tried to intimidate the union members who were celebrating the feast of St. John with bonfires and shoots into them hurting their leader. The movie then tells in flashbacks the story of the movement and the living conditions of the miners. Among other interesting things, the film puts the role of women in a prominent place in the movement and recreates the events with a poetic beauty; it also includes in its documentary-like structure the testimony of the survivors who actually play their own roles in the film.

El Coraje del Pueblo coincided with the few months of populism in the military regime that ended with another coup from a right-wing faction of the army. After this many filmmakers left the country, including Sanjinés; others such as Antonio Eguino and Óscar Soria, however, remained in the country. Since they could not really continue making the type of films that were allowed in the past, they opted for a different strategy—they would make films that touched on social issues, but present them as just more conflict for the protagonists. Eguino's first movie was *Pueblo Chico* (*Small Town*, 1974), a story about a young, idealist man who returns to his hometown after studying abroad and tries to change the conditions of the peasants; he fails to gain the people's trust and also alienates the local bourgeoisie; these problems, however, are nothing compared to his sentimental and amorous troubles. After *Pueblo Chico*, Eguino directed *Chuquiago* (1977), a similar movie in its treatment, but much more complex in its social commentary.

The film intertwines four stories about people from different classes whose lives cross in La Paz, the capital city of Bolivia. Isico, an Indian boy who speaks no Spanish, has to move to the city in search of a better life; Johnny, a working-class kid, wants to move up socially and hangs out with middle-class kids until he is denounced and rejected for not belonging to the same class; Carlos, a middle-age bureaucrat, dies on his way home after a wild night out; and Patricia, a rich girl, gives up the revolutionary dreams she had in college when she marries into her own class and returns to the comforts of a petite bourgeoisie existence. Despite its sporadic melodramatic episodes, the film ends on a sour note when we see Patricia and her husband driving to their honeymoon destination while in the background, on the hills, we see

Isico carrying a heavy burden. The film became one of the biggest hits of Bolivian cinema and the public went to see it with almost desperation; it remained in circulation for several months. In 1984 Eguino filmed a project he had had for a long time, *Amargo Mar* (*The Bitter Sea*), a film about the war of 1880 with Chile in which Bolivia lost its access to the sea. The result was not as good as anticipated, and the complexity of its focus—the political maneuvers that the leading classes have always done behind closed doors not always in favor of the country, but looking after their own interests—weakens the plot.

Also representative of the cinema of the 1980s was Paolo Agazzi who directed *Mi Socio* (*My Partner*, 1982), a film also about the differences between classes and, in this case, regions, in Bolivia. A truck driver travels from the high plateau to the tropical lowlands facing cultural, and social, differences so marked that it makes the case for the impossibility of the dream of national unity. Agazzi also directed *Los Hermanos Cartagena* (*The Brothers Cartagena*, 1984), a conventional film about fraternal rivalry in a politically explosive climate; similar in its interpretation of irreconcilable national differences to *Chuquiago*, the film was also a hit. It is interesting to mention that the issue of the irreconcilable class and cultural differences of the country symbolized by an impossible love has been at the core of Bolivia's modest film industry. In fact, the first films made in the country were *La Profecía del Lago* (José María Velasco Maidana, 1925), a film about a high society lady who falls in love with her Indian servant, a film that was censured for moral reasons; and *Corazón Aymara* (*Aymaran Heart*, Pedro Sambarino), a melodramatic view of the life of the Aymara Indians from the same year.

Similar to *Corazón Aymara*, *La Gloria de la Raza* (*The Glory of the Race*, Luis Castillo, 1926) is a film about the destruction of the Aymaran culture as told by an Indian from the region of Lake Titicaca to an archeologist. In addition, *Wara-Wara* (1929), a superproduction for its time, is about the relationship between an Aymaran princess and a Spanish soldier with the conquest of the Inca Empire as background; in this film, according to Schumann, "artists, poets, and members of the most select sectors of the local bourgeoisie participates as extras."[19] Talking pictures did not arrive in Bolivia until late, but the first attempt to have a sound movie was *Hacia la Gloria* (*Towards Glory*, 1932), a melodrama about a rich boy who is abandoned by a river at birth and is rescued and raised by a family of peasants. The boy eventually becomes a pilot and is hurt on a mission; he ends up injured in a hospital where a nurse recognizes him as her own son and prevents him from marrying his own sister. Although the film was announced as a talkie, it had a rather primitive system of records with sound effects. The film was a disappointment; today only fragments of it survive.

Evidently Bolivia has not had a long tradition or a very well established film industry; nonetheless, it has produced some important films. In the Latin American context, it is particularly important for its revolutionary and political cinema, and also for being the first country to deal with the indigenous cultures on film. In recent years Bolivia has been presenting regular films in festivals around the world, and these films show a variety that was not so evident in the past. One example of this new cinema is *Lo Más Bonito y Mis Mejores Años* (*The Most Beautiful and My Best Years*, Martín Boulocq, 2005), a charming and lighthearted film about a young man who in order to leave his provincial town of Cochabamba has to sell his only valuable possession—an ancient Volkswagen—with the help of his best friend Víctor and his girlfriend Camila. This is a very nice example of a more urban cinema dealing with the modern aspirations of Bolivia's youth. Also worth mentioning are *El Corazón de Jesús* (*Jesus's Heart*, Marcos Loayza, 2004), a black comedy about bureaucracy, health insurance, infidelity, and mistaken identities; and *El Día que Murió el Silencio* (*The Day Silence Died*, Paolo Agazzi, 1998), another black comedy about a handsome stranger who arrives in the quiet town of Villaserena with a pair of speakers; for a small amount of money, the villagers can broadcast anything they want, from gossip and local music to love declarations and "social service" announcements with obviously funny and even bizarre consequences.

PERU

To say that the Peruvian cinema industry has not had the same success as other Latin cinemas is an understatement. However, even though Peruvian movies have not been as technically accomplished, consistent, or famous as Mexican, Spanish, or Brazilian, some coproductions during the 1960s and 1970s, particularly with Mexico, played an important role in the development of a film tradition that now has been taking shape more as an industry. Unfortunately the majority of those coproductions were not artistically or technically ambitious enough to interest foreign markets. This of course does not mean that Peru did not have a film tradition before, because in fact the years from 1955 to 1966 were marked predominantly by the activities of the so-called Cuzco School, a group revolving around the Cine Club Cuzco and dedicated to the promotion of films, but also to the production of documentaries. Those years were also the years of intense protection of the fragile emerging industry by the *Ley de Fomento a la Actividad Cinematográfica* (Law of Incentives to Film Production), a law established in the early 1970s during the leftist military regime of General Juan Velasco Alvarado, which among other things guaranteed a space for the exhibition of Peruvian films under more favorable conditions and promoted cinema as a social tool, just as the Cuban revolutionary government had done in the 1950s or the Mexican government had also done after the revolution in the 1930s.

Velasco Alvarado's cinema law also offered tax breaks to producers; as a result, the production of films, shorts, and features incremented considerably to the point that "in 1979 there were eighty film companies that made 178 short films and 12 feature films."[20] Many of these films focused on the displacement of poor peasants from the provinces to the urban centers and their interaction with a national culture, a social issue of vital importance for Peru and many other Latin American countries in those years. However, they never developed a film movement compared to the revolutionary efforts of the cinemas of Bolivia or Cuba. But in many ways this attempt can be considered a desire to follow the new Latin American cinema, at least inasmuch as they reflected the problems of the nation and denounced the exploitation of the Indians and peasants by the local oligarchies. All this, however, changed radically in 1975 when a right-wing faction of the army rebelled against Velasco Alvarado and declared Francisco Morales Bermúdez the new president. Velasco Alvardo decided not to resist the coup and stepped down.

With this turn of events, a new repressive government declared an open war on any activity it considered subversive; therefore, many of the films produced previously were censured, even though they were not really very political, with the exception of *Allpakallpa* (Bernardo Arias, 1974). Of the School of Cuzco, perhaps the most important film was *Kukuli* (Luis Figueroa, César Villanueva, and Eulogio Nishiyama, 1961); based on an Indian legend, it "tells of a confrontation between a peasant and a nukulu—a mythological bear—because of their love for the same woman."[21] The film was beautiful and poetic with almost no dialogue, and the little there was was in an Indian language. It also used the rough landscape as background. Nine years later another film was produced in Peru; this film has been consistently appearing in the list of favorite Latin American films of many critics and scholars, as well as the public in general—*La Muralla Verde* (*The Green Wall*, Armando Robles Godoy, 1970). Despite its flaws, the film is an excellent exercise in poetic narrative and an exploration of the intimate and troublesome relationship between civilization and the wild, so embedded in the South American mind. The film was well received in festival circuits and was honored at the Chicago International Film Festival.

Also from the 1970s is *Los Perros Hambrientos* (*The Starving Dogs*, Luis Figueroa, 1976), based on a novel by Ciro Alegría. This film did not want to idealize the Indian peasants, so it presented them as a brave and dignified people in conflict with the interests of big landowners as well as of other groups of the ruling class. Other films appeared around the same time that also wanted to start a national cinema; some of them are *Kuntur Wachana* (*Where Condors Are Born*, Federico García Hurtado, 1977), *Laulico* (Federico García Hurtado, 1979), *Yawar Fiesta* (*Yawar Celebration*, Luis Figueroa, 1980), and *Tupac Amaru* (Federico García Hurtado, 1984), the first historical superproduction in Peru. Also from those years were *Muerte al Amanecer* (*Death at Dawn*, Francisco J. Lombardi, 1977) and *Muerte de un Magnate* (*Death of a Tycoon*, Francisco J. Lombardi, 1980), two interesting police dramas that look at class and ethnic relationships and their problematic connection with the judicial system. García and Figueroa were unable to continue producing films consistently and had to turn to television to earn a living.

That was not the case of Lombardi who, on the contrary, managed to develop a commercial career in filmmaking that has given him and his country some international reputation. Some of his most representative films are *La Ciudad y los Perros* (*The City and the Dogs*, 1985), a film based on the novel by Mario Vargas Llosa, that looks at the brutality of military schools; *La Boca del Lobo* (*The Lion's Den*, 1988), a film about the "dirty" war in the Peru of the 1980s when the rebel group Sendero Luminoso (Shining Path) challenged the official government; *Caídos del Cielo* (*Fallen from Heaven*, 1990); *Bajo la Piel* (*Under the Skin*, 1996); *No Se lo Digas a Nadie* (*Don't Tell Anyone*, 1998), a story about a young man in search of his sexual identity far from home; and *Pantaleón y las Visitadoras* (*Captain Pantoja and the Special Services*, 1999), another film based on a novel by Vargas Llosa that is a funny, black comedy about the way authority functions in the army, using sexuality as a metaphor. The movie and the novel are based on a real event and tell the story of Pantoja, an army captain who never questioned authority, not even when he was put in charge of providing his men serving in the jungle with prostitutes to keep them in order.

Lombardi is by far the most accomplished filmmaker from Peru so far, and he has kept a constant production of films into the new millennium. His most recent films are *Tinta Roja* (*Red Ink*, 2000), a film about the way in which corruption becomes institutionalized and brings down everything in its path; *Ojos que no Ven* (*What the Eye Doesn't See*, 2003), a political thriller about the last years of infamous president Alberto Fujimori, one of the most corrupt South American presidents in recent memory, told through the intertwining of different stories. His latest film, *Mariposa Negra* (*Black Butterfly*, 2006), is a film in which he again charges against the high spheres of power and corruption in Peru. Gabriela (Melania Urbina) is a young schoolteacher whose life changes when her boyfriend is brutally murdered. Devastated and humiliated when a tabloid tries to distract public opinion (her boyfriend was a prominent judge fighting corruption) by spreading rumors that he had been killed in a crazy night out with a male lover, she focuses on clearing his name, running head on against Peru's power elite. In the process she meets and becomes friends with the journalist who wrote the newspaper piece; she soon becomes her confidant. Other films have been presented as Peruvian, particularly one touching on the current issue of migration, *Soy Andina* (*I Am Andian*, Mitchell Teplitsky, 2007). However, this film, which is about a young girl who returns to Peru after years of living in the United States, her birthplace, in search of her identity, is an American independent film.

OTHER TRADITIONS

The limitations we have mentioned so far are even more dramatic in the countries that have almost no film tradition, such as El Salvador, Guatemala, Panama, Dominican Republic, Costa Rica, or even Puerto Rico. But as in the case of Bolivia, Chile, or Peru, in recent years most of these Latin American countries have produced films that have been received favorably by their own audiences as well as at international festivals. Ecuador has never been able to develop a cinematic tradition, despite the fact that Sanjinés tried to inaugurate a filmmaking tradition there in 1977 with *¡Fuera de Aquí!* (*Get Out of Here!*). Before that only *Se Conocieron en Guayaquil* (*They Met in Guayaquil*, Alberto Santana, 1950) is worth mentioning, in part because it was the first talking picture produced in that country. After *¡Fuera de Aquí!*, important to mention is *La Tigra* (*The Tigress*, Camilo Luzuriaga, 1989), an interesting drama about three orphan sisters who witness the brutal killing of their parents; one of them decides to avenge their deaths by killing the assassins and any men that come her way. In the 1990s *Ratas, Ratones y Rateros* (*Rats, Mice, and Thieves*, Sebastián Cordero, 1999), a realist look at the life of delinquency and urban marginalization in Ecuador, gave some hope that an industry could finally be possible.

In the new millennium some films have continued to feed this hope although they have also showed that they have a long way to go. One example of this is *Fuera de Fuego* (*Offside*, Manuel Arregui, 2003), a story about a young man, Juan (Manolo Santillán), desperately trying to leave his homeland in search of better conditions. He plans a robbery in order to get the money for his dream of migrating to a foreign county seeking better luck. Part social drama, part thriller, the movie stems from the possibility of the robbery going wrong and therefore crashing Juan's dreams and life. It is interesting to mention that the picture has the look we have become accustomed to with music videos and commercials; because of that, it could be easy to export to other cultures and it may end up opening some doors for the cinema produced in Ecuador. The other example worth mentioning is the interesting road movie that, like so many in the continent, serves as an excuse to travel through different landscapes and social backgrounds, *¿Qué tan Lejos?* (*How Much Farther?*, Tania Hermida, 2006). The film focuses on Esperanza (Tania Martínez) who has come to Ecuador from Spain in hope of finding an exotic and affordable vacation spot that is still somehow familiar. On her way to Cuenca, a colonial town in the mountains, she runs into Tristeza (Cecilia Vallejo). Because Tristeza needs to get to the town to prevent her boyfriend from marrying somebody else, she decides to hitchhike when the bus in which they are traveling is stopped by a strike. Esperanza decides to join her and the two girls then come across an array of characters and situations that serve as the excuse to expose in a very unassuming way social and class relations while creating a realistic mosaic of life in that South American nation.

Another country with a very weak tradition of filmmaking is Uruguay, which as mentioned before, received the invention of moving pictures before any other South American country, except Brazil. The new invention, however, did not find the same reception here as it did in Brazil or Argentina, countries that developed an industry first. As also previouly mentioned, many Uruguayan actors and talented people thought it was easier to work in Argentina, just across the river, than to start from scratch. Nonetheless, some films were produced in Uruguay. The first important one was *El Pequeño Héroe del Arroyo de Oro* (*The Little Hero of Arroyo de Oro*, Carlos Alonso, 1929), a family drama about an alcoholic man who kills his wife and is confronted by his young son. In 1936 the first talking picture was made in the country; it was a conventional melodrama called *Dos Destinos* (*Two Destinies*, Juan Etchebehere), which was a flop at the box office. Later efforts to establish an industry failed as well, and the only decades with some significance, mostly because film was seen as a way of documenting the repression of the military government established in 1973, were in the 1970s and most of the 1980s.

In 1982 a film appeared that gave some hope of establishing an industry, if not at least of occasionally producing an important film with 100 percent national capital and talent. The film was *Mataron a Venancio Flores* (*They Killed Venancio Flores*, Juan Carlos Rodríguez Castro). Set in the 1800s and based on a real historical event, the film is no doubt allegorical of the situation of the country under a military dictatorship. Technically, the film had some problems that the director attributed to the Argentine laboratory where the film was processed, so he decided to remove his name from the credits. Still, the film is a commendable attempt. In 2003 a film from Uruguay circulated to great success in international festivals; it also appeared in some foreign screens and received very favorable critics and the approval of audiences. The picture had the strange title of *Whisky* (Juan Pablo Rebella and Pablo Stoll) and was an excellent story about an aging lonely man, Jacobo Koller (Andrés Pazos), faithful to his routine, finds himself in a predicament when his brother announces he will be visiting from Brazil. Jacobo, anxious to show that he is not a looser, asks Marta (Mirella Acuña), one of the employees at his sock factory, to pretend they are married.

Ironic, sad, and full of comic possibilities in its observations of everyday existence, the film is a marvelous example of a cinema with little resources, lots of talented people, and of imagination. Like Wesley Morris of the *Boston Globe*, I feel comfortable calling this film a comedy, although "none of what transpires among these three [characters] is presented with the broad strokes or winking nudges you'd get from another movie."[22] That is also true of their previous film, *25 Watts* (2001), the story of three slackers trying to survive a monotonous Sunday in a modern Montevideo. Considering that the characters are young men, the temptation of including lots of slapstick could have been very tempting; nonetheless, the film is spontaneous and shot in black and white, which gives it an aura of reality that can be seen as a realistic portrait of any Latin American city and its inhabitants. Another couple of films more recently have been circulating in festivals with mixed reviews; they are *El Baño del Papa* (*The Toilet of the Pope*, César Charlone and Enrique Fernández, 2007), a black comedy about a man who decided to build a toilet for the thousands of pilgrims that would visit his impoverished town where he lives when the Pope visits it; and *El Viaje Hacia el Mar* (*Journey to the Sea*, Guillermo Casanova, 2003), a gentle, sweet road movie about a man and his dog on a journey to see the sea for the first time.

Similarly to other South American nations, Venezuela has struggled all through the twentieth century to build a national film industry; like them it has also consistently failed. But, like Uruguay or Colombia, it has managed to produce some interesting films that have received international attention. And as in the case of Peru's Lombardi, there has been a name that has dominated the scene in Venezuela, Román Chalbaud. Chalbaud started making films in the 1950s and has continued consistently until now. His first famous film was *El Pez que Fuma* (*Smoking Fish*, 1977), a look at the criminal and marginalized underworld of the slums of Caracas centered on a brothel called "El pez que fuma." Other films by Chalbaud are *Carmen, la que Contaba 16 Años* (*Carmen at Age Sixteen*, 1978), a sort of updating of Georges Bizet's Carmen; *Bodas de Papel* (*Paper Wedding*, 1979); *Cangrejo* (*Crab*, 1982), a well-executed police thriller; *Cangrejo II* (1984), a sequel to *Cangrejo*; *La Oveja Negra* (*The Black Sheep*, 1987); *El Corazón de las Tinieblas* (*The Heart of Darkness*, 1990); *Pandemonium, la Capital del Infierno* (*Pandemonium, Capital of Hell*, 1997), and *El Caracazo* (2003), his moist recent film. *El Caracazo* tells the events of February 27, 1989, when a simple protest against an increase in ticket bus prices became a popular rebellion and a violent confrontation with the police that ended in a massacre.

Other recent films from Venezuela are *Florentino y el Diablo* (*Florentino and the Devil*, Michael New, 1995), a folktale about a man who defies the Devil in the form of nature to a singing duel; *100 Años de Perdón* (*Little Thieves, Big Thieves*, 1998) a comedy-drama about four friends planning to get even with the big banks as the result of the recent bank crisis in Venezuela; the title in Spanish refers to the saying that a thief who robs a thief deserves 100 years of forgiveness; *Amaneció de Golpe* (*Coup at Daybreak*, Carlos Azpurúa, 1998), about the frustrated coup attempt on the night of February 4, 1992, told from the perspective of several characters from different paths of life and the way it affects their lives. Also of interest are a coproduction with Mexico and Peru, *A la Media Noche y Media* (*At Half Past Midnight*, Mariana Rondón, 1999), a sort of metaphysical sci-fi film; *Punto y Raya* (*Step Forward*, Elia K. Schneider, 2004), a drama about the border between Venezuela and Colombia; and *La Pluma del Arcángel* (*The Archangel's Feather*, Luis Manzo, 2002), an allegorical tale, more magic realism than social commentary, about a stranger, Gabriel (Iván Tamayo), who arrives at a remote town in the 1930s and helps the people recover some of their dignity when he is put in charge of the telegraph; through it, he changes the lives of the people and encourages them to fight against the powerful local cacique.

Finally, a country that never really managed to establish a film tradition, not to mention an industry, but that has produced some interesting films is Guatemala. Two movies that received some attention in the past decades have been also received favorably by the critics and the international festival audiences. One is *El Silencio de Neto* (*The Silence of Neto*, Luis Argueta, 1994), which is a touching coming-of-age film about a kid from an upper class, who has to confront the hash reality of his troubled country from his sheltered life at first; however, despite his conservative family, Neto (Óscar Javier Alemngor) gives into his personal desire to explore and discover the country on his own. The other is *Lo Que Soño Sebastián* (*What Sebastian Dreamt*, Rodrigo Rey Rosa, 2003), which is the story of Sebastián (Andoni Gracia), a young man from Spain who, after inheriting some land in Guatemala, decides to go live in that country's rainforest. Once there, he has to fight to keep hunters and poachers off his land and to confront the local caciques and a corrupt system.

NOTES

1. Daniel Marranghello, *El Cine en Costa Rica, 1903–1920* (San José, Costa Rica, n.p., 1988), 54.

2. See María Lourdes Cortés, *El Espejo Imposible: Un Siglo de Cine en Costa Rica* (San José, Costa Rica: Farben Editorial Norma, 2002), 30–33.

3. Peter B. Schumann, *Historia del Cine Latinoamericano* (Buenos Aires: Editorial Legasa, 1987), 128.

4. Edda Pilar Duque, *La Aventura del Cine en Medellín* (Bogotá: Universidad Nacional de Colombia/El Ancora Editores, 1992), 16.

5. Ibid., 21.

6. Schumann, *Historia del Cine Latinoamericano*, 298.

7. B. Ruby Rich, "An/Other View of Latin American Cinema," in *The New Latin American Cinema*, ed. Michael T. Martin (Detroit: Wayne State University Press, 1997), 277.

8. Elena and Díaz López, "Preface," *The Cinema of Latin America* (London and New York: Wallflower Press, 2003), xiv.

9. "El Cine Debe Reflejar la Realidad del País," an interview with Juan Fisher, *Semana*, August 11, 2007, http://www.semana.com/wf_InfoArticulo .aspx?idArt=105526.

10. Umberto Valverde, *Reportaje Crítico del Cine Colombiano* (Bogotá: Editorial Toro Nuevo, 1978), 16.

11. Carlos Álvarez, *Sobre Cine Colombiano y Latinoamericano* (Bogotá: Universidad Nacional de Colombia, 1989), 32.

12. A. O. Scott, "History through the Eyes of a Frightened Child," *New York Times*, January 19, 2005, http://movies.nytimes.com/2005/01/19/ movies/19mach.html.

13. Timothy Barnard and Peter Rist, eds., *South American Cinema: A Critical Filmography, 1915–1994* (Austin: University of Texas Press, 1996), 223.

14. See Jacqueline Mouesca, *Plano Secuencial de la Memoria de Chile* (Santiago, Chile: Ediciones del Litoral, 1988).

15. Schumann, *Historia del Cine Latinoamericano*, 189.

16. Ibid., 196.

17. Ibid., 200.

18. Ibid., 70.

19. Ibid., 65.

20. Ibid., 274.

21. Barnard and Rist, *South American Cinema*, 279.

22. Wesley Morris, " 'Whisky' Is a Strong Shot of Solitude," *Boston Globe*, March 4, 2005, http://www.boston.com/ae/movies/articles/2005/03/04/ whisky_is_a_strong_shot_of_solitude/.

Bibliography

Acevedo-Muñoz, Ernesto. *Buñuel and Mexico: The Crisis of a National Cinema*. Berkeley: University of California Press, 2003.
———. *Pedro Almodóvar* (London: British Film Institute, 2007).
Alonso Barahona, Fernando. *Biografía del Cine Español* (Barcelona: Centro de Investigaciones Literarias Españolas e Hispanoamericanas, A.C., 1992).
Alvaray, Luisela. "National, Regional, and Global: New Waves of Latin American Cinema," *Cinema Journal* 47 (Spring 2008): 48–65.
Álvarez, Carlos. *Sobre Cine Colombiano y Latinoamericano* (Bogotá: Universidad Nacional de Colombia, 1989).
Aubert, Jean-Paul. "Le Cinéma de l'Espagne Démocratique. Les Images du Consensus," *Vingtième Siècle. Revue d'Histoire* 74 (April–June 2002): 141–151.
Aviña, Rafael. *Una Mirada Insólita. Temas y Géneros del Cine Mexicano* (Mexico City: Océano/Conaculta/Cineteca, 2004).
Barnard, Timothy, and Peter Rist, eds. *South American Cinema: A Critical Filmography, 1915–1994* (Austin: University of Texas Press, 1996).
Baugh, Scott L. "Manifesting La Historia: Systems of 'Development' and the New Latin American Cinema Manifesto," *Film and History* 34 (2004): 56–65.
Blanchot, Maurice. *The Infinite Conversation* (Minneapolis: University of Minnesota Press, 1993).
Cobos, Juan, *Las Generaciones del Cine Español* (Madrid: España Nuevo Milenio, 2000).
Cortés, María Lourdes. *El Espejo Imposible: Un Siglo de Cine en Costa Rica* (San José, Costa Rica: Farben Grupo Editorial Norma, 2002).
Couselo, Miguel Jorge, et al. *Historia del Cine Argentino* (Buenos Aires: Instituto Nacional de Cinematografía/Centro Editor de América Latina, 1992).

Davis, Catherine. "Recent Cuban Fiction Films: Identification, Interpretation, Disorder," *Bulletin of Latin American Research* 15 (1996): 177–192.

De Luna, Andrés. *La Batalla y su Sombra (La Revolución en el Cine Mexicano)* (Mexico City: Universidad Autónoma Metropolitana, 1984).

Denisson, Stephanie. "A Meeting of Two Worlds: Recent Trends in Brazilian Cinema," *Journal of Iberian and Latin American Studies* 6 (2000): 131–144.

Denisson, Stephanie, and Lisa Shaw. *Popular Cinema in Brazil 1930–2001* (Manchester: Manchester University Press, 2004).

D'Lugo, Marvin. "Almodóvar's City of Desire," *Quarterly Review of Film and Video* 13 (1999): 47–65.

Duque, Edda Pilar. *La Aventura del Cine en Medellín* (Bogotá: Universidad Nacional de Colombia/El Áncora Editores, 1992).

Elena, Alberto, and Marina Díaz López, eds. *The Cinema of Latin America* (London and New York: Wallflower Press, 2003).

Equipo "Cartelera Turia." *Cine Español, Cine de Subgéneros* (Valencia: Fernando Torres Editor, 1974).

Evans, Peter William, ed. *Spanish Cinema: The Auteurist Tradition* (Oxford: Oxford University Press, 1999).

Fornet, A., ed. *Alea, Una Retrospectiva Crítica* (Havana: Ediciones Letras Cubanas, 1987).

García, Gustavo, and José Felipe Coria. *Nuevo Cine Mexicano* (Mexico City: Clío, 1997).

García, Gustavo, and David R. Maciel. *El Cine Mexicano a Través de la Crítica* (Mexico City: UNAM, 2001).

García Riera, Emilio. *Breve Historia del Cine Mexicano. Primer Siglo, 1987–1997* (Mexico City and Zapopan: IMCINE/Ediciones Mapas, 1998).

Hershfield, Joanne. *Mexican Cinema/Mexican Woman, 1940–1950* (Tucson: University of Arizona Press, 1996).

Hershfield, Joanne, and David R. Maciel, eds. *Mexico's Cinema: A Century of Films and Filmmakers* (Wilmington, DE: Scholarly Resources, 1999).

Hopewell, John. " 'Art and Lack of Money': The Crisis of the Spanish Film Industry, 1977–1990," *Quarterly Review of Film and Video* 13 (1991): 113–122.

———. *El Cine Español Después de Franco. 1973–1988* (Madrid: Ediciones El Arquero, 1989).

Igler, Susanne, and Thomas Stauder, eds. *Negociando Identidades, Traspasando Fronteras. Tendencias en la Literatura y el Cine Mexicanos en Torno al Nuevo Milenio* (Madrid: Iberoamericana Vervuert, 2008).

Johnson, Randal. "Brazilian Cinema Novo," *Bulletin of Latin American Research* 3 (1984): 95–106.

———. *Cinema Novo X 5: Masters of Contemporary Brazilian Film* (Austin: University of Texas Press, 1984).

————. *Manoel de Oliveira* (Urbana and Chicago: University of Illinois Press, 2007).

————. "Nelson Rodrigues as Filmed by Arnaldo Jabor," *Latin American Theater Review* (Fall 1982): 15–28.

Johnson, Randal, and Robert Stam. *Brazilian Cinema* (New York: Columbia University Press, 1995).

Jordan, Barry, and Rikki Morgan-Tamosunas, eds. *Contemporary Spanish Cultural Studies* (London: Arnold, 2000).

Joseph, Gilbert, Anne Rubenstein, and Eric Zolov, eds. *Fragments of a Golden Age: The Politics of Culture in Mexico since 1940* (Durham, NC: Duke University Press, 2001).

Kinder, Marsha. *Blood Cinema: The Reconstruction of National Identity in Spain* (Berkeley: University of California Press, 1993).

————. "Pleasure and the New Spanish Cinema: A Conversation with Pedro Almodóvar," *Film Quarterly* 41 (Autumn, 1987): 33–44.

————. "Reinventing the Motherland: Almodóvar's Brain-Dead Trilogy," *Film Quarterly* 58 (December 2004): 9–25.

Maddison, Stephen. "All about Women: Pedro Almodóvar and the Heterosocial Dynamic," *Textual Practice* 14 (2000): 265–284.

Mahieu, José Agustín. *Panorama del Cine Iberoamericano* (Madrid: Ediciones de Cultura Hispánica, 1990).

Marranghello, Daniel. *El Cine de Costa Rica, 1903–1920* (San José, Costa Rica: n.p., 1988).

Marsh, Steven, and Parvati Nair, eds. *Gender and Spanish Cinema* (Oxford/ New York: Berg, 2004).

Martin, Michael T., ed. *New Latin American Cinema. Volume Two: Studies of National; Cinemas* (Detroit: Wayne State University Press, 1997).

Martin, Michael T., and Bruce Paddington. "Restoration or Innovation? An Interview with Humberto Solás: Post-Revolutionary Cuban Cinema," *Film Quarterly* 54 (Spring 2001): 2–13.

Maza Pérez, Maximiliano. *100 Años de Cine Mexicano* (Mexico City: ITESM/ MARCO, 1996).

Millán, Francisco Javier, *La Memoria Agitada. Cine y Represión en Chile y Argentina* (Huelva, Spain: Ocho y Medio Libros, 2001).

Mira, Alberto, ed. *The Cinema of Spain and Portugal* (London: Wallflower Press, 2005).

Monaco, James. *How to Read a Film: Movies, Media, Multimedia* (New York: Oxford University Press, 2000).

Monsiváis, Carlos. *Rostros del Cine Mexicano* (Mexico City: México Arte, 1997).

Mora, Carl J. *Mexican Cinema: Reflections of a Society, 1896–2004* (Jefferson, NC, and London: McFarland & Co., 2005).

Mora, Segio de la. *Cinemachismo: Masculinities and Sexuality in Mexican Film* (Austin: University of Texas Press, 2006).

Mouseca, Jacqueline. *Plano Secuencial de la Memoria de Chile* (Santiago de Chile: Ediciones del Litoral, 1988).

Nagib, Lúcia, ed. *The New Brazilian Cinema* (London: I. B. Tauris/Center for Brazilian Studies University of Oxford, 2003).

Noriega, Chon, ed. *Visible Nations: Latin American Cinema and Video* (Minneapolis: University of Minnesota Press, 2000).

Noriega, Chon, and Steven Ricci, ed. *The Mexican Cinema Project* (Los Angeles: UCLA Film and Television Archives, 1994).

Paraguaná, Paulo Antonio. *Mexican Cinema* (London: British Film Institute/ IMCINE/CONACULTA, 1995).

Peredo Castro, Francisco. *Alejandro Galindo, un Alma Rebelde en el Cine Mexicano* (Mexico City: CONACULTA/IMCINE, 2000).

Ramírez, Gabriel. *Crónica del Cine Mudo Mexicano* (Mexico City: Cineteca Nacional, 1989).

Ramírez Berg, Charles. *Cinema of Solitude: A Critical Study of Mexican Film, 1967–1983* (Austin: University of Texas Press, 1992).

Rashkin, Elissa. *Women Filmmakers in Mexico: The Century of Which We Dream* (Austin: University of Texas Press, 2001).

Rêgo, Cacilda M. "Brazilian Cinema: Its Fall, Rise, and Renewal (1990–2003)," *New Cinemas: Journal of Contemporary Film* 3 (2005): 85–100.

Reyes, Aurelio de los. *Medio Siglo de Cine Mexicano (1896–1947)* (Mexico City: Editorial Trillas, 2002).

———. *Los Orígenes del Cine en México: 1896–1900* (Mexico City: UNAM, 1972).

Reyes Nevares, Beatriz. *The Mexican Cinema: Interview with Thirteen Directors* (Albuquerque: University of New Mexico Press, 1976).

Schumann, Peter B. *Historia del Cine Latinoamericano* (Buenos Aires: Editorial Legasa, 1987).

Schwartz, Ronald. *The Great Spanish Films: 1950–1990* (Metuchen, NJ: The Scarecrow Press, Inc., 1991).

Shaw, Deborah, ed. *Contemporary Latin American Cinema: Breaking into the Global Market* (Lanham, MD: Rowman & Littlefield, 2007).

Smith, Paul Julian. "Transatlantic Traffic in Recent Mexican Films," *Journal of Latin American Cultural Studies* 12 (2003): 389–400.

Stam, Robert. *Tropical Multiculturalism: A Comparative History of Race in Brazilian Cinema and Culture* (Durham, NC: Duke University Press, 1997).

Stevens, Donald F., ed. *Based on a True Story: Latin American History at the Movies* (Wilmington, DE: SR Books, 1997).

Sutherland, Elizabeth. "Cinema of the Revolution: 90 Miles from Home," *Film Quarterly* 15 (Winter 1961): 42–49.

Talens, Jenaro, and Santos Zunzunegui, eds. *Modes of Representation in Spanish Cinema* (Minneapolis: University of Minnesota Press, 1998).

Todorov, Tzvetan. *The Conquest of America: The Question of the Other* (New York: Harper Perennial, 1982).

Torres San Martín, Patricia, ed. *Mujeres y Cine en América Latina* (Guadalajar, Mexico: Universidad de Guadalajara, 2004).

Trelles, Danilo. "El Cine Latinoamericano en la Batalla de las Culturas," *Cinemas d'Amerique Latine* 7 (January 1999): 161–165.

Valverde, Umberto. *Reportaje Crítico al Cine Colombiano* (Bogotá: Editorial Toro Nuevo, 1978).

Vaughan, Mary Kay, and Stephen E. Lewis. *The Eagle and The Virgin: Nation and Cultural Revolution in Mexico, 1920–1940* (Durham, NC, and London: Duke University Press, 2006).

Vernon, Kathleen M. "Melodrama against Itself: Pedro Almodóvar's *What Have I Done to Deserve This?*," *Film Quarterly* 46 (Spring 1993): 28–40.

West, Dennis. *Contemporary Brazilian Cinema* (Albuquerque, NM: Latin American Institute, 1984).

Index

About the Author

R. HERNANDEZ-RODRIGUEZ is an Associate Professor in the foreign language department at Southern Connecticut University. He has published three books, some book chapters, and several journal articles and book reviews. He has also participated in numerous professional conferences on film and culture in Brazil, Canada, Mexico, the Netherlands, Spain, and the United States.